Living with Koestler

Living with KOESTLER

Mamaine Koestler's Letters 1945-51

edited by Celia Goodman

St. Martin's Press
New York

Library of Congress Cataloging in Publication Data

Koestler, Mamaine.
  Living with Koestler.

  Letters from Arthur Koestler's second wife, Mamaine Paget, to her twin sister Celia Goodman.
1. Koestler, Arthur, 1905-   —Biography.
2. Authors, English—20th century—Biography.
3. Authors, German—20th century—Biography.
4. Koestler, Mamaine.   5. Wives—Great Britain—
Correspondence.   6. Goodman, Celia. I. Goodman, Celia.
II. Title.
PR6021.04Z634   1985   828'.91209 [B]   85-1803
ISBN 0-312-49029-1

First published in Great Britain by George Weidenfeld & Nicolson Ltd.

First U.S. Edition

10 9 8 7 6 5 4 3 2 1

Contents

List of Illustrations   *vii*

Acknowledgements   *ix*

Introduction   I

1945–6   23

1947   45

1948   72

1949   99

1950   124

1951   163

Postscript   193

Index   *195*

Illustrations

Nanny Michelmore, King and the twins, August 1924
A studio portrait of Mamaine by Harlip, 1937
Mamaine in Bavaria, by Celia, 1950
Celia, by Mamaine, 1949
Bwlch Ocyn
Arthur and Mamaine at Bwlch Ocyn (Photograph Pat English/Life
   © Time Inc 1947)
Arthur in Wales with Joe and Dina
Mamaine with Nellie, by Arthur
Verte Rive
Mark and Irene Sontag
Albert Camus
Richard Crossman and Emily
Dick Wyndham, 1948
Arthur and Mamaine at the Berlin Congress for Cultural Freedom,
   1950 (*Der Tag*, Berlin)
Island Farm
Arthur at Island Farm

Where no credit is given otherwise, the photographs were taken by
Mamaine, except for the first one.

Acknowledgements

In editing this book my chief debt has been to Arthur Koestler. I spent many hours questioning him about the people, events and organizations mentioned in it and he always dealt patiently and helpfully with my queries. He never objected to any of my editorial decisions or asked me to delete any unfavourable reference to himself – indeed for him to have done so would have been quite out of character. Cynthia Koestler also helped very willingly by supplying names that Arthur had forgotten. I feel deeply grateful to them both for their cooperation, and far more so still for their friendship, which enriched my life immeasurably up to the time of their death.

I am very much indebted to Storm Jameson and Diana Witherby for their invaluable advice, criticism and encouragement. I extend to them my warmest thanks. I also wish to thank Frances Partridge and my daughter Ariane for their most useful suggestions.

I should like to thank the following, all of whom have kindly supplied me with relevant information: Countess Gisela von Arnim, who generously gave me a book describing the events that befell her father Count Carl Hans von Hartenberg; Professor Mary A.B. Brazier, Frau Beate Bremmer, Mrs Miriam Camps, Mrs Cecilia Gillie, Mr John Grigg, Mr J.J. Hadey, H.R.H. the Princess of Hesse, the late Mr Robert P. Joyce, Mr Jon Kimche, Mr Andrew Knight, Mr Teddy Kollek, Mr Melvin J. Lasky, Mr and Mrs Donald Wayne and Mrs Ella Wolfe. I am especially grateful to Signor Matteo Spinola, who undertook some valuable research for me in Rome.

Finally, I gratefully acknowledge permission to reprint from *Encounter* the extracts from Mamaine's diary of 1 and 8 October 1947.

Introduction

It is now thirty years since my twin sister Mamaine Koestler[1] died and it never occurred to me until recently to publish any extracts from her letters or from the three short diaries she kept. Lately, however, I have come round to thinking that they may be of interest to others besides myself, and in particular to Arthur Koestler's readers, since they give a fairly full account of nearly six years of his life – from November 1945 to August 1951 – not covered by any of his autobiographical writings, and record a number of his opinions and preoccupations throughout those years. They also relate some curious and at times comic incidents concerning the intellectual worlds of Europe and the United States during that period with the vividness and spontaneity characteristic of contemporary records, as opposed to memoirs written many years after the events they describe.

To set them in context it is necessary to give a short account of Arthur's and Mamaine's backgrounds and of their lives up to the time of their meeting. These were as different from each other as they could possibly have been.

Arthur was born in Budapest on 5 September 1905 into a family of the educated middle class. His father, who came from an Eastern, perhaps Russian, Jewish family recently settled in Hungary and subject to fluctuating fortunes, had, by the time his only child was born, made sufficient money to enable him to finance a couple of cranky inventions, the second of which – a machine for making 'radioactive' soap – proved, strange to say, successful enough to allow him to run a viable business. Arthur's mother, who was also Jewish, came from Vienna, and she held in disdain the Hungarians among whom she lived for the first ten years of her marriage; she considered them socially inferior and would not let Arthur play with their children. When he was nine the family moved to Vienna, where he attended the Gymnasium, a secondary school specializing in science

[1] Born Mamaine Paget.

I

and modern languages, and subsequently the Technische Hoch-
schule, which, like most other continental Polytechnics, enjoyed
university status.

During his student years Arthur became a convinced Zionist and
one of the founders of the League of Zionist Activists. In the
winter of 1925, a year before he was due to graduate, he abandoned
his studies on a sudden impulse, and the following spring he went
to Palestine to join a kibbutz. After a probationary period in the
community, however, he was pronounced unfit for permanent
membership, possibly because he had revealed that he had never
intended to remain in it for good. For a year after this he scraped a
living through a variety of jobs, which included selling lemonade in
an Arab bazaar and working as an architectural draughtsman. A
friend rescued him from this precarious existence by recommend-
ing him for the post of Middle East correspondent of the powerful
Ullstein press based in Berlin, with its wide network of influential
newspapers and journals.

After working for them for two years in Palestine and one in
Paris he was transferred to Berlin as science editor of one of
Germany's leading newspapers, the *Vossische Zeitung* (he later
combined this post with those of foreign editor and assistant
editor-in-chief of the *BZ am Mittag*). He arrived in Germany on 14
September 1930, the very day of the Reichstag elections in which
the National Socialist Party achieved its first real breakthrough.
The economic state of the country was appalling: a third of the
work-force was unemployed and the workers were reduced to
hopeless misery. The dismal record of the Socialist Party during
the Weimar Republic showed that it could not be relied upon to
improve their lot or stem the Nazi advance. In his search for some
alternative Arthur turned to the study of Marxist dialectic. It
struck him with the force of a revelation. He felt that he had found
in it an ideology inspiring enough to counter that of the National
Socialists and a coherent political theory which, if put into practice,
could radically improve the future of mankind and bring about the
reign of social justice which he passionately wanted. On 31
December 1931 he joined the Communist Party.

He at once began to work for the cause. After a couple of months spent collecting information of no particular importance and passing it to a member of the *apparat*[1] his activities were revealed to his employers and he lost his posts on the Ullstein newspapers.

He was now free to fulfil his ambition to visit the USSR and see its achievements with his own eyes. The Party obligingly commissioned him to write a book extolling them, and he set off to collect material for it. According to his own account, so blinkered was he by his new faith that he travelled through the Ukraine at the height of the terrible famine of 1932–3, induced by collectivization, and witnessed the first show trials in Soviet Central Asia, without realizing their causes or implications.

In the meantime Hitler had come to power in Germany. It would have been useless as well as dangerous for him to return there, so he went to Paris, where for the next few years he continued the struggle against Fascism by means of various unpaid activities, such as editing an émigré journal, making contacts between French intellectuals and raising funds.

In 1935 he married Dorothy Ascher, who was at that time a member of the German Communist Party, but the marriage was shortlived, ending after a year in a friendly separation.

In August 1936 the Spanish Civil War broke out. Arthur immediately got a commission from the *News Chronicle* to go to Spain as a special correspondent: he was to investigate and report on the degree of Axis intervention in the conflict. Equipped with a safe conduct which he had procured by devious means from General Franco's brother, he went straight to the General's headquarters in Seville. He had only been there for a couple of days, however, before a former colleague at Ullstein's recognized him and denounced him as a Communist, so he had to make a hurried escape from the country. But even in this short time he had seen ample evidence of German military aid to Franco, and this he reported in a propaganda booklet which he published almost immediately after his return. He also testified to it before the Commission of Enquiry into Breaches of the Non-Intervention Agreement in Spain. He was thus taking a serious risk when he returned there the following year, again as correspondent for

[1] His only period as a 'conspiratorial character' – see letter of 4 August 1946.

3

the *News Chronicle*, to cover the war in Andalusia. When Málaga fell he was in the city and was unable to get away. He was arrested by Franco's Military Intelligence and put in jail in Seville.

He spent ninety-five days in prison, nearly all of them in solitary confinement. For the first sixty-five he was kept incommunicado and was allowed no exercise. Executions were being carried out three or four times a week between midnight and 2 a.m. and he could hear the warders taking the other prisoners out to be shot. He knew that many of them were mere boys, and their despairing cries left an indelible impression on him. Moreover, he lived in constant apprehension that his turn would come next, for in view of the fact that he was known to be a Communist and to have testified against Franco, and that he was under the special jurisdiction of General Gonzalo Queipo de Llano, of whom he had given a brief and unfriendly character-sketch in his recently published booklet, he had little doubt that he was under sentence of death.[1] In fact, thanks to pressure from prominent English politicians, he was set free in exchange for another hostage.

He had now been a Party member for five years. He had had doubts about its ethics, but these had not been sufficient to cause him to leave it, since, in common with other doubting members, he still believed it to be the vanguard of the working-class struggle and capable of reform only from within. But he now began to find many of its characteristics unacceptable. One was its misuse of language: the word 'freedom', for instance, was given a meaning that was the opposite of its accepted one. All decisions were imposed from above, the rank and file having no say in the formation of the Party line, and there was in fact no choice for members but to obey orders: their actions, their language and even their thoughts must be adapted to it. Since it was apt to take sudden U-turns, so that the enemies of one day were the friends and allies of the next, this required a high degree of mental dishonesty.

Moreover, in the USSR intellectuals were being abused and reviled. News began to penetrate to France of the arrest of many of Arthur's friends in the European and Russian Communist parties.

---

[1] He was never to be quite certain whether this was so. The delegate of the International Red Cross who negotiated for his release had been officially informed that Franco had signed the death warrant. On the other hand, shortly before his exchange the Foreign Office was told that his case was still *sub judice*.

Among them was his wife's brother, who, though a Party member, was politically naïve and indifferent. He was working as a doctor in a State hospital in the Volga German Republic when he was suddenly arrested and accused of having injected syphilis into his patients, of having undermined their morale by telling them that venereal disease was incurable, and of being the agent of a foreign power. He was never seen again. Another was the physicist Alex Weissberg, who appears in these letters. He was working in the Ukrainian Institute for Physics and Technology when, in 1937, both he and his wife were arrested. Weissberg was accused of having hired twenty bandits to ambush Stalin and Kaganovich and was sentenced to three years' imprisonment, but after the signing of the Soviet-German Pact he was handed over to the Gestapo together with a hundred other European Communists. His wife, who was a ceramist, was accused of having introduced swastikas into the designs of teacups, and subsequently of having hidden two pistols under her bed with the object of shooting Stalin at the next Party Congress. She spent eighteen months in the Lubyanka prison and was reduced to attempting suicide before she was eventually released, thanks to her Austrian nationality.

These and many other results of the doctrine that the end justifies the means caused a deep revulsion in Arthur and finally completely undermined his confidence in and loyalty to the Party. The last straw came at a lecture on the Spanish Civil War which he gave in Paris in 1938 to an association of émigré writers. Having refused to insert in it, at the request of a Party official, a sentence condemning the Trotskyist militia in Spain, POUM, as agents of Franco, or to submit his lecture to scrutiny, he included three phrases which he knew to be unacceptable to the Party: 1) that no movement, party or person can claim the privilege of infallibility; 2) that appeasing the enemy is as foolish as persecuting the friend who pursues the same aims by a different road; and 3) that a harmful truth is better than a useful lie (this last being a quotation from Thomas Mann). The non-Communist section of the audience applauded but the Communist half remained silent. A few days later Arthur wrote a letter of resignation to the Central Committee of the Communist Party.

That year he began to write his most famous novel, *Darkness at Noon*.

It was now that he met and formed an attachment to the sculptor Daphne Hardy, and they were together when war broke out. Two weeks later he was arrested, incarcerated for two nights in the cellar of a police station with fifty other people and then transferred to a large tennis stadium, the Stade Roland Garros, where he was confined with a thousand other 'undesirable alients'. Among them was Leo Valiani, who is also mentioned in these letters. An Italian from Trieste, he was thirty at the time of his first meeting with Arthur in the stadium, but he had already spent six years in prison for anti-fascist activities, which he took up again as soon as he was released. He appears as Mario in *Scum of the Earth*.

After a week in the stadium Arthur was transported with all the other detainees to a concentration camp at Le Vernet, a village in the foothills of the Pyrenees. Conditions there were extremely harsh – indeed the accommodation, hygiene and food were inferior to those in some Nazi camps. As winter came on the cold became intense, there were no stoves and hardly any blankets and the prisoners had to stand immobile in the frost four times a day for periods of from half an hour to an hour for roll-call. Like all the others, Arthur had no idea how long he would have to remain there. In the event he spent two and a half months in Le Vernet before international pressure brought about his release.

Back in Paris, he applied at once for a new identity card, as his had expired and without it he was an illegal resident and might be sent back to Le Vernet. He was told to return the next day, then in forty-eight hours, then in a month's time, and so on for four long months of acute psychological torture. Meanwhile the Germans were advancing on Paris and he knew that if he were not able to escape he would be deported to a Nazi camp. Finally, just in time, he was given the essential document and he and Daphne set off at once for the south, hitching lifts along roads thronged with refugees. Arthur had heard that the Foreign Legion was not particular about papers, so he enlisted in it under an assumed name and then proceeded with Daphne to Périgueux, where he was accepted in the army barracks as a presumed *soldat isolé* – that is, one who had lost his regiment in the retreat. But learning that the Germans were rapidly advancing southwards he rejoined Daphne and moved on to Bordeaux. There he left her in the care of an American journalist, who took her to St-Jean-de-Luz, where she boarded a ship for England. Arthur, who had been briefly arrested by a gendarme, was unable to accompany her, so he went south-west towards Bayonne and eventually found temporary refuge in a cantonment that had been set up in some ruined farmhouses at Susmiou. It was this village and the surrounding district that he revisited with Mamaine in 1950. In the late summer he deserted from the Legion and made his way via North Africa to Lisbon, from where, after a delay of six weeks, he was able to fly to England. He arrived with faked papers and, true to form, was immediately imprisoned in Pentonville until his identity could be established. This was a far cry from the death cell in Seville and the French concentration camp, and as the German bombers droned overhead he felt positively safe. After six weeks he was released, and he at once enlisted in the Pioneer Corps, the only army unit open to aliens. During the two months that elapsed before he was actually called up he hastily set down his recent experiences in France in *Scum of the Earth*, the first book he wrote in English. Membership of the Pioneer Corps entailed unskilled labour such as digging trenches and building road blocks. He was soon discharged from it, and instead lectured to the Army, wrote propaganda films, leaflets to be dropped over Germany and talks for the BBC, besides doing occasional stints in the Auxiliary Ambulance Unit. In between these activities he began writing another novel, *Arrival and Departure*.[1] This was followed by a collection of essays, *The Yogi and the Commissar*, which he finally completed in December 1944.

Daphne Hardy, who had been doing war work in Oxford during the first part of this period, joined him in London in 1943. At the end of that year, however, they decided to part company, although they remained close friends until Arthur's death.

Mamaine's life up to the time when she met Arthur was conventional and uneventful. Her origins and upbringing, so different from his, were the same as mine, as we were identical twins. Both our parents came from families of the English country gentry, and although they were not related they happened to have the same surname – Paget –

[1] Published in 1943.

before they were married. Our paternal grandfather's forbears had been principally distinguished in the previous generation by military prowess, but he, being a younger son, had gone into the Church and had become Vicar of Hoxne, a village in the north of Suffolk, where his five sons were brought up. His wife was the daughter of Robert Eden, Lord Auckland, who, as Vicar of Battersea, established evening classes for the poor, at which he himself lectured in anatomy. He was chaplain to William IV and Queen Victoria and became Bishop of Bath and Wells. His brother, whom he succeeded to the title, was Governor-General of India, and his sister was the novelist Emily Eden, author of *The Semi-attached Couple* and *The Semi-detached House*.

Our mother's family came originally from Leicestershire, but she was brought up in Derbyshire, where her father owned a coal-mine. Her name, Georgina Byng Paget, included a reference to her descent from the ill-starred admiral who was shot after the defence of Minorca, thereby provoking Voltaire's *bon mot* about 'encouraging the others' and causing him to comment that if Byng were not sufficiently close to the enemy, the French admiral had fought at exactly the same distance away from him.

Our mother was the only one of the five children in her family who seriously wished to acquire some education, but for a girl from her social background in the late Victorian era this was out of the question, so she had to make do with local adult lecture courses. Later she wrote poems and stories, and she was, I believe, a competent pianist.

We were born on 7 September 1916. Our parents had by then been married for twelve years but they had no other children, an earlier daughter having died in infancy, and our mother, who longed for children, was already forty-two. She succumbed to complications, and died when we were a week old. Our parents' marriage had been a very happy one and our father never got over her death: he remained desperately lonely for the rest of his life. Perhaps it affected us also – at any rate we languished and appeared to be going to die too. Our father hastily had us baptized at home, giving us the names Mamaine and Celia Mary, but we survived and were christened again in church. I do not know who looked after us for the first few months of our lives,

8

but when we were four months old a nanny was found for us. Her name was Ellen Michelmore. She was the daughter of a Devon farmer and must then have been about sixty years old. She was tall and held herself very straight, and she always wore a dress made of thick brown material which came down to her boots. Her hair, which was loosely pinned up, was white, thin and wispy, and her skin, tanned by wind and sun, was finely wrinkled, but her face was very beautiful. She was a person of great honesty and integrity and she possessed an innate nobility of character which was reflected in her appearance, giving her an air of grave distinction. Our father, who was himself devoid of triviality, greatly admired and respected her, and we grew to love her deeply.

We lived in East Suffolk, in a house which stood back off the lane that runs between the villages of Melton and Lower Ufford. The garden, which was bordered to the north by this lane, was surrounded on the other three sides by fields, ploughed in winter and in summer bearing crops of wheat or sugar-beet. To the left of the drive a narrow wood extended past the house to where a number of flower-beds, unkempt and overgrown, flourished in summer with a profusion of coral-coloured zinnias, orange eschscholzias and pale yellow evening primroses. The wood consisted mainly of limes, poplars and other deciduous trees, from whose branches owls hooted and screeched at night, while wrens nested on the ivy-clad trunks of the poplars and hairy caterpillars fed on the leaves of the lime trees and were collected, together with their food supply, by us. The River Deben, which flows through Melton to the harbour at Woodbridge, could be seen from the far end of the garden, and to the west of the house, beyond yet another field, stood a clump of Scotch pines. From their canopies, silhouetted at evening against the setting sun, came the soft cooing of woodpigeons.

Our father was now a very solitary man. Although he was on friendly terms with most of the people in the village he seldom invited them to the house, and he hardly ever had anyone to stay. The only person who came at all regularly was a Welshwoman named Alice Edwardes who acted as companion to an invalid sister of our mother's called Meg. At first they used to come together, but after Aunt Meg died Alice Edwardes still continued to visit us, and when our father eventually became too ill to look after us she took charge of us for a while. All in all we owed her a very great deal. Quiet, grave, intelligent and cultured, she conveyed an impression of great stability,.and we were very fond of her.

From an early age we loved music more than anything else, but we had very little opportunity to hear any. Our father possessed a pianola with a number of rolls, among them several arrangements of symphonies (these were our favourites), the Waldstein Sonata and the Spinning Song from *The Flying Dutchman*, which we never tired of hearing, and when we were five we were allowed to play these ourselves. Hymns and psalms in church on Sundays and the piano pieces played at our weekly dancing classes (which were held at Boulge Hall, where Edward Fitzgerald once lived) was the only other music we heard.

We detested dolls, apart from two beloved sheepskin ones, rather larger than us, with suede faces, and the only time we were lent a dolls' pram we turned all the inmates out and filled it with books. But we loved babies and longed to have one in the family. However, it appeared that as our mother was no longer alive we never could. Like all children, we asked where they came from, and we were told that they fell from heaven into their mothers' arms, but this only puzzled us still further, for how, we wondered, could our mother possibly have caught both of us at the same time? The answer came out pat: the district nurse had been on hand to catch one of us while our mother caught the other one. 'And what does she do with the babies she catches if their mothers die?', we asked. 'She gives them to whoever wants them most', our nanny replied. This new light on the district nurse's profession gave us an idea: the next time she caught a baby might she perhaps be willing to sell it to us? We saved up our pocket money until we had sixpence and when she came to the house we offered it to her in return for her next spare baby. We were both chagrined and surprised when our offer was greeted with roars of laughter, for we saw nothing wrong with our reasoning and did not suspect that the premise was false.

We lived simply. Our father employed only two servants – a cook named Mabel, who saw as little of us as she could manage, and a gardener named King, a sturdy, good-natured, ruddy-faced man with a dark moustache who usually wore a straw hat on his bald head. The house was lit by oil lamps and heated by coal fires, there was no telephone and our father did not possess a car or a wireless (the 'crystal set' which he eventually acquired never worked). By way of pets we had a mongrel dog, a bullfinch taken from a nest in the garden, and numerous guinea-pigs, whose breeding activities filled us with wild excitement. When we were seven we began taking lessons for an hour a day from the retired village schoolmaster, who walked up from Melton every morning to teach us. This was the only education we had until we went to boarding-school at the age of eleven, and it was also almost the most rewarding we ever had.

Our father, who was fifty when we were born, was a gentle man, kind, humorous and witty, though given to bouts of melancholy. We considered him the most delightful companion: we used to whoop with joy if he offered to come for a walk with us or to take us for a picnic. He would entertain us with long stories of his own invention in which we featured as boys (since that was what we longed to be), or make bows and arrows for us, weighting the arrows with elder-wood. He would carve bulrushes into candles by the river at Ufford, play patience with us on winter afternoons, sing or whistle songs from the Gilbert and Sullivan operas to us – he was said to be able to 'whistle well enough to go on the stage' – photograph us with his tripod camera, developing and printing the photographs himself, and allow us to write stories on his typewriter. But his health was never good, and when we were seven he began to develop alarming symptoms. He went to London to consult a specialist and returned in an extremely depressed frame of mind. We somehow gathered that he had been told there was no hope for him. Soon after this we overheard him saying to a man from the village: 'When I die you must take over the bowls club.' These words and our interpretation of the specialist's verdict filled us with acute anxiety. We had always been prone to suffer from chest ailments and we now developed asthma. From then on until our father's death five years later a deep fear that he might soon die clouded our happy lives.

Fifty years ago English children, with the exception of those who won scholarships, were strictly segregated into different social classes for the purpose of education, so it doubtless did not occur to our father to send us to the village school, but even had it done so, by the time we reached the age of eleven he was too ill to keep us at home much longer. We were sent to a small boarding-school at Buckhurst Hill on the edge of Epping Forest. We looked forward to going, because we were very sociable, but the reality did not correspond to our expectations. Not that there was anything in the least grim about the place, but – like other English boarding-schools, I presume – it deprived its pupils completely of privacy, quiet and solitude, in spite of the fact that most children need all of these. During our first term we were utterly miserable and intensely homesick and we often fell ill, probably from a desperate, if subconscious, desire to obtain some solitude at any cost. But illness and pain are far worse than lack of privacy and we always recovered very quickly, partly, I believe, owing to an effort of will.

During our first term we ceaselessly dreamed of returning home to nurse our father, but we never did go home and we were not able to look after him: he had sold the house in Melton and we spent our first holidays, which were the Easter ones, at Hindhead, where, to our dismay, we found him too ill to see much of us. When we had gone back to school he entered Chiswick House, then a private mental home, as a voluntary patient, because he believed that his illness might affect his mind. On the few occasions after that when we saw him it clearly had not done so.

In the summer holidays of that year Alice Edwardes took us to Haslemere to attend the Dolmetsch Music Festival. The early music, played on contemporary instruments or reproductions of them, enchanted us, and we did not worry about the standard of performance since we had never heard any other. I can still remember some of the works that were played then. We were also fascinated by the entire Dolmetsch family and immediately wrote a 'novel' – really a long story – about them. That autumn, and for the whole of the Christmas holidays, we stayed with our mother's only brother, Jack Paget, and his wife and two daughters in Roehampton. Our nanny was still with us, and she took us to visit our father at Chiswick House, where he showed us the magnificent deodar trees and the small gardens in the French and Italian styles that had been laid out in the grounds. In the Christmas holidays he came to see us once at Roehampton. This was the last time we saw him: the following March he died. We were then twelve years old.

Our first emotion on learning of his death was a sadness more intense and overwhelming than any other in life. Our second was one which I believe is not uncommon in children who have been dreading the death of one of their parents for a long time: a feeling of relief. The worst had happened and we were still alive! But beneath this, on a subconscious level, we suffered, I now realize, from a profound sense of abandonment and from the terrifying feeling that the entire framework which had supported us during the whole of our lives until then had suddenly been withdrawn, leaving us, as Henry James put it in a different context, 'howling in space'.

It had been arranged that after our father's death we should go and live with our Uncle Jack and his family. Our hearts sank at the prospect of being transplanted into a world so different from the one in which we had been brought up. Our uncle was exceedingly rich, and it is no reflection on him or on our aunt to say that the milieu in which they lived was never congenial to us and we always felt strangers to it.

Uncle Jack's house was about a mile from Richmond Park. It had been built in the present century but in the Queen Anne style, and it had a large and pleasant garden. Behind the house a terrace with rose beds at one end of it led to a wide lawn covered with apple trees and bounded by a hedge, and beyond this a small shallow swimming-pool was sunk into the middle of a second lawn. Although nothing in the house was pretty – the furniture was all rather ugly imitation Queen Anne and there were no good pictures – it was extremely comfortable, and in the drawing-room there was a Blüthner grand piano on which we were allowed to practise when our uncle and aunt were out. Whereas our father had employed three people to run his house, tend his garden and look after his children, our uncle employed eighteen. These included a kindly butler whose head was higher on one side than on the other, a peculiarity I have never seen in anyone else, and a nightwatchman whom Uncle Jack had taken on after a burglar had slipped into the house one evening during a dinner-party and pocketed one of his ties before being disturbed by departing guests.

Our aunt, named Germaine but known as Maimaine, was French and had been brought up in the kind of aristocratic society described by Proust, but, unlike the characters in his novel, she was entirely devoid of snobbery. In appearance she was tall, slim and elegant and her face, though it can never have been beautiful by conventional standards, was extraordinarily expressive and attractive, while her personality was one of the most fascinating I have ever come across. This was partly due to her keen sense of humour – she was a very amusing talker, and her strong French accent, which she never lost, as well as her idiosyncratic versions of certain colloquial expressions,[1] added to the charm of her conversation. She was a person of rare sweetness and warmth and was quite without affectation or vanity. Her daughters, Winifred and Anne,[2] have inherited her sweet nature: we were always happy with them and with her, and as we managed to avoid our uncle most of the time our relationship with our new family was soon perfectly harmonious.

Our uncle had been a regular soldier but had retired from the army many years earlier with the rank of major. He looked the part. Tall, straight and stiff, his face adorned by a moustache and an eyeglass, he corresponded closely in appearance to the accepted military conventions of the time, and he might have been considered handsome had he not been devoid of charm and – apparently, though perhaps not in fact – of humour. As it was, his most striking outward characteristics – to us children, at any rate – were the cold expression in his eyes and the unfailing severity of his gaze. Fifteen years older than his wife, he tyrannized over her and his children, and any attempt to thwart his will, or his discovery of any act that contravened it, was liable to incite him to an outburst of violent rage, during the course of which he would impose the worst punishment he could think of upon the unfortunate person who had provoked it. In those early days we only saw his cold, hard-hearted and vindictive side and perceived in him no redeeming features, but he had, in fact, some good qualities. Although, in spite of his great wealth, he used to effect all kinds of minor economies (which caused us to nickname the house Poverty Hall) and was occasionally inexplicably mean, he was also

[1] For instance, 'in death's store' instead of 'at death's door'.

[2] Now Winifred Hope and Anne Reid.

capable of great generosity, deriving from a real consideration for the sufferings of the sick and the underprivileged. Moreover when he was no longer in a position to tyrannize over others – that is, during the war, when he was a guest in his elder daughter's house instead of being master in his own – he mellowed considerably and even became almost endearing. He began to show a genuine affection for his wife, and used to take his five-year-old grandson for daily walks – something he had never done for his own children.

Uncle Jack was a vegetarian, a theosophist and a believer in re-incarnation, astrology and fortune-telling. He was also a British Israelite – in other words, he felt convinced that the British people were the Lost Tribe of Israel – and his solution to the problem of Palestine was original in the extreme: he devised a scheme for sending the Prince of Wales out to rule over that country and had it printed in pamphlet form under the title 'The Paget Plan: a Prince for Palestine'. He used to hand it out to people whom he believed to be Jewish, but as he was completely incapable of distinguishing Jews from Gentiles he often gave it to the latter, to their utter mystification. On the subject of reincarnation he was usually reticent, but he did once come up with the hypothesis that his daughter Anne was a reincarnation of William Pitt. He had a portrait of the younger Pitt in the dining-room and he measured the skull, compared the measurements with Anne's head, and decided that they were identical. Soon afterwards, during a lunch party, he called Anne into the dining-room, propounded his theory, and quoted a saying of Pitt's. 'Do you remember saying that in the House?', he asked her hopefully. She was unable to pretend that she did, so the experiment was not repeated.

Uncle Jack was a staunch and unquestioning conservative. We, on the other hand, were by nature left-wing, and as soon as we began to take an interest in politics we became, in theory, socialists, or rather, to use a less ambiguous term, social-democrats of a moderate and un-doctrinaire kind. We never held communist beliefs and indeed knew very little about the Communist Party. Naturally our uncle never suspected that our views were opposed to his, because he assumed that anyone he knew personally was bound to be a Tory. If we had told him that we were not, and if, in that event, he had been able to credit his ears, he would, I think, have regarded us as traitors to our class.

Six months after we had gone to live with him and our aunt we were moved from our first boarding-school to another one in Essex, this time near Malden. We learned nothing at all there, because we were in no mood for concentration. Every morning we made our way to the fields that lay beyond the grounds and wandered about in them until sunset or until we felt that our absence might be detected. Owing to the haphazard arrangement of the school time-table it almost always remained unnoticed, and we ourselves failed to notice until the end of the summer term that we had sunk nearly to the bottom of the form. Our desperate pleas to be taken away from this school were ignored by our guardian, the Public Trustee, but we were saved by the local doctor, who recommended that we should be sent to the mountains for the sake of our health. Our aunt promptly discovered a *pensionnat de jeunes filles* on a hill above Lausanne and took us out there the following term. We liked our new Swiss school from the day we arrived. The girls were of all nationalities, but Americans predominated, and their friendliness and lack of malice delighted us from the start. So did the civilized surroundings. There were no dormitories, and our bedroom looked out across the Lake of Geneva far below to where at night the lights of Evian sparkled on the distant shore. Because this was a finishing-school the education was very limited and several important subjects, including science, mathematics and the classics, were omitted altogether, but as we stayed there much longer than most of the other girls we were eventually put into a class by ourselves and allowed to choose two subjects that were not in the main curriculum. We chose music and 'philosophy', that is, the history of philosophy. The tuition was sound enough, but it did not do much to remedy the state of profound ignorance in which our two English schools had left us. Lord Melbourne is reputed to have said 'What's all this damned nonsense about education? – the Pagets have got along very well without it', but he was not thinking of us, and the meagreness of ours proved a permanent disadvantage.

Mamaine had good reason to bewail her lack of it, especially in those fields in which Arthur was particularly well informed. However, she had always been an avid reader, so by the time they met she was reasonably well read in English and French literature, and although her knowledge of German was limited she returned again and again to her favourite German poets, especially to Hölderlin. She was also familiar with a good deal of music through having attended concerts regularly, collected records and studied the piano for many years. Towards the end of her life she began to learn ancient Greek and found herself to be an ardent Hellenist, though she never visited Greece. She did not possess a scientific mind, but she was interested in several branches of science and made a few small attempts to pick up a rudimentary knowledge of them: in the last months of her life she was planning to study the physiology of the brain and wrote asking Arthur to recommend some books on the subject, which he did; and she was always fascinated by ornithology. Finally, though not herself a thinker, she was keenly interested in ideas and this, combined with her eagerness to learn about a wide range of subjects, caused her to find the company of Arthur's friends extremely stimulating.

Although we were at times profoundly bored in our Swiss school, especially when illness prevented us from going home for holidays, on the whole the three and a half years we spent there were happy and peaceful. We left in the summer of 1935 and six months later were on our way to Florence to learn, not Italian, but German in a *pensione* run by a Professor Aschaffenburg, who had held a unique chair in forensic ballistics in a German university. He and his wife and three daughters were cultured and musical. The other guests were all German Jewish refugees. They were much older than we were and were very kind to us, and we immediately felt at ease with them, as we always did subsequently in any similar milieu. We soon got to know a number of Italians of our own age, and we met and made friends with two twenty-three-year-old Germans – a doctor named Hans Hahndel and Wolfgang von Leyden, who was then working for a doctorate in philosophy and who later became Reader in that subject at Durham University and a well-known expert on Locke, whose shorthand he succeeded in deciphering. With these two companions we explored Florence from Fiesole to the Porta Romana, beyond which Wolfgang lived in a house surrounded by vineyards. That winter, besides the galleries, the churches and the occasional outings to Siena, Pisa and San Gimignano, there were regular orchestral concerts in the Teatro Comunale, while the famous Lener Quartet was giving a series of recitals in the Sala Bianca of the Palazzo Pitti. We were in Florence from the beginning of January until mid-March and it was bitterly cold, but the sky was nearly always blue and the scent of mimosa hung in the air and penetrated even to our room overlooking a courtyard in an old palazzo in the Via Giuseppe Giusti. It was one of the happiest periods of our lives. The only cloud on the horizon was the prospect of returning to England, since our wish to work for university entrance had been overruled in favour of the custom known as 'coming out'.

When the time came for this and we had been duly presented at Court and had gone through certain rigmaroles considered by our uncle essential to the role of a débutante – their object was to be seen in the 'right' places at the 'right' time – we went to at least one dance, if not two, every night throughout the 'Season'. When these were given in crowded London ballrooms there was a certain sameness about them, but when they were held in country houses, their gardens hung with lights and the air scented by the gardenias that the girls often wore in their hair or pinned to their dresses, they were very enjoyable. However, as the days were spent in making up for lost sleep or attending lunch-parties to meet other young girls there was no time to do anything else, so for us, at any rate, that summer was every bit as frustrating as we had feared it would be.

The following year the number of social events we had to attend greatly diminished and we had time for other activities, so we began to take piano lessons from Joseph Cooper, who was then living in Blackheath and working for his career as a concert pianist. We kept these lessons up until the war, and many years later were fortunate enough to be able to study with him again.

We now at last began to meet people whose interests coincided with our own. Although we were, so to speak, starting from scratch, this was not difficult in London. We went regularly to concerts in the Queen's Hall and in the three recital rooms in Wigmore Street and Bond Street, visited art exhibitions and joined the London Library. There were, in addition, two places where we spent a lot of our time. One was Tickerage Mill, a charming small red-brick house on the bank of a stream in lovely Sussex countryside. It belonged to Dick Wyndham, a totally original man who had moved from his *grand seigneur* background and created there a circle of his own consisting principally of writers and artists (he was himself a painter and published three books). Among those of his friends whom we first met at that time were Sacheverell Sitwell, Matthew Smith, Cyril Connolly, Peter Quennell and Constant Lambert. Our other haunt was in London, the old Café Royal, which was then a very different place from what it is now. In the front half of the huge downstairs room, which was furnished like a French café with bare tables and leather-covered seats, only coffee, served in glasses, and drinks could be had. This part was frequented by taxi-drivers, artists, musicians, writers and the man-in-the-street, and after dinner it was always full. The atmosphere was pleasant and congenial: people would wander over to join their friends at other tables and then return to their own. The far end was run as a restaurant, while on the balcony that extended round the whole room were tables laid for two or four. Coffee and drinks alone could be had here too, but the smaller tables were also much in demand for tête-à-tête dinners.

When we were twenty-one we left our uncle's house and went to live in London in a small studio house off the Fulham Road.[1] We still spent much of our time together. We had a piano and each contrived to practise on it for about four hours a day – not sufficient for us to acquire more than a very modest technique; we spent many weekends roaming in the country around Tickerage and we went abroad together for several holidays, two of them with our friend the archaeologist Seton Lloyd.

Two observations about our relationship as identical twins are relevant to these letters. Firstly, as we had all the same characteristics, though in slightly different proportions, there could be no question of pretence or insincerity when we wrote to each other. Secondly, our tastes were the same in everything from food to music and so were our reactions to people, landscapes and indeed to everything. This is why Mamaine often did not trouble to comment in her letters to me on whatever she had read, seen or heard: she knew that if I was familiar with it my feelings about it would be identical to hers. It may be objected that, for instance, most people who understand the language of music will have the same emotions on hearing a work of indisputable worth (though I am not certain that this is so). But not everyone reacts in the same way to *all* music, *all* poetry and *all*

---

[1] Arthur stayed there for six months during the war, when we let it to Cyril Connolly.

painting as we did. I will give one trivial example. On her return from Israel Mamaine sang to me an old Russian waltz which she had heard boatmen singing on the Dead Sea. It struck us both most forcibly as at the same time sad, lovely and comic. I do not believe that many other people would have reacted in exactly that way to this simple tune.

When the war broke out we parted company, but in September 1940 we were reunited for a few months when I transferred from a hospital where I was nursing to another in which Mamaine had signed on. At the end of that year, however, we both returned to London and Mamaine began to work in the Ministry of Economic Warfare, where she remained until the end of the war, mainly doing research for C. E. ('Tom Brown') Stevens, the Roman historian and Fellow of Magdalen College, Oxford, who was then engaged in war work at Bletchley.

Arthur was now also living in London, and he and Mamaine first met on 10 January 1944 at a party which Cyril Connolly gave in his flat in Bedford Square. They were instantly drawn to each other and began straight away to meet regularly. At first their relationship did not always go smoothly, but they both felt that it was to be an important one for them. Then, on 12 June 1944, Mamaine noted in her diary: 'Got back from work to find a box of records and letter from Arthur saying that his family had been deported to Poland.' Arthur's father had died many years earlier, but his mother was still alive, and at first he believed that she was among the members of his family who had been sent to Auschwitz. Under the shock of this news he broke off his relationship with Mamaine and went to stay in a friend's country house. Three weeks later he heard that his mother had not after all been deported, but he later learned that her sister and the latter's two teenage children had perished in the gas chambers.

Towards the end of August he returned to London and he and Mamaine began to meet frequently again. He was now working extremely hard, often till two or three in the morning, on *The Yogi and the Commissar*. By the beginning of December it was finished, and as Mamaine was due for a week's holiday they went together to Merionethshire, where Arthur had already been for a couple of days to look for a house to rent when the war was over. They stayed in the Oakley Arms, a small hotel in Maentwrog, near Blaenau Ffestiniog, which was to become very familiar to them later on. They found two friends of Arthur's already staying there: the novelist Storm Jameson, who, as president of the PEN Club, was working tirelessly for the cause of refugee writers, and her husband the historian, writer and publisher Guy Chapman. On 17 December Mamaine noted in her diary: 'Last day of my holiday. We were both very happy all the time. Went for long walks, played Russian billiards, sat up drinking with the Commandos, looked for a house for Arthur. Back to London.'

Two days later Arthur set off for Palestine, ostensibly as a correspondent for *The Times* but in reality because Chaim Weizmann had asked him to try to win the terrorist groups over to partition. He remained there for eight months, during which he and Mamaine wrote to each other regularly. On 12 August 1945 Mamaine's diary reads: 'Arthur arrived from Palestine . . . very brown, with a bag full of arak and brandy. Dined at Scott's. Felt very elated and rather tight. A. said he would like to marry me but (a) cyclic neurosis (b) refused to have children. I said I would like to too but refused not to have children. . . . Very happy.'

Arthur did not, in fact, ever suffer from 'cyclic neurosis' or from any psychological traits of a pathological nature, but at that time and for a year or two afterwards (to judge from Mamaine's letters) he appears to have believed that his intermittent bouts of depression were congenital. His second objection to marriage had a more real foundation. He rightly surmised that children would seriously interfere with his work and thus prove an intolerable source of irritation to him. Mamaine was passionately fond of babies and children and longed all her life to have some of her own, but she soon realized that this was a question on which Arthur could not compromise with any hope of success. Her strong maternal instinct therefore never had any outlet, since, to my deep regret, she did not live to know my children.

After a period of uncertainty on her side caused by this dilemma and by her growing awareness of Arthur's mercurial temperament, and a spell of low spirits induced in him by the necessity of writing about terrorism in Palestine, they decided to go and live together in the house in Merionethshire that Arthur had found the previous winter.

He had chosen Wales because of the preference for mountain scenery that he derived from his childhood in Austria. He always liked to spend part of every year in the country, but it did not mean as much to him as it did to Mamaine, who loved it intensely. She was fortunate in being able to live in it for most of her time with him while also enjoying frequent spells of social life, for she loved people too and friendship meant a very great deal to her. There were, of course, drawbacks. For an East Anglian the Welsh climate was depressing and debilitating, and for someone as *enracinée* as she it was often a strain to live with a man for whom it would have been, at that time, anathema to put down roots. But she did her best to adapt to Arthur's rather nomadic style of living, and, after the comparative isolation of the first two years in Wales, she found the variety and interest of their lives together a compensation for the lack of a settled home. She became accustomed to moving on every few years, although when they settled in the United States she was never able to overcome a feeling of exile and a longing to return to Europe.

The house Arthur had rented was called Bwlch Ocyn (the name means Ocyn's Pass). It is a long low grey stone farmhouse half a mile from Manod, near Blaenau Ffestiniog. On one side of it a path leads up from the village, while on the other it is surrounded by a remarkably beautiful panorama of mountain peaks, hills and wide valleys. The room which Arthur and Mamaine used as their sitting-room was very high; it had a wide, open fireplace, and almost the whole of one side of it was taken up by a huge uncurtained window overlooking this view. All the downstairs floors were paved with stone, and the roof was of slate.

Arthur and Mamaine set off from London by car on 19 August and arrived at Bwlch Ocyn the following afternoon. At first they felt 'miserable because the house looked all wrong and we couldn't think how or where Arthur would work'. But after 'a couple of days shifting furniture about and making plans' they cheered up. They soon acquired a seven-weeks-old Welsh sheepdog puppy and some hens, for which Mamaine used to cook up meal in a large saucepan; she planted some bulbs, and was amazed to find that Arthur did not know what daffodils, narcissi or crocuses were. Thus they settled down in what was to be their home for the next two years, and from this point Mamaine's letters continue their story.

C. M. G.

Cambridge
1984

·1945- 46·

6.11.45

Bwlch Ocyn,
Blaenau Ffestiniog,
North Wales

Dear Twinney,

Ever since I left London I have been trying to find time to write to you, but I have been very busy. First of all, having Tom Hopkinson[1] to stay, which was extremely nice, naturally altered our smooth routine, and involved rather more cooking than I would otherwise have done. He stayed till last Thursday, and on Friday evening Polanyi arrived.[2] Also K and I had to fetch a man and force him to whitewash the ceiling almost at pistol point. Nearly every day I have to bully and nag the workmen in an effort to goad them into some sort of action, and when I succeed they usually do the thing all wrong. They are very unpleasant too, I now think. I am sure they all hate me, and I have decided that strength through fear is better than *Kraft durch Freude* as far as my relations with them are concerned.

We have arranged the house differently now: K is back in his little room, plus his books; next to that is the big sitting room in which we sit after dinner, then comes the hall where we eat and out of that opens a little panelled room which is now MY sitting room. It is awfully nice and quiet and is next to the kitchen with a communicating door, so that I can, so to speak, read in it while stirring the stew with one hand. This is most convenient, as you can imagine. Even now I am in the middle of cooking an enormous ox's heart, which can be heard sizzling away.

Relations with K could not be better, and he has made several encouraging remarks such as that he has never lived so well with anybody else, and that he can't see what can go wrong with our *ménage*. Also he keeps saying how happy he is and we are – isn't it wonderful? I do wish you would come and stay. We are not going to

23

have any more guests till Christmas, when we *might* have George Orwell, Tom Hop[kinson] and his wife and child, and you. None of these have definitely said they will come yet. But of course you can come any time. If we achieve so many people we can billet some of them in the pub.[3]

I have decided that in view of Edmund's last letter I can't very well go to the States without risking feeling rather guilty when I get there, so have told him this.[4] K might go when his play comes on, but of course that would look rather silly if it is an awful flop, which personally I expect it to be. It is not a very good play really, but K says it might be good theatre.[5]

My latest idea is to try to go to Switzerland after Christmas for two months on health grounds. Do you think this is possible?[6] It would be lovely if we could both go, but I suppose that is out of the question on account of your job.[7]

Love from
Mamaine

[1] H. T. (now Sir Thomas) Hopkinson, writer and journalist, was editor of the weekly illustrated magazine *Picture Post* from 1940 to 1950.

[2] Michael ('Misi') Polanyi was at that time Professor of Physical Chemistry at Victoria University, Manchester.

[3] George Orwell, his adopted son Richard (then nineteen months old) and Celia were the only guests at Bwlch Ocyn that Christmas.

[4] Mamaine had met Edmund Wilson in April 1945. He had fallen in love with her and had asked her to marry him. On 4 October he wrote to her from New York: 'I do need an intelligent secretary for a couple of months, but of course what I really want of you is YOU, and if you come – since you don't want to marry me – you ought to have a clear recognition of the practical and emotional problems involved.'

[5] *Twilight Bar* was put on in Baltimore and Philadelphia but it did not reach New York, and Arthur did not go to the United States then.

[6] For several years after the war stringent foreign currency regulations were in force.

[7] Celia was working as editorial assistant to *Polemic*, a bi-monthly magazine dealing with contemporary thought and edited by Humphrey Slater. Bertrand Russell, George Orwell, A. J. Ayer and Rupert Crawshay-Williams were among its contributors.

4.1.46   Bwlch Ocyn*

Dear Twin,

My God, we have had a cold spell (but no fog). We spend all day in

* Addresses are given in full only at the first change.

Arthur's little room, which is very snug, working (we get through about 25 pages a day but it is very tiring) and have dinner in front of the fire in the sitting room.

I like this life as it lets me out of cooking; as a matter of fact we have been right out of food lately, and have been living on goosefat, bacon, the fish you brought and occasionally some eggs, noodles and Oxo. So there was not much cooking we could do anyway.[1]

On New Year's Eve we wanted to go to the Oakley for dinner with Polanyi, but Arthur got stuck with the car in the garage, it got somehow up against a wall and we simply couldn't get it out. So after trying for about an hour or more we went back into the house and tried to make up our minds what to do, as by that time we felt the Oakley to be the most desirable place on earth, and also felt we couldn't bear to miss the Sylvester Abend celebrations. We had just eaten the cold duck's carcass and decided to go there by bus and hope for a lift back when K suggested that we should go to bed in the sitting room where there was a blazing fire and he would make bacon and eggs. So we sighed with relief and did that. What did you do?

Love from
[no signature]

[1] Food rationing did not end until 1951.

11.1.46   Bwlch Ocyn

Dear Twine,

I have permission to take money to Switzerland, so now I only have to get visas for Sw. and France (which shouldn't be difficult), then I can go. Isn't it wonderful? I will therefore come to London some time next week, probably Friday, and stay in my flat. So try and keep some time free for me over the weekend.

Life has been very pleasant lately except for an awful spell of highbrow social life with Polanyi, the Crawshays[1] and Bertrand Russell. The latter came to lunch with us and we nearly broke our necks trying to get some food for him, as K had invited him just when we had nothing.[2] Misi Polanyi dined with us and we with him, and he and K had endless conversations about the weight of various particles, the mismic field, the impossibility of formulating any extrapolation which would predict the movements of electrons or God knows what. What with this, a dash of semantics, more physics, and emergent vitalism with Russell, a discussion with the latter on politics came as a great relief to my weary brain. But my inferiority complex about my ignorance and general dumbness is worse than ever.

Love from
Twin

PS. No major rows with K since you were here, things seem to be looking up!

[1] Rupert Crawshay-Williams, philosopher, and his wife Elizabeth lived on the Portmeirion estate near Penrhyndeudraeth.

[2] Bertrand Russell was living at Llan Ffestiniog with his third wife Patricia ('Peter') and their nine-year-old son Conrad. In her diary entry of 10 January 1946 Mamaine wrote: 'K discussed with Russell his project for a new League, which he also discussed with George and Tom. Russell seemed to agree with K's ideas, though he didn't want to be involved and said he thought the first step should be a conference of any 12 people with special qualifications, who should discuss what to do to prevent an atomic war.' This scheme came to nothing.

Mamaine spent the last week of January 1946 and the whole of February in Switzerland, visiting Zürich, Gstaad, Bern, Lausanne, Château d'Oex and Basle. She stayed eight days in Paris on the way home, arriving in London on 9 March. She was met by Arthur, who had remained in Wales for part of the time she was away and had spent the rest of it staying with friends in London. After a few days they returned to Bwlch Ocyn, arriving there on 13 March.

23 January 1946. Left Victoria at 9 a.m. Arthur came to see me off. Met Silone and Nenni on the boat and lunched with them, also travelled to Paris with them.[1] We arrived at midnight. I talked quite a lot to Silone on the boat and train. He said he had spent a good deal of time ill and in prison and it had given him a chance to think about the meaning of life; and that he wants to write Spina's reflections in prison.[2] Also said he thought that 'il ne faut pas isoler la Russie' and that a western bloc would at this time seem aggressive towards Russia. Didn't discover what his alternative was.

[1] Pietro Nenni, leading Italian Socialist and for many years editor of the Italian Socialist Party's paper *Avanti*, was Minister for Foreign Affairs in 1946.

[2] Pietro Spina is the hero of Ignazio Silone's novel *Bread and Wine*.

[Postcard]
Samstag den 9.2.46

Hôtel Bellevue,
Bern

Dear Celia,

Would you please try and get hold of a copy of *New Bats in Old Belfries*[1] for Edmund, as I'm afraid by the time I get back it'll be sold out.

Went to an incredible dinner-party and ball last night in a club modestly called Le Cercle des Grandes Familles where I danced among others with Mr [later Sir Clifford] Norton, the British Minister here and with a pompous gent called le Chef de Protocol, whose job in life is to decide who goes through doors first, etc. This hotel is wonderful, the bath in my bathroom would hold 3 people; I'm afraid it must be awfully expensive. May I stay a few days with you when I come to London?

Love Twine

[1] Poems by John Betjeman.

[Postcard]
Lausanne (wagon restaurant) Saturday 15.2.46

Dear Twinny,

Yesterday I lunched with Tzara,[1] who asked me to go to Vienna with him as a guest of the Government (?Russian); he is a Stalinist of the deepest dye.

Love Twin

[1] Tristan Tzara, the French Dadaist poet.

Monday 18.3.46   Bwlch Ocyn

Darling Twinney,

My God it was cold when we arrived back here: I put on twice as
many clothes as I ever wore in Switzerland, and yet I shivered for two
days. Now thank God it is warmer. But I must say coming back here
from Switzerland makes one realize what an austere life K and I lead.

I work hard on secretarial work for K, and now I am going to start
helping him with his book.[1] We have got (today for the first day) a
servant, who is obviously moronic, paralysed in one arm and hardly
understands any English! Mrs T. takes all morning to wash up three
plates, and the whole thing is very unsatisfactory. Did you hear K on
the wireless? He was awfully good I thought, but he was horrified by
what he calls his strong German accent, which he says he never
realized was like that. Can you come up the Thursday before Easter?
and stay till Tuesday.

Love
Mamaine

[1] *Insight and Outlook* (1949). It is dedicated 'To Mamaine for her remarkable patience with this book
and its author'.

Sunday 24.3.46   Bwlch Ocyn

Dear Twin,

Today is a wonderful spring day, very hot sun and curlews
whistling away. I have spent most of the morning wandering about
with my new camera taking photos of the house. I have discovered a
wonderful beach not far from here where there are all sorts of waders
to be seen at low tide; when you come up we must go into this. There
are lots and lots of tiny lambs in the fields, very sweet, skipping about.
I work jolly hard but today is a day off for me. I have twice seen
buzzards near here, the other day I saw about 6.

When oh when are you coming to stay?

Love
Twin

6 April [1946]. Guy and Alix de Rothschild,[1] Freddie Ayer and Celia to stay. Everything went well, the weather was good, K good-tempered, food edible.

[1] Baron Guy de Rothschild, head of the French branch of Rothschild's Bank, and his wife Alix. While he was returning from the United States during the war to join the Free French his ship was torpedoed and he spent five hours in the water before being rescued. At the time of the attack he had been reading *Scum of the Earth* and he vowed that he would make Arthur's acquaintance as soon as he reached England. His cousin Dr Miriam Rothschild brought them together and they became friends.

Monday 8 [April 1946]. Freddie, Celia, Arthur and I dined with the Russells. Russell was extraordinarily charming and witty. He said that as the Catholic population of America was increasing by leaps and bounds the States would one day be Catholic-controlled, and we should then be faced with a new choice: Stalin or the Pope.

Sunday 14 April [1946]. K has hatched a new plot to save the world from the Russians: Russell agreed to it so we (K and I) drafted a petition about it.

17 April 1946   Bwlch Ocyn

Dear Celia,

Life has been very pleasant here lately, the weather has continued good, and last Sunday it was really hot so we climbed up Snowdon taking our lunch. It only took 2 hours to get up and 2 hours to get down, but the last bit was rather steep and we were puffing and panting a good deal, indeed Arthur could hardly make it – I got up five minutes before he did! Imagine, we haven't had the slightest row since before you were here. It is like that, one has bad spells and good spells.

The Russells called on us one day and Russell said he did want to see more of us and to continue his discussions with Arthur, which we both thought very flattering. Then we dined with them at the Oakley, getting there 1 hour late as the clocks had changed and we didn't know it, and had a pleasant evening.

We also had a *very* good dinner party with the Sontags[1] and another man, it was extremely *gemütlich* and enjoyable. Sontag is really nice.

He went into ecstasies over my picture and said if I would paint one for him I could have any of his I liked, which is a very unequal bargain as his are quite good.

Love

Twin

[1] Mark Count Sontag von Sontag, painter, was an Austrian anti-Nazi refugee. He and his English wife Irene were close neighbours of Arthur's and Mamaine's and soon became good friends of theirs.

23 April 1946   Bwlch Ocyn

Dear Twinnie,

The weather continued good here and we have had quite a nice time. On Sunday we dined with the Sontags and Henry Winch (a huge man who lives at Portmeirion) at the Oakley, and when we took the Sontags back to their house I ran the car into a ditch (not at all my fault), so as nobody could think how to get it out we had to stay the night. The Sontags produced some tea and cider and bread and salami and we had a sort of midnight feast and it was great fun. They lent us a lamb, aged ten days, which we are bringing up on a bottle. When it becomes a ram we will give it back to them. It is very minuscule and sweet and runs about after one.

We dined with the Russells the other night and Russell told us a lot of hair-raising stories about American capitalism and reactionaries. I will tell you as many as I remember when I see you. He said he thought the Americans are at the stage the English were in 1868, for exactly the same thing happened to him in New York as happened to his father in Devon in 1868, viz., a scandal because he said there ought to be easier divorce and adultery should not be frowned on quite as much (in his father's case, he had suggested that the question of birth control might be investigated). After this Russell lost the job he was to have had in an American university and couldn't get any other one!

He told me that Lord Odo Russell, after having to cope with a drunken Shah of Persia at a party, remarked: 'La nuit, tous les Shahs sont gris.'

Peter Russell [Lady Russell] came in after dinner last night (Russell has gone back to Cambridge) and immediately had a blazing row with Arthur, as a result of which she left in a huff after five minutes.[1]

Love,
Tw.

[1] This row was over Arthur's insistence that the discussion of what Mamaine called his 'world-saving plan' should be strictly confined to Russell and himself. Peter Russell objected to this, and Russell upheld her objection. Arthur also expressed doubts as to whether she had reported Russell's views correctly.

30 April 1946   Bwlch Ocyn

Dear Twiney,

We lost our lamb completely, wasn't it sad, I think somebody must have pinched it.

I did two pictures, of which one was very nice. It was of the Sontags' house, and the Sontags adore it so I am swapping it against one of Mark's pictures. A very good bargain for me. They came to dinner the other day and we had great fun, as K tried to make some Austrian Knödels [dumplings] with jam in the middle and he and Sontag went off in the middle of dinner to cook them, but they swelled for some reason to the size of footballs and the jam quite disappeared and they tasted like cannon-balls – Kanonenknödeln, as Sontag said. This gave us all hysterics.

Everything is going well except for the mountains of correspondence Arthur gets which I have to answer – yesterday there were 21 letters and today lots more. It is a stinking bore. It makes us both frightfully bad-tempered.

Darkness at Noon has sold over 70,000 copies in France already and the Communists got Joliot-Curie to speak against it in public.[1] The MRP[2] weekly had front-page headlines the other day saying 'De Gaulle in his country retirement is reading *Le Zéro et l'infini*'. Lots more books by Arthur are soon coming out in France, so if we went over money would be no difficulty.

Love from
Mamaine

[1] Frédéric Joliot-Curie, the French physicist and joint winner with his wife Irène (*née* Curie) of the Nobel Prize for Chemistry in 1935, was a Communist. He won the Stalin Peace Prize in 1951.

[2] The Mouvement Républicain Populaire, the Gaullist party. *Le Zéro et l'infini* is the title of the French translation of *Darkness at Noon*.

12 June 1946   Bwlch Ocyn

Dear Celia,

Daphne and Henri have been staying here since last Thursday and are staying till Monday.[1] Daphne is very nice indeed and I get along fine with her. But K has been in an absolutely fiendish temper, so life has hardly been worth living. I told him before they came that if I felt like doing some housework while they were here he was not to interfere, as I refused to have Daphne spend her entire holiday cooking and washing up; so I begged K just for once to desist from his nagging on this subject. But has he done so? Not for one minute. I would go on strike if it were not that poor Daphne and Henri must eat. For once I really do feel that K is being rather selfish: it doesn't really interfere with his life in the least if I occasionally work in the kitchen, which is miles from his room, but he talks as if he couldn't have a quiet moment for clattering pots and pans. I am quite determined not to have K dictate how I shall spend every minute of my day, nor at what time of day I do which work, and I told him that if he wanted *me* to make an effort not to (for instance) make a fuss when he drives the car when he is drunk (which the other evening led to his ditching it), then he must make an effort himself not to nag me about every single meal we ever have.

However, this is only because he is doing hellish work correcting endless French versions of his books and play, and therefore can't get on with his book; by Thursday he should have finished and then his temper will improve – I hope; otherwise I shall soon retire to a mental home.

Love,
Twin

[1] Daphne Hardy, the sculptor, had been Arthur's companion from 1938 to 1943 and had translated *Darkness at Noon* into English. She married the graphic designer Henri Henrion.

4 August 1946   Bwlch Ocyn

Dear Celia,

I have done an awfully nice little picture, which I am terrifically
pleased with. It is of the house and mountains (more or less). God it is
pretty (I think).

Arthur came back [from a few days in London] on Thursday with
Brenda Willert[1] and her little girl Wanda, aged 10, who are staying till
tomorrow. Wanda is very sweet and very enthusiastic about
everything from the mountains to the dogs; she looks just like Paul.
Arthur loves her and is very good and funny with her. I got a chicken
and a duck and Brenda brought two pheasants, so we have had lots to
eat.

We went to Portmeirion the other night and after dinner had drinks
with the Russells in a private sitting-room they have. We have now
made up our row with them: they started the reconciliation by asking
me if we would have dinner with them (about a fortnight ago). If it had
been Arthur he would probably have said, yes on condition that you
take back everything you have ever said, or something, but needless to
say I didn't take a firm line of any kind, rightly or wrongly, but just
said yes, so now we are all palsie-walsies again. Well, we had a nice
evening, except that Peter provoked Arthur so much that half way
through he went off, and was discovered later haranguing against
women with Jim [Wiley] and Teddy Wolfe.[2] Russell talked to me
most of the time. Arthur said this was because he (Russell) has a crush
on me; he also has a theory that M . . . H . . . is in love with me, so I
said you have an *idée fixe* that every man not demonstrably homo-
sexual has a crush on me, and Arthur said, well it is so. Then he made
a little speech about how when he looked at all the other women he
knew (giving examples of some exceptionally frightful ones) he
couldn't help thinking that he had got a winner. Of course I was
terrifically pleased about this, which is why I am telling it to you. He is
very sweet these days and yesterday he said I was getting prettier every
day: wasn't it encouraging? Russell was very interested when I told
him about Freddie's appointment[3] and said how much he liked
Freddie and admired him as a philosopher. Today the Russells and
Conrad came over to tea.

Next weekend the Crossmans[4] are coming, in fact they are staying
for a week, and Teddy Kollek perhaps, Arthur's Palestinian friend.[5] I

do hope he will come as I like him so much. He brought back three little bottles of Lelong scent from Paris for me, which pleased me tremendously.

About Palestine, Arthur takes a pretty poor view, as you can imagine: he thinks the Government are trying to make it into a sort of Crown Colony and that they are antagonizing everybody in the process, including the Americans. But I have not discussed it much with him as it depresses him so much to think about it.

How funny Solly Zuckerman saying Arthur was a 'conspiratorial character', but it is the last thing he is.

You know all those stories about Arthur's Ma starving in Budapest and dreaming of sardines? Well when he asked her about it she said 'The chief thing was I got so sick of the monotony of the food – always the same old thing day after day.' So Arthur said 'What thing?' and she said '*Always* ragout of goose, and *always* done in the same monotonous way, with cream sauce'![6] She had got hundreds of food parcels and never said anything about it.

Oh I am enjoying life so much just now.

Love from
Mamaine

[1] The Hon. Mrs Paul Willert.

[2] James Wiley managed Portmeirion for Clough Williams-Ellis; he was the owner of Bwlch Ocyn. Edward Wolfe, the painter, lived at Portmeirion.

[3] A. J. (now Sir Alfred) Ayer had recently been appointed Grote Professor of the Philosophy of Mind and Logic at University College, London.

[4] Richard Crossman, Labour MP, was a member of the Anglo-American Palestine Commission, 1946. The following year he published *Palestine Mission*.

[5] Teddy Kollek was at that time trying to persuade the Labour Government to carry out the decisions of the Labour Party concerning the Jews in Palestine, free immigration for survivors from concentration camps being foremost among them. Arthur was able to help him by putting him in touch with a number of influential people in England, including Aneurin Bevan and Harold Macmillan. He is at present Mayor of Jerusalem, a post he has held since 1965.

[6] But see letter of 7.7.48.

10 August 1946   Bwlch Ocyn

Dear Twinnie,

The Crossmans are staying here, they arrived yesterday, and are both extremely nice. It is therefore very pleasant having them, except for the extra work, which may or may not turn out to be considerable. Arthur of course doesn't understand that when one has people to stay one simply has to do *something* about it, such as stewing some fruit and coping with food and shopping, and they have anti-social meals like tea which take hours, especially when one has to make coffee at the same time for Arthur. However, Mrs Crossman is a sweet person and very willing to lend a hand, she plucked a chicken and skinned a rabbit this morning, thus saving me hours of work, as I am so slow at that sort of thing. If only I could abandon some of my secretarial work while the Crossmans are here, but I am doing more than ever, since Arthur has discovered that he can write his book much quicker if he dictates it to me: I do not mind this except when I am worrying about other things.

Love,
Twin

16 August 1946   Bwlch Ocyn

Dear Twin,

The Crossmans are going tomorrow. It will seem extraordinary to be alone again. The other evening we all went over to dinner with Lady Lloyd George, as Basil Liddell Hart[1] was staying with her and wanted to see the Crossmans. Her house, which is at Criccieth, is absolutely beautiful from the front: a perfect little square house of white plaster with one mansard window in the middle, date 1700. At the back it is not so good. But it has a very nice library-sitting room with a lovely view over the bay, and a wonderful garden.[2] Lady Ll. G. (who was Lloyd George's secretary until she married him) is very charming and only about 45–50.[3] So this was most enjoyable. Another evening I took the Crossmans to dinner with the Russells – I may have told you this – and Russell made a sort of pass at me, which was pretty awful, though it only consisted of holding my hand and making fine speeches.

The story about K's book and the French CP may be roughly true, and he doesn't mind this being known. Sales have now reached 200,000.[4]

K has been in an unmitigatedly good temper for as long as I can remember; the Crossmans say the whole time that they simply can't understand why people say he is difficult and quarrelsome!

Love from
Mamaine

[1] Basil (later Sir Basil) Liddell Hart, strategist and author of numerous books on military history, including histories of the First and Second World Wars.

[2] The back of the house, including the library-sitting room, had been rebuilt by Clough Williams-Ellis, the creator of Portmeirion.

[3] She was in fact fifty-seven or fifty-eight.

[4] Celia had heard that 'the French Communist Party had orders to buy up every single copy of *Le Zéro et l'infini* immediately and they were all being bought up and there was no reason why it should ever stop being reprinted, so in this way K was being enriched indefinitely from Communist Party funds.'

Doggerel written by Mamaine to celebrate the anniversary of her and Arthur's arrival in Bwlch Ocyn. Dated 30 August 1946

POEM FOR AN ANNIVERSARY

Bwlch Ocyn, Manod, Blaenau Ffest-
Iniog, Merionethshire – you've guessed:
'Tis the abode of ARTHUR K.
One year ago this very day
K, who from sunnier climes had come
To make in CUMBRIA his home,
Arrived with MERMAID to begin
With her a life of care-free sin.

    ★ ★ ★

The antique house a little room contained
New-built when K his needs to JIM explained;
Here K did work; and, seeking not prosperity
Nor fame, penned volumes destined for posterity.
Also, as he sat writing at his desk,
Hastening to complete th'appointed task,
He found that here a slate, there a loose pane
Left him exposèd to the wind and rain.
But soon JOHN OWEN JONES and MR LLOYD
From dawn till dusk were steadily employed

Mending a broken window, door or slate
To give protection from the Welsh climate.

Often at evening, with his trusty Hounds
JOSEPH and DINA, K would tour the grounds
And from some pinnacle or knoll inspect
Th'autumnal hills with crimson fern bedeck'd.
Or, if in sorrowful mood, he'd take the car
All cares to banish in PORTMEIRION's bar,
Where he would find HENRY, TEDDY AND JIM
Eager to drink and talk and jest with him.
Apricot brandy, orange curaçao,
Gin, rum and whisky there did freely flow;
The Sage LORD RUSSELL would with K rehearse all
The arguments against the Universal,
Or, while they watched young CONRAD's lively antics,
RUPERT and K would talk about Semantics.
And when, the evening over, he did wing
His homeward way, K to himself would sing:

> *Biology, neurology,*
> *Aesthetics and psychology*
> *Ethics, epistemology,*
> *The art of terminology*

I'll study, and with them I do resolve
The riddle of the Universe I'll solve.

As time went by, attracted by its fame,
Many a pilgrim to Bwlch Ocyn came.
ROTHSCHILD and CROSSMAN, ORWELL, CELIA, FREDDIE,
BRENDA and WANDA, DOMINIQUE[1] and TEDDY.
Many a cheerful evening thus was spent
In eating, drinking, music, argument,
With DICK and ZITA, EMILY their poodle,
MARK and IRENE (and th'atomic Knoedel).

★ ★ ★

So from now on each year will ARTHUR K
And MERMAID drink together on this day;
Where'er they be, they will this happy date
With wine and song together celebrate.

[1] Dominique Aury, editor of the literary journal *La Table Ronde*. She translated two of Arthur's books into French.

22.9.46   Bwlch Ocyn

Dearest Twine,

Everything is going well except that Arthur is having difficulties with his passport, about which he anyway has an archetypal neurosis, having been through so much scum-of-the-earth stuff; I hope it will all come right, as his play is coming on in Paris at the beginning of next month and he does want to be there for some of the rehearsals –which have already started.

Today we got some lovely toys from Woolworths and have been playing with them most of the afternoon, outside. For the first time it isn't raining, or only occasionally. There are terrific floods every-where – yesterday afternoon the bridge over the river just before the Oakley (Maentwrog Bridge) was unnavigable (in a car)!

I can hardly wait to come to London to see you. I have an idea: we are coming in our car, and will have the October ration unused, so it might be the chance for us[1] to go to Suffolk for a weekend in it, *if* the weather improves slightly. It has been too awful here. Yesterday K and I went to our char's husband's funeral and were nearly blown and washed into the grave.

We had a lovely evening with the Hughes[2] at their house last night. Arthur got rather tight and on the way home along the sand (they live on the estuary opposite Port Meirion) he kept falling down; once he walked off a wall where he thought there were some steps and there weren't; then he disappeared into a hole, and shortly afterwards was seen up to his waist in the sea! It was all great fun.

The real object of this letter is to say that we have decided to visit K's mother[3] (who wants to meet me, bless her heart) on the evening of our arrival – Sunday – so I shan't be able to dine with you, but let's definitely do so on Tuesday.

Love from

M.

[1] I.e. Mamaine and Celia.
[2] Richard Hughes, the writer, and his wife.
[3] Arthur's mother had recently arrived in England from Budapest.

On 26 September 1946 Arthur and Mamaine drove to London.

Monday 26 Sept. [1946]. Dinner Crossmans with Arthur, Elizabeth (Crossman's secretary) and Teddy (Kollek) at the Moulin d'Or. Dick had just been having a long talk with Attlee about Palestine, in which it became apparent that Attlee didn't know much about it and wasn't even sure what he'd said on the subject. Dick thought he'd convinced Attlee, or that A. was anyway beginning to think, that he'd been wrong in rejecting the Commission's report and backing, or appearing to back (for Attlee didn't seem to realize that his statements had been thus interpreted) the policy of the Palestine Administration.

On 1 October Arthur went to Paris, and Mamaine joined him there on the 17th. She noted in her Diary on this date:

Paris by air. Met by Arthur, very depressed: we had some calvados in various cafés and later a wonderful evening dining in Montmartre, going to cafés and *bals musettes*, then to the Lapin Agile,[1] where I nearly cried with excitement at the songs they sang, and finally we ate oysters and drank Alsatian wine in a bistro called Victor on the Bd. de Montmartre at 4.30 a.m. Arthur is having a bad time with some of his old German friends who are unsuccessful and penniless and regard him as *arriviste*. But my enthusiasm got him in the end.

[1] A *chansonnier* where traditional French songs were sung.

Wednesday 23.10.46   Hôtel Montalembert,
                                                     Paris 7ᵉ

Dearest Twinnie,

   On Sunday we started the day at 10.30 a.m. in the Flore with Sartre
and Simone de Beauvoir, Kaplan (of *Partisan Review*), Teddy Kollek
and his wife, Sylvester and Pauline [Gates] and Arthur's friend Leo – a
not very successful *salade russe*.[1] Then Arthur and I lunched with
Sylvain [Mangeot] and Darsie Gillie[2] until 4.30, when I piped up and
insisted on having one hour off between lunch and dinner – Sperber,[3]
with whom we were dining, was calling for us at 6 – and we adjourned.

   We had a date with Sartre and S. de Beauvoir in Sartre's flat at
10.30. There was nobody else there except the four of us and we had a
most enjoyable talk. Sartre is simply charming and while he is talking
one feels that existentialism must be the thing, though always without
having much idea what it is. He and K get on very well and we both get
on like a house on fire with Simone de Beauvoir. We are dining with
them on Sunday, and I was supposed to be lunching with them and
the Camus today, but didn't go as I felt too tired.

   Tonight K and I had planned an evening *à deux* and Sartre had
given us seats for *Huis Clos*,[4] but we got involved with an old German
friend of K's, who got very drunk here and had a *crise de nerfs* and
could not be moved, so we got hold of his girl-friend and I talked to
her while K very angelically coped with the poor chap, till about 10. I
had had hardly anything to eat all day, but didn't feel hungry; K had
been drinking lots of brandy. We went next door to the Pont Royal bar
but could only get bread and honey, so I left K there with Simone de
Beauvoir and two other people and went to bed. But I can't sleep and
K shows no sign of coming in, which worries me rather as he must be
terribly drunk by now (3 a.m.), hence this rambling letter, as I can't
think what else to do.

   Of all the people I have met with K I like Sperber best (and Sartre).
Sperber is really fascinating, he is small and about K's age, with grey
hair, and vaguely like Pierre Blanchar in *Crime et Châtiment*; and I
am relieved to find that I get on well with him, as he is rather
frightening and one easily might not. Most of K's friends talk German
with him, including Sperber, so I am putting in a bit of practice on
that too, though I generally speak French.

K's play is coming on tonight and is going to be a God-awful flop, which is sad for him. He is worried about himself because he is always unhappy here, and is being 'psychoanalysed' by Sperber to the extent of pouring out his soul to him. I gather that there is not much hope for K, and I am really more worried about this than anything else. He says he is so much more of a manic-depressive – mostly depressive – than he used to be. But he still says I am his only prop, and though I have not been much good in that direction lately I intend to go on trying.

Oh the amount of money we have spent – I just don't know how much – but the food everywhere is wonderful.

Love,
Twin

---

[1] Harold Kaplan, American writer, was then working in Paris for the US Information Service and contributing regular Paris Letters to the New York literary periodical *Partisan Review* under the maiden name of his wife, Celia Scop. Sylvester Gates was a banker of wide intellectual interests; Leo Valiani an Italian writer and politician: see Introduction, letter of 19.2.48 and footnote to letter of 10.2.48.

[2] Sylvain Mangeot was foreign correspondent of Reuter's. Darsie Gillie was Paris correspondent of the *Manchester Guardian*, 1945–66.

[3] Manès ('Munjo') Sperber, novelist, essayist and Adlerian psychoanalyst. Arthur had first met him in Berlin in 1930 and had worked with him on the editorial committee of the weekly Paris anti-Stalinist journal *Die Zukunft* in 1938.

[4] Sartre's play, staged in England under the title *In Camera*.

26.10.46   Hôtel Montalembert

Dear Twinney,

I want to tell you all about our dinner with Malraux last night. He is very rich and has an enormous and flashy flat in the *banlieue* at Boulogne s/Seine; thither we went in a hired car. We were ushered in to a huge room, twice as high and three times as big as Drayton Gardens,[1] with two pianos made in one at one end (his wife is a professional pianist) and a large alcove for dining. It is horrible and very bare and *ungemütlich*. The walls are white and hung with large modern paintings and reproductions of Piero della Francesca (Malraux says he is more interested in art than in literature and thinks Piero della Francesca the greatest painter of all); the lighting, though indirect, is rather hard, and various graeco-buddhist, cretan and other sculptures, mostly oriental, stand about on pedestals. We were given some whisky but not invited to sit down, however I did so on one of the few chairs in the room; neither K nor Malraux sat down *once* during the whole evening, except for dinner.

The dinner started with oysters, and the Malraux had the bizarre idea of drinking whisky with them, till I said that this would very likely cause the immediate death of all, whereupon they suggested gin fizz! But in the end we drank Pouilly-Fuissé. Then roast chicken soaked in brandy with prunes and slices of lemon, then a very good chocolate cream.

Malraux is fascinating but not in the least attractive; K, who is rather in love with him, was very astonished and relieved when I told him this. He obviously has an ex-ophthalmic goitre, for his eyes protrude and he talks non-stop to the accompaniment of curious sounds at the back of his nose and throat – a kind of tic. He looks younger than he is (45) because he has no grey hair and is tall with a good figure. He talks in a kind of telegraphese which is very hard to follow; indeed I couldn't keep up at all some of the time, and K said nobody can, and he (K) has to take time off by not listening to Malraux's anecdotes, otherwise the effort of concentration is too great.

I need hardly say I enjoyed the whole evening immensely. Particularly fascinating was the spectacle of K and Malraux together – K unusually humble and hardly able to get a word in edgeways, Malraux obviously very anxious to impress K, show off to me, etc. His wife, who is young, not bad-looking and an excellent pianist, played some of the time, but Malraux never stopped talking to listen for more than a few seconds. He talked mostly about politics – he is *franchement Gaulliste* (as is K with certain reservations) – and a bit about painting and music, saying that if he had known I liked music he would have played me some very old music on records he had but had lent to somebody, and told a few stories about e.g. ancient kings, queens and generals, which were rather ostentatiously learned and difficult to follow (at this point K let up for a rest!). He gives the impression of being very inhuman and impersonal, and it is difficult to see how anyone ever establishes an intimate contact with him; this is also K's opinion, though he knows Malraux well and they get on with each other.

This morning K recovered from his flat lots of MSS, including one or two whole books, which he thought the Germans had taken![2]

Love,
Mamaine

[1] 102A Drayton Gardens, London, a small house which Mamaine and Celia rented for a few years from the age of twenty-one. The main room was a large studio.

[2] These included half of the German text of *Darkness at Noon*.

Friday 1 November 1946   Hôtel Montalembert

Dear Twinnie,

Just a line to tell you about my life in Gay Paree. Yesterday evening K and I went out to dinner with Sartre and Beauvoir and the Camus. We went first to an Arab bistro to eat some Arab food; then we went to a little 'dancing' with blue and pink neon lights and men with hats on dancing with girls with very short skirts. Here for the first time in my life I danced with K, and also saw the engaging spectacle of him lugging the Castor[1] (who has I think hardly ever danced in her life) round the floor while Sartre (who ditto) lugged Mme Camus. From there we went to a posh Russian night-club called Schéhérazade. Here one is plunged in almost total darkness and a great many violinists wander round playing soulful Russian music into one's ear. At first everybody except K was very much against this place, but after a while they all started to enjoy it no end. Sartre got very drunk almost at once, Beauvoir also got drunk and wept a great deal and K got drunk too (we drank vodka and champagne, both in large quantities). Francine Camus (who is extremely beautiful and nice) also got tight. Camus and I did not get drunk, though we nearly did.

It was very difficult to get K away from the Schéhérazade (where, incidentally, somebody pinched my notecase containing 13000 francs and £4, which I had given to K as the money was his); but finally at about 4 we got going and went to a bistro where we ordered *soupe à l'oignon*, oysters, white wine and various other things. By that time Sartre was simply roaring drunk, and awfully sweet and funny. He kept pouring pepper and salt into paper napkins, folding them up small and stuffing them into his pocket. He said that he had to give a lecture today at Unesco; Camus said 'Alors tu parleras sans moi', and

Sartre said 'Je voudrais bien pouvoir parler sans moi.' It was really great fun and everybody was terribly nice to me, they kept saying Mamaine must have a first prize for niceness and sweetness and everything else, and drinking toasts to me, and so on.

Finally we left (I suppose it was about 7, anyway it was broad daylight) and after that it took me till 8.30 to get K home – we wandered along the river, which looked incredibly beautiful with those lovely lemon-green and yellow poplars with their black trunks, and the houses reflected in the water and the early morning light, and K got very sentimental and wept profusely. We slept all day.

Love
Twin

[1] Simone de Beauvoir.

Arthur now returned to London and then to Wales. Mamaine remained in France and went for a short holiday with friends to the Pays Basque. She then spent a few days in London before returning to Bwlch Ocyn.

•1947•

20 January 1947   Bwlch Ocyn

Dearest Twinnie,

At last the weather has improved, and yesterday Arthur and I went
for a walk up Cnycht, taking our lunch. The day before we drove into
Bangor where we bought lots of food which one can never get here,
such as lobster, plaice, a chicken and some endives, thus spending a
fortune but having great fun. Also, wonder of wonders, we found a
shop where they sell Army cast-offs and I got a lovely green
mackintosh belonging to some women's service for 30/-, no coupons.
Imagine my joy, as I have wanted a mackintosh, which I really badly
need, for years. K also got a sort of blue battledress top for 12/-. I have
had no time this week to continue with my studies,[1] as it has been a
very bad week for correspondence and other chores.

Yr.
Mamaine

[1] Mamaine was studying psychology.

[?Early February] 47   Bwlch Ocyn

[The beginning of this letter is missing.]

. . . About our future plans: K is more and more keen on going to
America as soon as possible, and talks about it nearly every day. Thus,
last night we had one of our long arguments about and around this
subject, starting as usual with K running down the English, going on
as usual with me pointing out the horrors of American Capitalism and
the dangers of having de Gaulle in France, because once you get a
dictatorship, however mild, there's no guarantee that it won't get
worse; then K pointing out on the other hand the difference between
the dictatorships from Stalin through Hitler, Mussolini and Franco to
Kemal and Salazar and finally de Gaulle, who he believes is more or

less safeguarded from becoming very rabid by his character, about which K thinks one can now know something. The upshot of these arguments always is, that living in Europe means living in France or Italy, and in both these countries there is the dilemma between Communism and the opposite, and so on. My point of view is that as there probably remain only a few years in which life in Europe will be possible one should make the best of them. But the language difficulty for K is a real one – his English got much worse after he had been to France last time, and I'm afraid that our prospects of ever getting a house in France are receding, as I always supposed they would, to an ethereal dimness.

We haven't made any plans yet about our summer holidays – which will probably start in September if the book gets finished by then. For some reason I cannot get K really enthusiastic about the idea of going to Italy: he says he's too old to go to countries he doesn't know and whose language he can't speak, or some such balls. I simply can't bear it when people say they're too old to do this or that: it condemns one to behaving as though one were as old as they before one's time.[1] And if we don't go to Italy soon, when are we going to be able to go – especially if we go and live in the States, so far away? Now another thing: I think K may abandon his project of going (with me) to Palestine in November. Dick Crossman told him that he (K) would keep a better perspective for the next part of his Palestine novel[2] if he didn't revisit the country, and K thinks there is something in this; so do I.

K is turning poet in his middle age. I enclose a specimen of his translation, which as you will see does not indicate *beaucoup de talent*.[3] He now wakes me every day with a song, the words of which are as follows (composed by him):

> Rise and shine
> Sweetheart mine
> For the clock is striking
> Half past nine.

As it is usually half past eight, these words are generally omitted and only the tune (very out of tune at that) is sung.

Love,
Twin

[1] Arthur was then forty-one; Mamaine was thirty.
[2] *Thieves in the Night* (1949). Arthur had begun writing it in 1945.
[3] Nun hab' ich von früh bis spät amtiert
Und dabei ist es mir wieder passiert
Ich spürte das kleine, das dumme Vergnügen
Was abzumachen, was fertig zu bringen.

        (Theodor Storm)

I sat in my office from morning till dark
And again became victim of that ancient lark:
I felt that puny, foolish satisfaction
Of duty discharged, of completed action.

      (Translation by A. Koestler)

Wednesday 19.2.47   Bwlch Ocyn

Dearest Twinnie,

   I am spending this morning in bed in an effort to keep warm – I have to shiver all the rest of the day until dinner time when we get up a good fire in the sitting room.[1] K and I have now become so obsessed by the weather that we think of nothing else but how much longer it will last, how unlucky we are not to have more oil stoves, how lucky we are to have found one new one before both our old ones broke down, etc. We haven't of course had a bath for 3 weeks, and sometimes have a feeling that we may be beginning to stink. All water has to be fetched from K's lavatory, where it's so cold that the soap and nailbrush are all iced up (as K remarked last night, 'it's pleasantly cool in the peeing apartment'), and heated on the primus; the oil cooking stove doesn't work so I have had no oven for ages and probably never shall have again. But yesterday something very exciting happened: we got a food parcel from America containing 2 lbs of tinned butter and tinned bacon, a tin of salmon and lots of packets of noodle soup. Altogether this week we've been lucky about food, and about time too, for it does get one down sometimes, the eternal diet of corned beef, macaroni and tinned steak and kidney pudding. I am not writing all this to arouse pity in your breast, as I realize you are just as cold and badly fed as we are, but because there is nothing else to say about life at the moment.

Great News: we are having a telephone installed at last, and will probably have it by the middle of next week, so we can ring each other up! The number will be Blaenau Ffestiniog 55. Send me your hotel no. and we'll arrange a time and day to experiment.[2] It will make a great difference to our lives here.

I have very little work to do these days as we now palm off a great many of K's letters onto Peters[3] to write, so I spend my spare time either sleeping or studying psychology. You have no idea how boring most of the latter is: endless arguments between different schools about things like which behaviour patterns are acquired and which inborn, about the details of perception and so on; but that is chiefly because I have been concentrating on the history of psychology, and it is only very recently that these basic problems have to some extent been solved. I enjoy doing it, though.

K is sweeter than ever, he never gets cross, though he has lost weeks of work through the cold: he's really wonderful, and thinks all the time about whether I'm getting tired or cold or bored, and tries to remedy it by making me stay in bed and sacrificing all available stoves, or thinking up some treat or cooking the dinner or whatever it is. No matter how hard he's working he always stops if I want him to start the car or bring in a sack of potatoes or mend the electric kettle in a hurry. I now see that his constant niceness creates an atmosphere of mutual affection and helpfulness which is what makes us both happy; I am fairly hard-working myself too, and try to do things for K as he does for me.

M.

[1] The winter of 1946–7 was an exceptionally hard and long one.
[2] Celia had recently gone to live in Paris.
[3] A. D. Peters, Arthur's agent.

Thursday 18 March 1947   Bwlch Ocyn

Dear Twinnie,

Teddy Kollek turned up on Saturday for the night and he and K just went on drinking Armagnac which Teddy had brought. Consequently K had a bad attack of anxiety neurosis the next day; and of course it was a perfectly dreadful day, for although it was, at last, thawing, there was a 90-mile-an-hour gale, and as we were frying our dinner on the sitting-room fire there was a loud crash and half the big 17th-century west window fell in on us, followed by lashings of rain. But we are well off compared with most parts of England, where people are rowing into their local pubs in boats.

The weather is awful – now it has gone back to rain and fog. All the sheep and lambs are dying. We took in a day-old lamb yesterday and it did all right till this evening, we put it to sleep in the shed with Joe [their Welsh sheepdog] but this morning it is dying. K has been in a bad temper for about a week, but is improving now. Anyway I take his outbursts much more philosophically than I used to. He got furious the other evening because he wanted to go to the Oakley and I didn't seem enthusiastic. The fact is, I never have the slightest desire to go out because I enjoy the evenings so much at home, listening to music on the third programme and reading novels, and it seems to me a waste of time to sit at a bar drinking and talking to boring people; but I quite see that K, who sits all day in his tiny room, occasionally feels like an outing, especially as he likes drinking, so off we went in the end and had quite a pleasant evening.

Yours,
Twin

Tuesday 24.3.47   Bwlch Ocyn

Dear Twinnie,

On Saturday we had the Sontags and Jim [Wiley] to dinner and drank a lot, especially K, who consequently suffered from the usual remorse and anxiety the next day. The result of our blind was that we slept almost the whole day on Sunday and couldn't even stay up till 10.15, when I wanted to hear a piece by Elizabeth Lutyens on the radio, so I still don't know what it sounds like. Well, to cheer ourselves up we had the usual discussion about where to live when we leave here. I said I didn't see why we shouldn't continue to live in England and go to France and Italy frequently. But of course K is fed up with living in England, for various reasons. He said he thought the Communists might come to power in France within the next eighteen months – he believes anyway that there will be a showdown between them and the Right – and that if they do he feels the atmosphere in England will soon become intolerable. He wants us to apply now for immigration permits and simply go to the States when our lease here is up, without having looked round first. He says, after all, there is always Mexico to travel to when one is sick of highballs and frigidaires. Well, we shall see; it is all very gloomy, isn't it?, but I now have such an absolute mania about this climate that I feel I'd almost rather live in California than in North Wales. You can't imagine what it's like never to see the sun for more than half an hour at a time. Yesterday was a moderately fine day, fine enough for me to do some gardening, but even so it snowed from time to time and there was a cold wind. K insisted on our dining at the Oakley, to my intense boredom. He has by no means recovered from his bad temper yet, but I have adopted the line that I simply take no notice.

Love from
Twin

22.5.47   Bwlch Ocyn

Dear Twinnie,

Poor K is in despair, his brain is simply not functioning at all, and he still can't get back into his work; it is over 2 months since he was working properly so you can imagine the state he's in, and how impossible he is. But it will come all right soon no doubt.

Did I tell you I have acquired an upright Bechstein? It has not arrived yet. I need hardly say that K did his best to prevent me from getting it and make me get some obscure and not half as good German piano, which he thought was mechanically better suited to the Welsh climate! He was awfully sweet about helping me to get a piano, and thought I was being unbearably obstinate in not wanting the one he thought I should have, which I dare say I was. But after all I am to play on it, not he.

Love,
Twin

Monday 26 May 1947   Bwlch Ocyn

Dear Twinnie,

The weather is lovely and has been ever since we got back. Of course it's not really hot, but it is sunny, and the country looks quite beautiful. But I very rarely go out of the house, as I don't have time.

Arthur is still depressed and morose. This mood seems to have lasted a long time – nearly three months, I should think. However, we now work all morning and from about 4 till 7.30 on the book [*Insight and Outlook*], which is making slow and steady progress. Also, Arthur has to interrupt and write a London Letter and an article on the Future of Socialism for *P[artisan] R[eview]*. I wonder whether Camus is also going to do the latter? I know he has been asked. Have you any news of him, especially about whether there is any chance of his leaving *Combat*? I feel very worried about his health after what Francine said.[1]

Love from
Twin

[1] Camus did leave *Combat*, the most important daily newspaper to emerge from the Resistance, early in June 47, when he and most of the other original directors and editors handed it over to one of its founders, Claude Bourdet. He had spent three weeks in the mountains earlier that year for reasons of health, but he had no serious recurrence of the tuberculosis from which he had suffered since he was a young man until 1949.

27 May 1947   Bwlch Ocyn

Dear Twinnie,

Misi Polanyi has just been to dinner with us. Today he was more interesting and slightly less woolly than usual, mainly because K made him talk about two subjects in which he is interested, namely extra-sensory perception (and allied topics) and religion. For believe it or not, K has now only one interest: mysticism. He also believes in miracles. He had lunch in London with 2 psychologists, one a specialist in miracles,[1] and the latter said 'There is no logical reason not to believe in them'; this is also K's view. There is a man called Dr Rhine in Duke University, US, who has demonstrated that if one is throwing dice and *wants* a six to turn up, it will do so by a significant proportion above the laws of probability, thus proving the influence of mind over matter. K is feverishly reading about Yoga. Of course he is greatly disappointed.

Apart from this, he has not yet recovered his normal interest in life, and yesterday complained that he hadn't been able to experience real rapture about anything for over a year – e.g. to really enjoy listening to music. He complained that he seems to get little or no stimulation from people. He bewailed the collapse of all his heroes, and said how awful it was to have nobody to look up to. I quite agree about this. I then said (though rather by the way) that I thought that, just as my attitude to things was (according to him) a negative one, so was his attitude to people – that neither people nor life could be said, objectively speaking, to be very wonderful – all depended on one's attitude to them. The reason I said this was because I fear for myself, living with K – his cynicism and pessimism are so overwhelming, and besides he has such *mauvais caractère* he brings out all mine; I mean, we are both getting awfully bad-tempered.

However, I will say one thing for K: he has more moral courage than anybody I've ever met. He said so himself last night, but I've often thought it. As a rule, when one objects to his statements on politics, etc., one finds afterwards that one's objections are based on purely conventional ways of thinking and on a cowardly refusal to face the facts of the situation. At the same time, I combat a certain anti-rationalist trend in his thoughts which he doesn't realize he has.

Sorry for this boring diatribe. As usual here, I have a certain amount of time to think because I am so often alone, and generally use it to think of K or of the various moral problems concerning him. Again, I could write endlessly about this subject. But I don't dare to for fear of proclaiming moral principles which I won't ever live up to.

I will, instead, tell you about K's mother and Freud. K's mother, when she was here, one day said: 'I see you have all the books of that Dr Freund.' 'Dr Freund?' said K: 'Do you mean Freud?' 'Oh yes that's it,' replied his mother, 'I used to know him very well, when I was 17. *Er war sehr befreundet mit der Tante Lore* who kept a *pensionnat* for *jeunes filles* on the Franziskanerplatz in Vienna. *Ich habe alle seine Bücher bekommen*,'[2] she went on. 'What books?' asked K. 'Oh, one about *Jüdische Witze*, and one about dreams, another about psychoanalysis, or psychoparalysis as we used to call it – ha ha!' 'How did you come to see him?' 'Well, he was great friends with Tante Lore, and was very proud to be able to frequent our family (sic); and one day Tante Lore sent me to him, as I had a nervous tic.' 'So what did he do?' 'He massaged the back of my neck and asked a lot of annoying questions – anyway he was an *ekelhafter Mann, sehr unsympatisch*,[3] so I stopped going to see him.'

Then Arthur said 'That's very interesting – you know Freud was a very famous man.'

'Ach! but you don't know about my youth,' said his mother. 'I knew lots of famous people, many much more interesting than Freud – for instance . . .' and she cited several Austrian writers completely unknown to me but recognized by K as being third-rate writers of his young days! The idea of how different Arthur's, and consequently my, life would have been had his mother not stopped going to Freud is extremely fascinating.

Love,
Twin

[1] This was Eric Strauss, a psychoanalyst: he was a Catholic convert.

[2] 'He was a great friend of Aunt Lore, who kept a girls' boarding-school on the Franziskanerplatz in Vienna. I was given all his books.'

[3] A disgusting man . . . very dislikeable.

Saturday 31 [May] 1947   Bwlch Ocyn

Dear Twin,

Already things are going better. K and I really do get on awfully well. You know, we haven't seen a soul except ourselves and the tradesmen and Megan [their daily] since a fortnight, but we do not feel bored or get on each other's nerves.

What reaction, if any, to K's article on the New Trojan Horse which *Carrefour* reprinted from the *NY Times* almost a week ago?[1] We were rather dubious about having it done in France, as it is about France but written for Americans. It is very outspoken about the Communists. Now I do wonder why it is that even anti-Stalinist French writers like Malraux and Camus, who have done enough to put themselves definitely in the anti-Russian camp, don't go the whole hog while they're about it and denounce Russia *à haute voix* as K does.

They do, it is true, attack Russia indirectly but a) rarely by name and b) always with some counterbalancing attack on the US. This would be understandable if there was some chance of avoiding war by it, but the people in question must know there isn't, and that the only hope is to warn people what they're up against and what is going on.

Terrible things are going to happen in Palestine, I'm afraid; it seems to be all Bevin's fault.[2] Fancy leaving the country entirely to the military, who immediately say that journalists are non-essential and won't be given protection against terrorists. It looks as though they want to get witnesses out of the way before they start liquidating Jews in an attempt to wipe out terrorists. Do you know that so far they haven't caught *one* terrorist actually known to have killed somebody (39 people have been killed during the last year) and Gruener, the man they are going to hang, was merely involved in some sort of terrorist action.[3]

K *is* comic, the other day he wanted to go to London for 2 days and said he absolutely refused to leave me here alone. I said why on earth? and he said, Oh you might catch cold!! Even when I'd pointed out a) that I hadn't done so for a year and b) that there was no more reason why I should do so with him away he was adamant. The fact is of course he worries himself to death about everything. I quote this example to show you how neurotic he is about it. Can you imagine anything more absurd?

Yr

Twin

[1] *Carrefour*, a weekly journal and one of the few anti-Stalinist left-wing papers.
[2] Ernest Bevin was Secretary of State for Foreign Affairs, 1945–51. He was hostile to Zionism.
[3] Arthur sent Gruener a telegram from Bwlch Ocyn urging him to appeal for clemency, but he refused to do so and was hanged.

3 June 1947   Bwlch Ocyn

Dear Twinnie,

It is still lovely and hot here, though overcast and thundery a good deal of the time. This latter aspect of the weather gets K down, but I am too delighted by the heat to mind about it.

Everything is very peaceful, and K's brain seems to have regained some of its former properties, in any case he is writing in a missing chapter of the book at great speed, which gives me some time off.

If you see Camus please tell him that I spoke to Arthur's agent [A. D.] Peters about *Caligula*, and he is going to get the translated MS from Jamie[1] and write to Camus when he has done so. He is very willing to take it on, and is I believe particularly good about plays. Tell C that Peters is an extremely nice and efficient man whose opinion e.g. about actors can be trusted. When will *La Peste* be out?

It is impossible for me to concentrate on this letter as I had hoped because K is wandering up and down outside my window grinning to himself, and keeps stopping to tell me some joke and ask me whether I think it's funny enough to put into his book.

Love,
Twin

[1] Hamish Hamilton, the publisher.

Monday 16.6.47   Bwlch Ocyn

Dear Twinnie,

Yesterday Beryl and Arthur[1] came to tea, with Mary Roberts,[2] and afterwards we went down with them for dinner at the Oakley. The whole thing was rather a strain owing to the usual uncooperativeness of Arthur, who doesn't seem able or willing to discuss any subject on earth except language.[3] K made a great and noble effort, and at the end of the evening he tried to draw Arthur on the question of Jews, on the point: if you are a Jew who believes that Jews who want to be assimilated should be (as do both the Arthurs), but if you are with people who make anti-semitic remarks, do you or not feel bound to say that you are a Jew?, because if you want to be assimilated, i.e. not to be singled out from other people by your Jewish descent, it is obviously going the wrong way about it to emphasize the latter; but on the other hand, one cannot help (said K) suspecting oneself of moral cowardice if one doesn't, and feeling that in some ways one should. This seemed to me quite a reasonable problem, put by K without emotional bias; but needless to say Arthur W. simply said he didn't see the problem as he never felt the slightest necessity to say anything on such occasions. He said people have as much right to dislike Jews as to dislike potatoes, but obviously this is in some way begging the question, which is, that anti-semitic people are often anti-semitic for reasons entirely of prejudice and it is very harmful, neither of which is true of people who dislike potatoes. In this argument, as in all others, the Waleys, especially Arthur, show it seems to me a complete lack of sense of reality. For instance, though we kept off all questions connected with Russia, we learnt from Mary Roberts that they hardly think the Hungarian business[4] constitutes any problem, and that Beryl said the Americans were a much greater danger, because of their (economic) infiltration into the Far East (i.e. Bali and Java where Beryl wants to go). Now how anybody in their right minds can compare economic infiltration as a danger with police infiltration is a mystery to me.

Last week a man called Ciliga[5] came to stay two nights with us. He had written to K (whom he didn't know) asking if he could meet him, so we asked him up. He is apparently very well-known in anti-Stalinist Leftist circles, because he was formerly leader of the Yugoslav CP and was the first man to oppose Stalin from the Left. He was in prison in Russia for two or three years, and in Siberian exile for another three, then was released because (a) he had an Italian passport, in those days a help, and (b) they wanted to use him in an attempt to implicate Trotsky (it was just before the trials) by giving him messages for Trotsky. Ciliga took these messages in good faith, though he was no Trotskyist; but luckily it dawned on him in time that they had been given him by an *agent provocateur*. Then during the war he was in a Yugoslavian concentration camp, where he was at one moment put into a category which was due to be killed by being hit on the head and falling into a grave, and then being covered with quicklime ('S'ils nous avaient fusillés, ça ce n'est rien,' he remarked, for he is a wonderful man who takes everything including being shot absolutely for granted); but he was reprieved for some reason so has survived. He is a peasant from Pola, in Istria (?), and K and I took a great liking to him. He ate the most enormous amount and talked non-stop, in atrocious French, but everything he said was very interesting.

Love from

Twin

Couldn't you come up soon? I'd pay half your railway fare.

[1] Arthur Waley, the oriental scholar and translator of texts from classical Chinese and Japanese literature, and his lifelong companion Beryl de Zoete, expert on Balinese and Indian dancing. Arthur Waley was Jewish.

[2] Mary Roberts ran the Oakley Arms.

[3] An unfair comment: Arthur Waley had an exceptionally wide range of interests and was usually willing to talk about them. But there were times when he was not willing to talk at all.

[4] In a move to split the Hungarian coalition government of the Smallholders Party, the Socialists and the Communists, and so engineer a takeover by the Communist minority before the withdrawal of Soviet military forces, the Soviet Union had accused the Prime Minister, Ferenc Nagy, a moderate member of the Smallholders Party, of an anti-republican conspiracy and he had been obliged to resign. This was in contravention of the Yalta agreement not to interfere in the internal affairs of states under Allied control.

[5] Anton Ciliga, one of the first Yugoslav dissidents. Author of *The Russian Enigma* (1940), first published in France in 1938 under the title *Le Pays du grand mensonge*. He turned up to stay with Arthur and Mamaine bringing as his only luggage a briefcase containing one detachable collar.

There is a gap in the letters here because Celia did visit Mamaine and Arthur in Wales, and in August Mamaine went to London.

10.9.47   Bwlch Ocyn

Dear Twin,

We have been working at very high pressure since I got back from London – from 9 in the morning or earlier till 8 or 9 p.m., at top speed, with a 2-hour break for lunch. At the end of the day we are both quite *gaga* and conversation regresses to monosyllables repeated on a sound-association basis. We hope however to get the book ready for the typist by the 20th. We now propose to spend a week in Paris and then return here. At one moment I thought the whole trip had fallen through; I volunteered to give it up – you can imagine with what feelings – I'll explain how it happened when I see you. In Paris I shan't be free for one second to see any friends whom K doesn't feel like seeing, so I look forward to the trip with quite a lot of apprehension; still, it is better than nothing. Italy seems too far to go for a week, and we don't want to stay away for a month as we're going abroad again in December.

Love from
Twin

Paris, 1 October 1947. Dinner Malraux. We met them in the bar of the Pallas-Athénée (an enormous luxurious bar full of glamorous *demi-mondaines* in extravagant clothes). Malraux spent twenty minutes at least studying *La Semaine à Paris* and finally decided that we should dine at the Auberge d'Armailhès. We drank vodka and ate caviare and blinis and balyk and *soufflé sibérienne*, and M. got very tight, so that it was even more difficult to understand what he was talking about than usual. However we did understand him to say that in using his reputation as a man of the Left to help the reactionaries he was taking a big gamble, in which he believed he would succeed; but if he didn't (i.e. if de Gaulle, once in power, did not act as Malraux thought he should) he would feel he had betrayed the working class and there would be nothing left for him but to *se faire sauter la cervelle*. When K said 'What about the General's *entourage*?' Malraux replied 'L'entourage du Général, c'est moi.' We thought this rather silly, but were later told that Malraux is in fact the only man who dares to give de Gaulle advice, who sees his speeches before he makes them, etc. Towards the end of the evening he started talking the most awful nonsense, particularly when he asked K about his psychology book, and then, instead of listening to what K said, started telling him the meaning of certain psychological terms, all of which he got wildly wrong. At this point K mentioned Bergson, whereupon Malraux went right off at a tangent and started talking at full speed about Bergson; after a bit he said 'Je suis le plus grand philosophe du monde.' 'Do you mean *you* are, or are you quoting Bergson?', asked K bravely. 'Non, c'est moi qui parle,' replied Malraux – but we didn't feel quite sure, and I don't think he knew himself by that time, what he was talking about. He then turned to me and asked me whether, as *une anglaise*, I thought that T. E. Lawrence had '*de l'accent*'. I said I didn't know what he meant by that, and he said, no, I do use the word in a rather

58

special sense. He explained, but in such a way that both K and I understood different things: I thought – and still think – that he was talking about Lawrence's *style*, K understood a reference to personality or something else, I forget what. Malraux also told us some rather long historical anecdotes about ancient Persian princesses and princes which I remembered his having told us on a previous occasion; but as K always seizes such opportunities for a short rest, he still hasn't heard them. Madeleine [Malraux] was very beautiful and charming.

8 October 1947. Dinner *chez* Camus, we all took food and drink, and K and I, after careful marketing in the rue de Buci, brought a cold roast chicken, a lobster and some champagne, as although there were lots of other delicious things to be had, we felt French people would not think them worth eating. However we did take a few shrimps and clams for ourselves, which indeed everybody else spurned, except Mlle Labiche.[1] The other guests were: Sartre and Simone, Kappy and his wife, and Celia. K started talking about the 'iron curtain' which has separated the French intellectuals from Anglo-Saxon culture since 1939, and said what a pity it was that, through no fault of their own, they were ignorant of all the latest developments in e.g. psychology, biology, neurology; also, most important, that they were unacquainted with the semanticists and in particular had never read *The Meaning of Meaning*.[2] We told how we'd met Merleau-Ponty's wife, who is a doctor and helps at brain operations, in the Mephisto, and K had asked her whether she'd ever seen an operation on the third ventricle and whether she knew about Forster's syndrome,[3] and how she'd obviously never heard of it; and said we found it curious that Merleau-Ponty, who writes books about psychology, shouldn't have primed his wife to look out for this. Sartre and Camus expressed polite regret at their ignorance, but didn't sound very sorry about it; they said they didn't think ventricles existed in the brain, only in the heart; and they further thought that psychology and the empirical sciences had nothing whatever to do with philosophy, and consequently they weren't interested in them. I was not surprised at this, having already been told by Camus (who got quite worked up about it) that nothing of any interest had ever come out of laboratory work, and that it was particularly unlikely that anything worth while had ever been done in American laboratories.

Later in the evening, when all had drunk quite a bit and the Kaplans had left, Sartre started attacking Kappy in violent terms. He accused Kappy of being anti-semitic and anti-negro and anti-liberty. Of course we knew he wasn't any of these things, and K got so cross that he let fly at Sartre and said who are you to talk about liberty, when for years you've run a magazine which was *communisant*,[4] and thus condoned the deportation of millions of people from the Baltic States and so on? Sartre was a bit taken aback by this, and as the atmosphere had anyway become intolerable we left. Afterwards we could not quite think how we had got from the subject of Kappy to this very violent attack on Sartre, and K wrote Sartre a letter of apology, to which Sartre replied with a very nice letter; so all was well.

[1] Suzanne Labiche, later Mme Agnély, was Camus's secretary from 1949 to 1960.
[2] By C. K. Ogden and I. A. Richards. It was first published in 1923.
[3] Forster, a neuro-surgeon, had a patient who broke into a manic flight of words, mostly punning and rhyming, whenever the third ventricle of his brain was stimulated.
[4] *Les Temps Modernes*, published by Gallimard.

9 [October 1947]. Had drinks with Petitjean,[1] Camus, Sperber and le Père Bruckberger[2] in aid of K's campaign, which of course is doomed to failure, to de-atomize the *hommes de bonne volonté* of the Left. While we were still alone with le Père Bruck, he told us the following story about [François] Mauriac and Camus. Bruckberger and Camus were the only two writers to resign from the *Comité des Écrivains*[3] after the Liberation, when it became merely a communist instrument. One day at a dinner, or meeting, Mauriac, who was anxious to get Camus back into the Comité, said to him 'Why did you resign?' Camus said 'It's for me to ask you why you didn't resign – and I'll tell you why you didn't: because you were afraid.' Mauriac said 'You're quite right.'

As K has by this time become obsessed by the question of sins of omission (the French intellectuals who don't open their mouths against the Communists and Russia) he said to le Père Bruck that it had occurred to him that Original Sin really meant sins of omission.

[1] Armand Petitjean, writer, a friend of Arthur's.
[2] Father Raymond-Léopold Bruckberger, Dominican, author and editor. He was formerly active in the Resistance and was a friend of many of the writers who frequented the district of Saint-Germain-des-Prés.
[3] The Comité National des Écrivains started as a clandestine organization during the occupation. Camus resigned from it in 1944 because of its pro-communist orientation.

10 [October, 1947]. Lunch Calmann-Lévy,[1] Pierre Bourdan, Sperber, Raymond Aron.[2] Talk mostly about the usual subject, viz., whether if de Gaulle comes to power it will help the Communists by pushing over to their side hesitant elements, or whether he will be able to crush the Communist fifth column or seriously weaken it, e.g. by replacing Communist cadres in factories. Bourdan thought the former, K the latter; Aron said it depends how much time he has in power.

In the evening we went with Aron to the [Guy de] Rothschilds to meet Walter Lippmann,[3] but he had to leave almost at once, so there was not time for much talk. K said, the main problem is, if war is inevitable should one make a preventive war, and if not why not? He said that personally he was convinced it was inevitable, but wouldn't advocate a preventive war because of the chance that one might be wrong. Lippmann said he didn't think war was inevitable. He said he thought our aim should be to get the Red Army out of Europe and behind the 1945 frontier line and to keep it separate from the Comintern. Aron said, even if you get the Red Army out of Poland half the officers in the Polish Army are really Russians. Lippmann said it depends whether one believes in national resistance. Aron said there can be no resistance against a dictatorship.

[1] Arthur's publisher.

[2] Pierre Bourdan, leading political commentator, broadcaster, journalist and junior minister in Ramadier's government. Raymond Aron, one of France's most distinguished political thinkers and academics. He was then writing for *Le Figaro*.

[3] Walter Lippmann, the influential American columnist.

4.XI.47   Bwlch Ocyn

not a proper letter – one will follow in a few days, if I have time.

Dear Twinnie,

I dreamed last night that you were in a nursing home, the owners of which were secretly poisoning you, so that you became iller and iller without suspecting the cause; also, they hid you; but I managed to discover you, and was about to call the police in to liberate you, but uncertain whether I should be in time, when I awoke, and read a few pages of Proust by candle-light to calm my anguish. As I have not heard from you for ages, I wonder if this dream is true? I wish you would write to prove it false.

Did I say, do get Edmund [Wilson]'s new book *Europe without Baedeker* and read about me: unfortunately it is a bad book so my immortality is not assured; but perhaps that is after all just as well, particularly as he very clearly hints that I was his mistress, which God forbid! I am called 'G'.

I am enclosing an article by Burnham (which *please return*) and a beautiful and instructive article about the dances of BEES.

Love from
Mamaine

4.XI.47   Bwlch Ocyn

Dear Celia,

The point I wish to make clear is that the two fields may be compared to two steps of a staircase, of which in this case one is higher than the other; or rather to two ascending notes in the scale. Perhaps we shall simplify our meaning (for it is important to understand this point, even at the risk of pedantry and tediousness) if we say that the two juxtaposed contexts, which, as we have already seen (cf. Chapter x) are connected by a junctional concept (we shall have occasion to return to this point in more detail in Chapter xx), must, to produce the desired effect, be situated on an ascending hierarchy, of which the peak represents the integrative values of the archetype in question, while its base represents the pre-verbalized symbolic image in the 'collective unconscious'. In other words, the 'upper' or 'higher' of the two fields, as defined by its selective vector (cf. Chapter xxx), must be nearer to the peak of the hierarchy than the 'lower' operative field.

I hope you like the above passage, because it is rather typical of Arthur's book [*Insight and Outlook*],* the final pages of which we are now correcting at the rate of 5 pages a day.

He is also writing that piece he thought of in Paris, in which Le Petit Vieux Ivan Pavelitch, leader of the Existenchiks, and Simona Castorovna and other friends play their parts. It will be fairly long, about 8,000 words I should think – would it be at all in the style of your magazine?[1] It is pretty violent politically, but will make the fame of any mag which publishes it; however better not say anything about it to your people, except very vaguely, as K has by no means decided who he would like to print it. The main trouble is, however, who will? So you might let me know your thoughts on this.

I am afraid he is starting a period of very bad temper, but perhaps it will blow over. I just try to shut my eyes and ears and withdraw into my shell. I feel pretty dismal and there is no news, which is why I haven't written for so long (except today, earlier). I long to hear about your life, so do write soon.

Yours
Twin

* no it's not as bad as that really!

[1] Celia was collecting material for *Occident*, a tri-lingual magazine of arts and letters published in Paris for which she was working as editorial assistant.

11.11.47   Bwlch Ocyn

Dear Twinnie,

We had (you will be surprised to hear) quite a pleasant evening with the Crawshay [-Williams] and the [Richard] Hughes at the Oakley (Mary [Roberts] has left and there are new people there who seem nice). Yesterday I drove over to the Hughes' house (which is on an estuary opposite Port Meirion) to take K's French story for Diccon's [Richard Hughes] secretary to type. To get there one has to walk for at least 20 minutes across fields, but when you do arrive it is rather beautiful, right on the sands and with a big view of the mountains, sands, sea and islands. That brings to an end the account of the events in our life since I last wrote.

I am now in pretty good form, and K and I are again getting on well, though the poor fellow has been having slight gastric flu or something (maybe I've got it too) and is consequently pathologically irritable and flies right off the handle several times a day. He is very apologetic about it and says I am angelic; but if so it is because I know he can't help it. It is this tranquil life which has, as I knew it would, restored my morale. We work every morning from 9 to 1 together on K's book;

from 1.30 to 2.30 or 3 I read and sleep; I then sometimes take the dogs for a short walk, do a few chores in connection with dinner and other things, make tea, and subsequently work alone on K's book or his mail; if I succeed in getting this finished by six (which I don't often, especially as I go shopping twice a week, which takes half the afternoon) I play the piano till 7; I haven't had time to practise since I've been back, but am plodding slowly along and do terrifically enjoy playing. At 7 I stop work and do chores: feeding dogs, cooking, laying the table, fixing stoves and fires if not already fixed; at 8 we eat and about 10 or 10.30 I go to bed. In this way I have always more to do than I have time for, and consequently the days go smoothly and quickly – altogether the whole thing is most satisfactory. As I have no desires, at any rate concrete ones, I don't think much and am having a rest from my usual mental and moral struggles.

It seems likely that UNO will come to *no* decision about Palestine at this session, in which case K and I won't go there. So *if* you hear of a house in Provence, or indeed anywhere else in France except the North, which we could take for Jan and Feb please let us know. K would quite like to go near Paris, but I don't want to and am still propaganding for Italy, as I think it's silly to go to France when Italy's just *half* as expensive.

K and I have just been reading Philip's book[1] and like it very much – K thinks it is a 'glorious failure', I think it is rather brilliantly written, don't you?

Do tell us exactly what de Gaulle is going to do, and what is going to happen in France.

Love
Twin

---

[1] Philip Toynbee's novel *Tea with Mrs Goodman* (1947).

Tuesday 18 November [1947]   Bwlch Ocyn

Dear Twinnie,

I never seem to have much time to write these days, and haven't now, but a few lines will serve to keep you *au courant*. It is extremely cold here, and has been snowing; the mountains are covered with snow. Though we have acquired some new heating pipes and stoves it seems quite impossible to keep the house warm – it is just icy. I don't think I shall ever be able to play the piano again without my fingers dropping off with cold, because the big music room really is quite unheatable; but as I never have time it probably doesn't make much difference.

I am terribly depressed, chiefly because life with K seems to get more and more difficult. Lately he seems to have been nagging more than usual; perhaps not; perhaps I am less able to react well than formerly. The dogs are a constant source of trouble, and I have vengeful dreams of drowning them all, which of course I shan't carry out. K now refuses to let them come into the house except in the evening, and I am very sorry about this because I love having them with me when I am working alone, and think it very beastly for them to be alone out of doors all day; dogs hate being alone without people for long. When I told K I had specially begged to be allowed a pet dog, in the form of Jenny, he said all right I could have Jenny indoors – but as Joe is usually away in the village that is terribly unfair on Pupsie, who looks in at my window crying pitifully, so I finally put Jenny out and then they are alone and so am I. Yesterday we had a great shouting match and I threw a saucepan full of mashed potatoes at a wall, but for one thing I disapprove of this sort of thing, and secondly it wears one out emotionally and gives one a headache. At the same time I am getting on well with K, really, and he is not in a really bad mood. I do have moments of feeling quite gay and happy, but they are usually soon hit on the head by some new row from K.

It now seems almost certain – in fact I think quite certain – that we won't go to Palestine after Christmas; for one thing they have refused to renew K's passport. I don't know where we will go, though.

I am reading a very good *Histoire des Jacobins* by Gérard Walter. He has apparently written books about Robespierre, Mirabeau, the Terror and lots of other subjects connected with the French Revolution, and I recommend this one because it is obviously very accurate.

I'm sorry this is such a boring and gloomy letter. As a matter of fact life is not so bad as I make out, but it is not so good as I could wish either. Anyway, I enjoy more than anything hearing about your colourful life, so do tell me about it as often as you get a chance.

You can tell your boss that your excellent approach was responsible for K's giving his piece to *Occident* (or don't they want it?) because I'm sure that's true.[1]

> Love
> Twin

[1] See second letter of 4 November 1947. Arthur's fragment about French 'fellow-travelling' intellectuals was printed in *Occident* in 1948 under the title 'Les temps héroïques'.

Monday 24 November 1947   Bwlch Ocyn

Dear Twinnie,

Yesterday evening we went to the Oakley and played poker with the new owners – a young man and his wife called Johnston. K loves poker and finds it very relaxing, and he needs mental relaxation, so I foresee a good many poker evenings in store for us. Tonight we have to go and dine with Henry Winch. It is terrible, I suppose, but I just dread going out here – it seems such a prize waste of time to sit for five or six hours doing something which bores one (I quite like poker, but not much) when one could be reading one of the many books one wants to read but never has enough time for. I know full well K would never spend one single evening with friends of mine who bored *him* – but one doesn't apply the same standards to men as to one's self, does one? And I think quite rightly, for I believe there is a justice of quite another kind beneath the apparent injustice of the lives of women with men, in which the latter always do what they want and never do what they don't want. But I can't be bothered to explain what this is now. In the meantime, one just has to suffer and try to look as though one's enjoying it; and certainly two evenings a week isn't too bad (three this week); but just at the moment I have an extra strong craving to read, and there are simply dozens of books I am dying to read.

I don't know whether you have seen in the French papers that the British have sabotaged by every means in their power the UNO decision to partition Palestine, so that it's not even certain whether the partition idea will get enough votes in UNO,[1] and if it does the British will arrange things in such a way that the Arabs get armed (by them) and the Jews are prevented from fighting till the last minute.

K is now thinking of going to France and perhaps Italy for the *Observer*, who have asked him to go to Germany for them; but I have no idea whether they will want him to go to France instead. If so, that would admirably solve his problems, as he could spend two months in France and Italy with some *raison d'être* and without feeling he was just sitting about eating and drinking while people were starving and cutting each other's throats. Until more definite plans are made I am not thinking much about what to do myself, except that I have at the back of my mind the idea that I might go and stay with the Joyces [see p. 78] in Trieste for a bit if they can have me. I don't think I want to go to Paris with K, but I have not said this yet and he may not go there himself anyway.

Do you think there will be a war soon? If not, why are the Russians letting the French and Italian CPs play their trump cards, which once they've done without success they will no longer be in such a strong position?[2] K thinks perhaps it is just the usual Russian way of abandoning the Comintern in other countries, to which they have never given adequate support. But it *might* be that the Russians don't mind risking another general war – which they would do in the case of civil war in France and possible American intervention. What do you think? Do let us know what people in France think of the present developments there: find out what *le farfelu* A[rmand] P[etitjean] thinks, if you see him and can understand what he says.[3]

Sorry I always write such gloomy letters – I *am* awfully gloomy because I am so worried about my future life with K, which I am determined to make a success of if it's humanly possible. But all sorts of things happen to change one's life in one way and another, don't they?, and I suppose that after a year or two of gloom some change for the better may occur.

Love
Twin

[1] It did, by 33 votes to 13, with 10 abstentions, including Britain.
[2] The Communist Party was organizing widespread strikes in France, and to a lesser extent in Italy.
[3] *Farfelu* was an adjective then in common use among Gaullists. It derived from André Malraux's short book *Royaume-Farfelu* (1928) and may be roughly translated 'amiably crazy'. Armand Petitjean spoke in an intense and involved way.

Dear Twinnie,

Further to my letter of yesterday (as they say), Henry Winch's dinner turned out to be great fun: it consisted of us and the Sontags, and a great deal of food and drink was consumed. The end of the evening was like the end of all evenings where K is present, namely a struggle between me, on behalf of myself and the rest of the company, and K, on behalf of himself, in which I try to persuade him to go home and he refuses. I very much sympathize with K, because the fact is that he simply has an Eastern constitution, like Russians, Hungarians and Slavs always do, which makes him not only able but anxious to stay up ALL night once he gets going; and of course he is generally frustrated by the Westerners, who want to go to bed at a normal hour. As for me, since my constitution is in this respect the opposite of K's, I suffer from midnight on like Rubashov after several weeks of third degree. In vain I think of T. E. Lawrence and remember his endurance as he paced the desert on his camel for days without sleep (but he suffered hell doing it): there always comes a time when I feel I just can't stick it any longer.

I was, however, consoled last night by the fact that in the course of the evening I made a discovery, which, if true, is, as you will see, of great significance for us. It is rather difficult to explain as you haven't read K's book, but I will try.

You know K has this theory about the Tragic and the Trivial planes, the former consisting of all sorts of ultimates and irreducibles, the latter of everyday life and habit. He points out in his book that it does occasionally happen, though it is exceptional, that people are suddenly forced to live for long periods more or less on the Tragic plane: this was the case with RAF pilots who faced great danger and imminent death all the time. In order to ease the strain, they so to speak projected a trivial structure on to the Tragic plane, by calling fatal accidents by slang names and referring to their best friend's death as 'he's had it' or 'he's been'. In this way they managed to trivialize even death, and thus were able to stand the strain. Now K believes that the artist is a person who lives on the line of intersection between the two planes, but instead of projecting the Trivial on to the

Tragic, as the pilots do, he does the opposite, namely sees the Trivial in the light of the Tragic, that is to say in terms of the underlying realities of the trivial experience (I don't know whether I explain this well enough).

Now my discovery is – if it is a discovery – that the definition, which we have always sought but never found, of what exactly makes some people 'deeper' than others, is precisely that they live nearer to the intersection-line of the Tragic and Trivial planes than other people, and are more often aware of the tragic perspective of ordinary events, or, if the word tragic seems misleading, of their deeper, more archetypal significance. It is only because I never take the things that happen to me at their face value, but always see them in terms of my life as a whole and what I take to be its significance, that I can keep going and take an interest in life at moments like the present when everything seems to be going wrong. Well what do you think of this theory? Does it seem to explain anything?

Love
Twin

2 December 1947   Bwlch Ocyn

Dear Twin,

Just a hurried line to say that the *Observer* men, who are here now, have agreed with enthusiasm to Arthur's plan, so DV we shall come to France some time early in Jan, with the car, and then probably go on to Italy. Isn't it WONDERFUL? Don't, however, say anything about it to anybody until later, in case some awful hitch arises.

Life has changed for the better, as you can imagine, since the UN agreed on Partition in Palestine. We had a great day of rejoicing and celebration and drank solidly all day, including some champagne which I procured. On the Tragic plane K and I always get on admirably – it is only the Trivial plane which sometimes gets us down!

Love
Twin

12 December 1947   Bwlch Ocyn

Dear Twinnie,

Delighted to hear things are looking up for you. I hope it lasts. For me too they are definitely better, in fact very good. We are working in the hall on the big table, in front of the fire, on the final MSS with final corrections – it should be finished within a week. However, we work long hours so I have no time for more than this scribble.

The Crossmans are coming for Christmas and will stay a week, which I greatly look forward to. They are going to bring a turkey and I have ordered a goose, so we shall have a great feast.

We have a RADIOGRAM with automatic change: it arrived yesterday, rather bashed about, and K immediately accused me of having broken it while unpacking it – which actually was quite impossible and made me very cross; but he later withdrew the accusation. It is wonderful, we can now listen to the 3rd programme with ease, and at last can play the gramophone in comfort.

Love,
Twin

19 December 1947   Bwlch Ocyn

Dear Twinnie,

Last night we finished packing up the MSS, and had a lovely dinner to celebrate, with our 1916 claret from Llandudno Junction. K said he felt so happy he could hardly speak, and I did too, though with me it took the opposite form. We have both been working so hard on the book with the feeling that it really was almost finished. K is generally very easy to work with. Actually we have had absolutely no time for anything else at all, except an hour's reading after dinner; and we got into the state where neither of us could sleep at night for the book turning over in our heads. The other night I dreamed that we were working on it and K said 'Oh darling, you've completely spoilt that diagram' – for I am terribly bad at doing diagrams; I woke up and a second later K said in his sleep '*Darling*, you've done that diagram all wrong' – he had been dreaming exactly the same thing as me. Last night we had to wake up and eat some cake and apples to clear our brains. K simply can't wait to know whether his book will turn out to be good or mostly balls – it is such a gamble for him, as he has spent two years on it and will probably spend another two on the second volume. But I do feel sure it is a *wonderful* book, even if parts of it do turn out to be wrong.

Love
Mamaine

•1948•

Paris. Arr. 7.1.48 midnight.

9 [January] 1948. K told me he had been to see Malraux, now official *chef de propagande* of the Gaullists, and was beginning to see that Malraux's position was untenable. He said M. talked awful nonsense and had to see in everything great dramas and tragedies. He told K he desperately needed 10–15 million francs for his propaganda, and K, thinking it important to strengthen Malraux's wing of the Rassemblement,[1] of which, he says, the other wing contains dreadful Jew-baiting fascists, mentioned it to Guy [de Rothschild] before dinner. But Guy said his family couldn't fork up this money. During dinner Malraux rang K up at the Rothschilds and said, don't say anything to them about the money as I have just got, from the Rothschild family, 5 million for the *caisse commune*. Great *dégonflage*.

[1] The *Rassemblement du Peuple Français*, formed by General de Gaulle in April 1947.

13 January [1948]. Met the Malraux and took them to the Rothschilds for drinks and dinner. Malraux was more extraordinary than ever. He talked without stopping from the moment he got there for about 1½ hours, with his usual brilliance but saying some very odd things. He has now given up his former line about de Gaulle being *un homme de gauche*, and K says that in spite of Malraux's new job his 'left wing' has clearly lost to the right wing of the Gaullist movement. Now his line simply is that the General is wonderful, and once he is in power (which is *certain* to happen soon) everything will be different. Alix [de Rothschild] asked him in what way de Gaulle would act differently as regards economic measures from the present govt., and M. replied 'Oh of course we can't *do* anything different, only the *climate* will be quite different.' He gave as an example what Christ might have said if asked such a question by Pontius Pilate: 'Après moi, les mères esclaves avec leurs enfants ne seront plus seules.' In

72

other words, the same thing done by different people – and, according to K, who now knows more about it, not very desirable ones.

K announced to me that he didn't think he could write his articles at all. He said he felt that the only things he could say which would be worth saying, and which he'd believe, might turn out to be irresponsible. Said he had discovered what an influence he has in France (with trade union people, etc.) and has the *frousse*! Felt *very* depressed as I feared our trip to Italy might not come off.

15 January [1948]. Decided with K to go to Italy next week, and 'do' that first. Party at Nora Beloff's.[1] K brought an industrialist, a syndicalist and a *chef de cabinet* of the general staff; I took the Kaplans. *No* quarrels with K so far, which is wonderful, but I am depressed and longing for Italy. Read a book of Jean Grenier's till 6 a.m. last night, which cheered me up a bit.

[1] Nora Beloff, author and journalist, was Paris correspondent of the *Observer* at that time.

16 January 1948. Dined with Sartre at the Escargot, then we went to three '*endroits*' near the Carrefour Vavin and talked and drank a bit. Very nice evening once we'd got past the stories about the Russian girls and their various *ménages* with Sartre and Castor. Of course one keeps having to stop short with existentialists because they don't admit a psychological (much less physiological) approach to anything; and whenever we got held up in this way Sartre told me to read *L'Être et le néant* and I told him I shouldn't understand it if I did. However, from time to time I found it possible to say that I'd 'choisi' something, and on these occasions we were in full agreement. Had promised to ring Arthur and let him know where we were, but Sartre's face fell when I told him this so I put it off, and finally K didn't come – he was at Malakoff listening to Gaullists – including Malraux – making speeches, and said M. was a brilliant speaker. K seems still very Gaullist, though now thoroughly against de Gaulle himself. I'm doubtful as ever, but haven't had a chance to talk to K about it yet.

22 January [1948]. Lunch Sartre, Escargot. He was furious with K because the night before, after a party which I had left early, K and a man called Barbereau, a RPF type, charming, 'farfelu' and very brave (he is a Compagnon de la Résistance) had met S. de Beauvoir in a bar, and K had introduced Simone as 'la femme de Sartre', whereupon Barbereau had said (being drunk, at 3 a.m.) 'ça ne fait rien, parce que Sartre, c'est une rigolade' and then told how Sartre had been to offer his service to the Gaullists two days before he'd made a speech on the radio attacking de Gaulle. Of course this was obviously ridiculous, Sartre being very anti-Gaullist, and K had said so, but had treated the whole incident as a joke. So Sartre thought, 'Why should he make a row in defence of Kappy and not in defence of me?' However, not having been there I refused to discuss the matter, and we talked of other subjects – the fear of dying (which neither of us has), *l'existentialisme* (which S. promised to explain to me in detail) and other things. In the afternoon, worked with K on his articles. After dinner K went off to meet Sartre, in order to make up his quarrel with him.

The following day Arthur and Mamaine left by car for Italy.

Florence 3.2.48   Hotel Berchielli,
                                         Lungarno Acciaiuoli,
                                         Florence

. . . Unfortunately K loathes Florence, so we have not had a nice time here. He thinks the atmosphere is stuffy and anachronistic, no doubt he's right, though I still love it, it is so beautiful; but K says he can't live on stones alone. Our contacts here have worked out badly, and K has been for the first time since we left Paris in a stinking temper – the only thing to do is to go on to Rome, so we are leaving on Thursday. Yesterday I went up to Harold Acton's villa in the afternoon, it is incredibly beautiful and full of lovely pictures.

                                         Love,
                                         Mamaine

10.2.48
Albergo Eliseo,
Via Porta Pinciana,
Rome

Dear Twin,

We had a very enjoyable time in Florence once K recovered from his initial bad temper. We went up to Fiesole, which was unbelievably beautiful, and we also dined with the famous art historian Berenson. Unfortunately at this dinner K got a fit of amnesia, so he kept getting the names of painters quite wrong and talking about Piero della Francesca when he meant Simone Martini, and so forth, with the result that his conversation was quite unintelligible.

On Thursday we left Florence and motored to Arezzo for lunch; there are some Piero della Francesca frescoes there we wanted to see. After lunch we motored slowly on to Perugia. The country we went through was simply wonderful, I've never seen such lovely country – very undulating and bright green from the young wheat which grows under the olive trees. So I enjoyed this very much, especially as it was sunny and warm. We stayed the night in Perugia and went on the next day to Assisi, where we lunched, then on to Rome. Of all these wonderful places – for they are all lovely towns in perfect country – Assisi was the one I liked best: it is on a hill (they all are) with a terrific view, it is very quiet and peaceful and from the back one can walk in the country along little lanes through olive groves.

In Rome we met Arthur's friend Leo Valiani and his wife, also Carlo Levi and a man called La Malfa who is said to be a very good politician, and dined with them.[1] Since then I have been sight-seeing a good deal, both with the Valianis and with K, and on Sunday we drove out with the Sprigges[2] to see the Lake of Nemi, which is lovely – it is a tiny lake with hills all round, on whose shores Frazer's *Golden Bough* begins; we sat on a terrace in the sun looking down on it and ate a delicious lunch. Then we went to tea with the Ruffinis, who live not far from there.[3] At dinner with the Valianis we met Darina Silone, who looked very miserable and pathetic. She slaves away all day at translating to earn a few sous, because for some reason they are penniless. We went with her and an Italian to a sort of *boîte*. Silone was away but has now returned and we are dining with them tonight. We also lunched with Darina yesterday in a restaurant where there is a table reserved for socialists where one can just go and sit with anybody who happens to be there.

We went to a very smart night-club where all the women were wearing dresses which at least came from Jacques Fath, but they were not very pretty women so the dresses seemed rather wasted. They all wear little heelless pumps, even with evening dress. Needless to say, no sooner had we installed ourselves – after a long search – in this rather nice hotel than K announced that he loathed Italy passionately and had always known he wouldn't like coming here, but I had dragged him, and so on. Actually of course he enjoys himself madly most of the time. He is on good form and very sweet. But to tell the truth I quite look forward to leaving Rome, where there is rather too much social life for my liking, and going to Trieste, whither I shall go I think when I leave here, which will be on Saturday week. After that may I come and stay with you?

I am not sure whether this letter conveys how much I am enjoying myself: the whole trip is just bliss for me and I wish it would go on for months. Everybody here speaks French so I haven't had much occasion to practise my Italian, but although at first it seemed lamentable it is already improving and I am capable of carrying on some sort of conversation, indeed I am quite pleased with myself.

K will be back in Paris by the end of the month, but only for a few days I think – he sails for the States on March 13th and will be away about 6 weeks or more, so I have plenty of free time left. I'm *so* glad I'm not going.

Love
Twin

[1] Leo Valiani, writer and politician; one of the leading contributors to the *Corriere della Sera*, created Life Senator by President Pertini. Carlo Levi, novelist, painter and former doctor, author of *Christ Stopped at Eboli*. Ugo La Malfa, politician, one of the leaders of the non-Marxist left; in 1946 he founded the Partito Repubblicano.

[2] Cecil Sprigge, writer and expert on Benedetto Croce, and his wife Elizabeth, biographer.

[3] Attilio Ruffini, Sicilian politician (Christian Democrat) and author of several books about Catholic values in the Resistance, in which he, Leo Valiani, La Malfa, Carlo Levi and Ivan Matteo Lombardo (see next letter) were all active.

Wednesday 19.2.48   Albergo Eliseo

Dear Twin,

It is good to think we shall soon be staying together. Where? I am going to Trieste next week, I don't know yet how long I shall be staying there; it is supposed to be an awful place and one can never go out because the Free Zone is only about a mile or two round the town. Supposing I stay a week or ten days, could we I wonder meet after that in the *midi*, say at Arles, and spend a week there before going back to Paris? Needless to say I have no French money at all, but can probably arrange to borrow some. I would stay in Italy a little longer if I had more lire, but we are running out.

I have been having a fine time here, I must say. On Sunday we drove out to Tivoli, which is some way outside Rome, with Darina Silone and Leo [Valiani] – Silone thank God had gone to Milan. Near Tivoli is a big ruined Roman villa called Hadrian's Villa – it consists of perhaps a square mile or so of ruined walls in the midst of lovely olive groves and cypress avenues. Behind it is a valley with a little river fringed with tall reeds, some vineyards and fruit trees and little straw peasants' huts; and behind that some hills with the usual rock villages perched on them. It was warm and sunny, and the blackcaps were singing away. We lunched there and went up to the Villa d'Este. It was a wonderful day.

Leo is really a fine chap, I simply love him and admire him no end. He spent 6 years in prison and two in concentration camps, then was parachuted into Italy and became a leader of the North Italian partisans and took part in lots of actions with them. As for Darina, she is really a pet.

I've seen more of the handsome Pietra,[1] who is really a nice chap; of Ivan Matteo Lombardo,[2] who's one of the most likable politicos here; and of various other Saragatians. Tomorrow we're going to drive out with the Ruffinis to see some Etruscan things 100 kms. from Rome, in Tuscany. On Friday we're leaving. K is still on excellent form and so am I. We never quarrel, it's wonderful.

Love,
Twin

The Etruscan frescoes at Tarquinia are *wonderful*. Off to dinner with

Cerletti, an old psychiatrist who has made a revolutionary discovery, K says.[3]

[1] Italo Pietra, journalist, editor of *Il Giornale* for many years.

[2] Ivan Matteo Lombardo, Socialist politician and economist. He left Nenni's branch of the Socialist Party in 1948, and eventually joined Saragat's.

[3] Aurelio Cerletti, neurologist. He had evolved a theory that in a crisis the brain secretes an emergency hormone.

Arthur now set off for a lecture tour of the United States to raise money for the International Rescue and Relief Committee. This was an organization that had been founded in the beginning of the war to help refugees – principally, but not exclusively, intellectuals – at first from the Nazis and then from the Iron Curtain countries and Spain. It was Arthur's first visit to the United States. He returned to England on 9 May.

Meanwhile Mamaine went to Trieste to stay with Bob and Jane Joyce. Robert P. Joyce, by career an Officer in the American Foreign Service, and a former member of the Policy Planning Staff of the State Department, 1949–53, was at that time Political Adviser to the Military Governor of the Free Territory of Trieste, then under the Security Council of the United Nations.

Sunday 29.2.48   Piazza Scorcola 1,
                                                   Trieste

Dear Twinnie,

Sorry not to have written sooner, but no time. I am sorry you got the idea that I was returning next Thursday, because I'm not: it is very nice being here and Jane has begged me to stay on and either go with her to Cortina, in the mountains, where she is going at the end of the week for a few days, or remain here with Bob till she comes back. I have chosen the latter, as I don't really want to go to the mountains, and look forward to a few days of quiet here in this lovely flat, which incidentally possesses a wonderful piano which makes one sound like Rachmaninoff. I'm terribly sorry after all the trouble you've taken to borrow a flat.

When we left Rome we stayed a night at Viterbo and then drove through Siena to Florence. It was marvellous getting to Florence again after Rome, and funnily enough K thought so too and became quite converted to Florence. We stayed there with an Englishman and his wife who have a villa at S. Domenico, on the way to Fiesole. It was very cold and there was a good deal of snow around, but nevertheless K insisted on our trying to get over the pass between Florence and Bologna without chains, though everybody said this was impossible and I strongly opposed it. Of course we soon got stuck, and I popped into some peasant houses near by to try and get some rope. While K and various other men whose cars were stuck behind ours because of the narrow road tried to fix the rope, I sat by the fire with one of the peasant women and ate pieces of rabbit cooked in oil out of a pot and drank a glass of wine. Then off we went, only to arrive at a part of the road which hadn't been properly swept; so as we had to wait an hour we went and had lunch, consisting of sausages obviously made of cat, in a mountain pub. Then on we went again, through a frightful blizzard and thick fog and finally by a miracle got over the pass. By that time the rope had transferred itself from the wheels to the brakes, which consequently no longer worked, so we slid down the other side with some rather terrifying skids. We spent the night in Bologna and drove on through Parma to Milan. Parma is a lovely and charming little town. We went into a café there for a cup of coffee and a grappa, and heard what we thought at first was the radio broadcasting some opera, but which turned out to be a workman singing Verdi arias to another workman in an incredibly beautiful voice, very softly. K and I both nearly wept, it was so beautiful and moving, and swallowed our grappas quickly and rushed out; and as we drove off the workers pressed their noses against the glass door and waved at us. We crossed the Po and drove through several villages with pretty baroque church towers.

Milan was hell, and the less said about it the better. We went to some parties of intellectuals which were pure suffering for me. Then I left K and went by train to Venice. I arrived at night and had to travel for half an hour in a gondola to get to my hotel; it was wonderful swishing silently through the canals all alone, past the pink gothic palazzi and under the high rounded bridges, but it was also bloody cold – I preferred the ride back to the station next morning in the sun.

Now for Trieste. It is a fascinating place, a curious mixture of

Italians, Slovenes and relics of the Austro-Hungarian Empire. This flat, for instance, is one of the latter. My bedroom contains a large white porcelain stove and a portrait of Franz Josef; and the salon next door has a painted ceiling, furniture upholstered in crimson silk, a chandelier, gilt mirrors and an open fire which is always blazing away.

Since I've been here I have been to a nightclub, a cocktail party, a wedding reception, a dinner party and a ball – we go about with some people who are more or less staying here, Cy Sulzberger of the *New York Times* and his wife, who is a sweet Greek girl called Marina.[1] Well, I'm afraid this is a dotty letter, but after a late night I'm not feeling very bright, and am in a hurry because it's 12.45 and I still haven't dressed.

Love
Twin

Dining tonight with the Commander-in-Chief at DUINO.

[1] Cyrus L. Sulzberger was at that time foreign correspondent of the *New York Times* and head of its Paris office. He had married Marina Ladas.

14.3.48   Piazza Scorcola 1

Dearest Twinnie,

I'm afraid you must be fuming against me for keeping on putting off the date of my advent; but please don't be. Time goes so fast here and there is so much to be done, and I am so blissfully happy, that I really could stay here for months. Everybody says Trieste is a dreary town, but I love it and love the country round it and the coast line – the sea is completely unspoilt and unriviera-ish. You can't think how wonderful Duino is; we're dining there again tonight.

The other day we drove out beyond Udine for lunch with some Italians who have a country house there and tea with others who have another. It is most enjoyable driving round in this country, which is flat and very fertile with the Giulian Alps forming a circle behind, very large and snowy. The little towns and villages are usually rather pretty: they are filled with the most incredible Communist posters: one we saw stated that Truman had said during the war that he would like as many people to get killed as possible. This was encircled by a blood-red line.

Since I last wrote I have spent 2 days in Cortina, in the mountains, with Jane. I ski-ed a bit but we seemed to spend most of the time either plodding across country on our skis or climbing very steep mountains carrying them. The snow was very bad too, half ice, half soup, so we came back on Friday.

I'm reading *Oedipus Rex* in an Italian translation[1] which Gastone lent me. It is a wonderful translation, I think; I'll bring it for you. I forget whether I've explained about Gastone:[2] he is an Italian diplomat, aged about 45, and he is quite wonderfully sweet and nice and amusing and intelligent and *cultivé*. I simply *adore* him and so does everybody, and fortunately he likes me I think and is an old friend of the Joyces and Cy S. so has been spending most of the time with us.

[1] By Salvatore Quasimodo.
[2] Gastone Guidotti was at that time representing Italian interests in Trieste. He was subsequently ambassador in Belgrade, Vienna, Bonn and London (1964–8).

After her stay in Trieste Mamaine spent a short time in Paris before returning to London on 4 May, bringing with her Albert and Francine Camus.

8.5.48   c/o Sonia [Brownell],
                                           London

Dear Twinnie,

Here is my news of the week, such as it is. We had a grim journey, because owing to my not having looked up the exact distance to the coast, combined with the Camus being late in starting and the car getting wobblier at every mile, we missed the boat at Calais and had to go on to Dunkirk, stay there till midnight, and get on a boat which arrived at 8 a.m. in Dover (fortunately it was calm). So we arrived in London worn out and furious – though in fact the Dunkirk part was rather fun and quite interesting – it is completely and absolutely devastated and very sad, and somebody there stole my big white case containing my trousers, red *nach-ski* shoes, two sweaters, two tins of precious olive oil and various other things. I had to get a new sweater and pants, which cost me nearly all my coupons.

Apart from that, Camus, Francine and I have been having rather fun. I have spent every evening with them except one, when they were in Oxford. There was a big *Horizon* cocktail party, followed by (for me) dinner with Adam, and a party at the [Hamish] Hamiltons consisting of the Camus, Michel St Denis, Michael Ayrton and others.[1]

I lunched in the House of Commons with Camus and Francine and the Crossmans and Maurice Edelman[2] and liked the latter very much. The lunch was a great success.

Yesterday I took Camus and Francine round the National Gallery in the morning and then we went with J. P. de Dadelsen,[3] his wife, Odile [de Laleine-Laprade] and her husband, who is a nice man called Michael Tweedie, to the Prospect of Whitby for lunch. Camus adored this. After lunch he and Francine and Dadelsen and I drove out to Windsor and around the Park in Dadelsen's car, and had tea in Eton. Then Dadelsen and Camus went up to Edinburgh, leaving me feeling very lonely and sad. It has been so nice having Camus about. He really is the nicest man on earth.

Arthur is coming back tomorrow morning, thank God. I am longing to get out of London and be settled back in Wales.

Love,
Mamaine

---

[1] Adam Watson, diplomat, later ambassador to Senegal and Cuba; Michel St Denis, the theatrical producer; Michael Ayrton, painter, sculptor, author and illustrator.

[2] Maurice Edelman, Labour MP. Author of *France: The Birth of the Fourth Republic* (1945).

[3] Jean-Paul de Dadelsen, poet and journalist. Author of two books of poems, *Bach en Automne* (1955) and *Collected Poems*, published posthumously in 1962. He had been London correspondent of *Combat* and at this time was working for the French services of the BBC. He was an old friend of Camus, whom he had first known in Oran before the war.

15.5.48   Bwlch Ocyn

Dear Twin,

It was pretty grim when K arrived back in the worst possible mood. He was tired and crotchety, but not I think seriously worried. So I tried to sit back and wait till he recovered, which he has now done – but it took a week, during which I despaired once again of ever being able to stick it out. The trouble of course with poor K is that he worries so much if anything goes wrong, or gets lost or broken, whereas I don't care a damn. I think he was more upset about my losing my suitcase than I was.

Wales is more awful than ever, the climate drains all my vitality, the problem of running the house efficiently with only half-wit Megan is insuperable and so is the food problem. But don't think I am unhappy. For it is good to be in the country and I want to read some books and do some work for a change. Also since the Americans recognized the Jewish State K's temper has improved.

He is in good form now so life is brighter, but he's still jolly difficult: last night he pointed out that a pile of books had been on a chair in the sitting-room for 3 days without my remembering it, and said this kind of thing would make it impossible for us to live together. At this I simply collapsed with laughter, but of course it is quite true, it is exactly this kind of thing which will get us down in the long run. Because I just don't notice piles of books, and never will. Well well!

We are migrating to the States, I mean emigrating, early next year, if I still find I can stick the prospect by then; the idea is to live in New England for 9 months of the year, and travel to Europe for the other three.

Do write soon with news of all our pals.

Love,
Twin

On 15 May 1948, the date of the last letter, the British Mandate over Palestine was officially terminated and the independent State of Israel proclaimed. It was at once invaded by the armies of five sovereign Arab states, which were strongly opposed by the Jewish defence force, Haganah, and war broke out. In these circumstances Arthur felt that he ought to be there. Mamaine encouraged him to go and said that she intended to accompany him. He acquired assignments to report on the situation for the Manchester Guardian, Le Figaro *and the* New York Herald Tribune;

he and Mamaine obtained visas, and they set off as soon as possible, arriving in Haifa on 4 June.

Tuesday June 6th 1948   Hotel Gat Rimmon,
                                                        Tel Aviv

Dear Twinnie,

Not much news so far, but I'll start all the same. The journey was uneventful. We got to Haifa about 4 p.m., I think, by local time, which is four hours ahead of English time. We stayed there a couple of nights in a very comfortable hotel on Mount Carmel, above the town. This was most enjoyable because cool, a balcony which we could work on, a garden of pines and eucalyptus, full of turtle doves and bulbuls (or Persian nightingales) – a local bird which has not very much to recommend it. The hotel was at the same time a convalescent home for wounded Haganah men and rather reminiscent of the war, because these chaps looked much like British soldiers on leave or convalescing; they were all very nice but mostly only spoke Hebrew and perhaps Polish, Hungarian or some such language; however, we talked to some and K had long conversations with them, as his Hebrew is quite fluent.

On Sunday we came on here by car; the country between Haifa and Tel Aviv is rather dull, but there are a few Arab villages which I stared at with popping eyes. The road passes within about four miles of the front, nevertheless there was no sign of fighting.

I must say Tel Aviv is pretty bleak: I was prepared for the worst, but it is uglier than my wildest fears. However, so far it is not too hot – about 85 in the shade I should think – and we have a nice room on the sea where there is generally a breeze; also it is interesting. We hope one of these days to go on a car trip round the country. Everybody is very suspicious of everybody else, and K and I are suspected of being agents of God knows whom and what; so is Alexis,[1] who turned up in our lives yesterday to our great joy. He lives just down the road and we had dinner with him last night. Needless to say he is absolutely charming and I nearly embraced him in my joy at meeting somebody so like Marina. K loved him too.

K is on fine form and no longer mad, so all is well for the time being.

We work quite hard, which is a good thing, as there is nothing else to do and no people to see. I haven't been in swimming yet, somehow the sea doesn't look very enticing, but I shall soon. As there is a censorship here I don't want to say much. Possibly there will be a truce soon – I hope so, as then we shall be able to go to Jerusalem. K is optimistic about the outcome. The British certainly have been INCREDIBLY bloody here, the things they did before they left make one's hair stand on end with horror. The Haganah and Irgun fight very well but the civilian population don't seem to have much feeling about civic cooperation. It is really not at all true that the Irgun are fascists, though a lot of the Haganah think so as they have been propaganded to that effect to stop them joining it.

Love from
Mamaine

[1] Alexis Ladas was a member of the United Nations Commission in Palestine. He was Marina Sulzberger's brother.

Saturday 26.6.48   Hotel Gat Rimmon

Dear Twin,

It is Sabbath, and the sea-front at Margate on a Bank Holiday is a prairie compared to the Tel Aviv sea front today. The Egyptians have broken the truce, so the wary Tel Avivers, who had lifted the black-out for a few days, it is believed as a result of a scheme of Arthur's, have re-imposed it. Everything is hellish. I haven't had a chance to write for some time as we went off last Saturday for a trip in a car with a Haganah guide called Schlomo and a rich industrialist called Mr Jerushalmi, in whose car we went. It was a marvellous trip, right round Galilee and up to the Syrian frontier, but I haven't time or energy to write much about it. We went to various kibbutzim, some on Lake Tiberias, which is below sea level and pretty hot; there I swam in the Jordan, green and glassy, and saw a wonderful big kingfisher with a brick-red head. Also we crossed the Lake (which as you should know is the Sea of Galilee) at night by full moon to visit a settlement on the other side, which is quite isolated. From the mountains behind it 'the Syrians came down like a wolf on the fold' (can't resist that quotation) and attacked the settlement, but were repulsed; they still sit so near that they could have shot at me as I walked alone through the settlement at 2 a.m. in the moonlight to an outpost where I had been lying among the guards and where something had dropped out of the pocket of my shorts. It was very romantic and beautiful, with jackals barking in the hills and occasionally stepping on mines outside the kibbutz, which went off with loud bangs. We went back across the lake to Tiberias at 4 a.m. Also we went up to a very isolated fortress settlement in the mountains, right in the north, where ten days previously some twelve Jews were killed by the Arabs, who attacked up a hill where the Jews (having arranged their positions badly) couldn't see them coming. The wild mountains, the slight stink of dead bodies emanating from their common grave and the indescribably strong stink round the corpse of a Syrian officer which was still lying on the hill-top, unburied and looking fairly horrible, made a macabre impression. After that we drove up Mount Canaan to Safed, a beautiful Arab town now largely destroyed, but in Jewish hands: there were previously 12,000 Arabs and only 1,500 Jews in the town, and some Arab irregulars from Iraq and Syria, but although the British handed over the fortress and other strong points to the Arabs on leaving, the Jews took the town after only a few hours' fighting.

We were away till Thursday, so missed all the shooting which occurred here over the Irgun ship.[1] It appears to have been simply awful, but no doubt you have read about it in the papers if you are still alive, which, not having heard one word from you since my arrival in Palestine, I am beginning to doubt.

There are rumours that Cy [Sulzberger] is to turn up here shortly; I don't know how true they are. It would be a treat to see a pal and if I could stave off a fight between him and K for a few days I would greatly enjoy talking to Cy.

Fortunately K's book is going well, and I now think that it may be quite good, as he has thought up how to do it in what I think is the right way; so he is on moderately good form, though disgusted by everything that goes on here. As for me, I am very demoralized still. But I have one consolation in the form of a Leica which K has given me very generously (it cost £90). It is a terrific thrill for me and though

I haven't really got cracking with it yet I intend to take some really good pictures. Indeed I love it so much I can hardly bear to be parted from it. Robert Capa[2] talked me into getting it instead of a cheaper kind of camera, and I must say it is wonderful.

Tel Aviv is not too hot yet, and probably never will be in this hotel as it is on the sea front where there is always a sea-breeze. But inland it really was pretty hot in some places; however, I am not so much got down by the heat as K, I think (except by the Khamssin, which drives one mad, but it is over for the summer I believe).

About the bird life: I have not got this taped yet, and probably never shall have much chance to do so; but there are a great many vultures, which sit and feed on the corpses of cattle and hover round above like aeroplanes going in to land; a great many hawks, some of species with which I am not familiar; and a good many bee-eaters, which are very pretty. Also some small black-and-white birds whose identity I have not established. Jackals are very common and as they always get run over by cars one sees a good few dead on the roads; hyenas also exist in the hills but are said not to be very common; and I have seen one wild tortoise and believe they must be fairly common. I wish I had a chance to go off alone in a jeep with a camera and field-glasses and prowl around; K and I are negotiating to buy a jeep, but even if we do one can't move far without no end of permits. We intend to go to Jerusalem and back before the end of the truce – if it hasn't already ended. We will try not to get stuck there, as communications with the outside world would be impossible.

Love from
Mamaine

---

[1] The Irgun ship *Altalena*, carrying 900 Jewish volunteers and a quantity of arms, was bombarded and set on fire by Jewish Government troops on 21 June 1948. For a full account of this disaster see Arthur Koestler's book on the Palestine question, *Promise and Fulfilment* (1949), pp. 245ff.

[2] Robert Capa, American photographer of Hungarian origin. He was particularly well known for his war photographs.

July 2nd 1948   Hotel Gat Rimmon

Dear Twinnie,

At last a wire from you, which I think might have been slightly longer; I am now here since a month without a single word of news of you – or for that matter anybody else on earth. However I suppose that is not your fault but the fault of the mail, which even from France takes a long time. Letters from England don't arrive at all, as the English Post Office won't accept them.

Yesterday I went to Jerusalem, and returned here today. K couldn't go as he had a gippy tummy, or perhaps slight dysentery. In Jerusalem I picked up a character called Keith Scott-Watson, who took me round, with the result that I saw what there was to see – not much, as one can't get by hook or crook into the Old City. The shelling there was pretty bad, I wouldn't have liked to have been there, also the civilians really have been terribly short of food for about a month preceding the truce. I went to see some people who live in a Greek monastery on the edge of the town, and we imbibed coffee there with an elderly Greek monk who was like something out of *Women and Monks*[1] – indeed now that he is cut off from the Patriarchate in the Old City his one idea is to go to a cabaret in Tel Aviv and see some girls, uncontrolled by his superiors. The Kimches[2] were also in Jerusalem and I dined with them and the editor of the *Palestine Post*, and this morning did some military sight seeing, during which at some points we were within 2 metres of the Arab positions. We had to be careful as they snipe like mad. Coming back one has to pass through a stretch of country which is in Arab hands, and is escorted through it by Arab Legionaries, who have the most glamorous costume imaginable, with yellow or red-and-white check head-dresses with black cords round, and jack-boots. K and I had thought of going and settling down in Jerusalem and letting ourselves be cut off there if the war starts again next week; but I dismissed this idea, as the complete isolation and absence of communication with the outside world is very depressing – I couldn't even ring Tel Aviv to find out how Arthur was or send a packet of cigarettes to a Scottish clergyman in a church on the edge of the town whom I visited yesterday afternoon, but who can only be got through to with special passes, and on foot.

Also, ghastly as Tel Aviv is, it has two compensations: (1) it is the centre of Palestine political life and there is really a lot going on here, especially since the *Altalena* show-down; (2) there is the sea in which one can swim every day if one has time. I have been TERRIBLY demoralized during the last week, but am better since my visit to

Jerusalem. How I wish Cy would turn up, though of course I wouldn't be allowed to speak to him alone, and together with K there would certainly be a row in no time.

One incident brightened our lives: we asked the French consul, Comte Charreyron, and his wife, who is rather attractive, to dinner, and felt very excited at the thought of an evening with civilized people. Before dinner, in the bar, Mme C. asked me if I was Jewish, then if K was, and then said 'It must be extraordinary to be married to a Jew, isn't it?' I was rather taken aback and baffled, but took no notice. Then at dinner she said to K: 'Do you mind if I ask your wife to dinner without you, because I'm giving a dinner-party of French journalists and haven't got any girls – it will be a Catholic dinner-party.' K said 'Okay' and I said 'Couldn't I bring K?' (thinking, if she's got 9 men and 2 girls she might as well have 10 men and two girls); to which she replied 'No, because you see it's to be a Catholic party.' I still didn't cotton on, but it became apparent that she simply meant that no Jews were to be allowed at it, and that was why she wouldn't have K, in spite of the fact that, as she kept repeating, she loved all writers and especially admired K! It was too comic for words, and we simply couldn't get over her obviously thinking it so natural that K or I couldn't possibly take exception to her request that I go alone. Indeed I didn't really believe my ears, while K thought it too strange and absurd to be worth while making a fuss about.

Love

Twin

[1] *Women and Monks*, a Russian novel by Josef Kallinikov.

[2] Jon Kimche, contemporary historian and journalist. Editor of the *Jewish Chronicle* and *Middle East Review* for fifteen years after the war, also of *The New Middle East* and most recently of *Afro-Asian Affairs*. Middle East correspondent of the *Evening Standard* until 1973. He wrote to me: 'I saw a good deal of Mamaine in Israel. She did most of the "leg-work" for Arthur's newspaper articles . . . Arthur was busy with *haute politique* . . . while Mamaine was out in the field. I recall the first trip to blockaded Jerusalem in convoy. Mamaine was in our taxi and displayed her usual cool when we had to pass through a not very friendly Arab Legion post at the entry to Bab el Wad. One Legionnaire checking our papers sneered at Mamaine "woman journalist! what next?" and stood by her car window playing with a live hand grenade.'
The editor of the *Palestine Post* was Gershon Agronski, later Mayor of Jerusalem (1955–9) under the name Gershon Agron.

7.7.48   Hotel Gat Rimmon

Dear Celia,

   Nothing in the least interesting has happened, and indeed things are getting worse, because whereas K has been on surprisingly good form since we've been here, and a pleasure to be with, he is now being got down by hotel life, lack of privacy, constant café music under the window and chatting people on the next balcony till midnight, blackout, expense and so on. Imagine, every week our hotel bill comes to at least £P80! So we have been looking for a flat, and succeeded at last in finding one, which we could have moved into today if its present inhabitant, an old woman of 73, could have got her exit permit to go to Czechoslovakia, where her daughter is very ill; but she has been refused one, so we are back where we started. Also, the truce is rather demoralizing, because nobody has any idea whether it will be extended or not, and both eventualities seem equally undesirable. K rants on night and day about Palestinian politics to everyone until I nearly go mad. When we go out on parties and Alexis is there he and I spend what little time we get to talk to each other quoting Eliot or Rimbaud or even Omar Khayyam as a form of escapism. 'Arthur demands that one should all the time be ten years older than one is', said Alexis to me in a desperate *cri de coeur*. Oh how I dream of rivers and willows, Woodbridge and the Vallée de Chevreuse, fishing at Stourbridge, Tickerage. . . !

   However, I foresee that we shan't be here longer than about the beginning of October, and I can hold out till then. What to do after that is indeed a problem. If as I believe one can't take a penny out of England to America this will mean that by going to America K virtually loses all his hard-won capital, with which he hopes to buy himself a house.

                                                               Love,
                                                               Twin

PS We have decided to move into the flat with the old woman and I hope it will be an improvement. This address is still okay – the flat is only two steps away. I forgot to say that it is now much too hot for comfort. Poor K suffers from this even more than I do. One sweats like a pig all day, has no energy and can't even get cool at night. The sea is too warm to do much good. There is no meat to be had in Palestine at the moment, with the result that in this hotel we have either duck, chicken or goose for every meal which we have here. It sounds ridiculous, but we can hardly stand it any more, it always tastes exactly the same – i.e. of nothing. A meal for one in the hotel costs 15/- so we only have one meal a day here – which we have to do – and go for the other one to some cheap restaurant, generally a little oriental-type place where we have more or less Arab food. So today we had at this place some humus (meal made of chick-peas), a little salad and some egg-plants and a cup of turkish coffee, which cost merely the equivalent of 6/- each! We have also probably bought an extremely old jeep in absolutely rotten condition, about which we don't feel particularly happy.[1]

[1] One night somebody attempted to steal this jeep, which was parked below Arthur's and Mamaine's bedroom window, but Mamaine, who heard the would-be thief tinkering with it, shouted at him in Hebrew 'thieves in the night' and he ran away.

July 21st 1948   Bograshov Street 3,
                                                 Tel Aviv

Dear Twinnie,

Cy turned up here the day before yesterday, to everybody's intense surprise, as we had given up hope of his coming. It is swell seeing him, and today I am going to have lunch with him alone so we will have a good talk. Altogether life has become slightly more tolerable during the last few days: for one thing, the air raids were really a terrible bore, as they went on almost all day and half the night and during each one life stops completely while everybody hangs about in halls and shelters. My reactions to them were exactly the same as to the London ones; of course these were much less bad, but on the other hand Tel Aviv is such a small place that the chances of the bombs falling on or near one are much larger, and as a matter of fact one often meets people who have been bombed out or wounded, which makes one feel it might after all happen to one. However, as I said, after the first adaptation reactions are the same, namely, not fear but apprehension, the boredom of deciding whether to go downstairs (we have a top-floor flat), a feeling of insecurity. So I was very relieved that the truce came and they stopped.

I don't think we shall be here after about the middle of October. What are you plans?

> Love from
> Twin

Soon after this Mamaine went to Cyprus for a week's holiday.

10.9.48   Bograshov Street 3

Dear Twin,

No news, I am just writing to say that I am okay, and since my return from Cyprus in very good form. I feel I shan't be here very much longer, and this gives me the strength to bear the remaining weeks or months.

We went to Haifa for two nights this week, and K got FRIGHT-FULLY drunk at the house of a psychoanalyst, whom he didn't know at all: then I abandoned him on Mount Carmel and he returned next morning in the company of a priest, who had discovered him sleeping under a tree and taken him for a tramp. K had explained that he was a famous writer, to which the priest replied 'Oh yeah?', or words to that effect. The priest then took him to a monastery, where he met another (English) priest (the first was French). K said to him that several young English writers had become converts to Catholicism, and the old priest said 'Oh yes, a fellow called Chesterton's one, isn't he?' I suppose he thought G. K. C. was still alive and only about 30.

Alexis had been in Rhodes since my return – our journeys crossed in Haifa as I was on my way back from Nicosia in a very small plane. Peter Bergson (if you know who that is) is out of jail.[1]

I do long to hear about Rome and whom you saw, not to mention whom you went with and stayed with, and so on. How is your Italian? My German is pretty awful and never seems to get any better – I talk it quite a lot here. My Hebrew is very elementary but I understand a bit now.

> Love,
> Twin

1948

[1] Peter Bergson was founder and chairman of the Hebrew Committee for National Liberation in the United States and one of the leaders of Irgun.

21.9.48   Bograshov Street 3

Dear Twinnie,

Just a hurried note to say I'm leaving here round October 1st–7th (depending on when there's a plane) and proceeding straight to England; there I shall do chores in connection with collecting our things from Wales and then return to Paris, about the end of October I suppose, to await the arrival of K, who will follow in the middle of November. We will spend a couple of months in France before going to America or wherever we go, separately or together as the case may be.

Oh how I long to be in Paris, and even more to see you. I am less depressed, but still frustrated. Life is the same as usual, except for the horrifying Bernadotte murder.[1] Do not get it into your head that it was anything to do with the IZL (Irgun) – they never do things like that and are no longer terrorists anyway.

Tomorrow we are dining with Begin, which may be interesting: at a press conference yesterday he said he thought that the Israeli Govt. should imprison all Britons here as retaliation for the British detaining illegally 1200 Israeli citizens in Cyprus. I was the only British subject there; K thought the idea an excellent one, said it would solve his domestic problems. Afterwards Begin said to some of his henchmen: poor Mrs Koestler, she's so sweet and charming and always has to hear people being bloody about the English. The night of Bernadotte's murder K and I went to a Sternist café to see what was going on, and a young man sat down at our table and told K that as all gois (gentiles) were enemies, the only good goi was a dead one. My hair stood on end with rage, and K protested on my behalf. It seems the chap was one of the commanders in Jerusalem, if not the commander. What a bunch of homicidal maniacs.

K is very anti-terrorist, anti-IZL, anti-Government and rather anti-Mapai (left-wing, pro-Russian tendencies). So he's depressed and melancholic. But we get on very well together these days.

Love from
me

[1] Count Folke Bernadotte, United Nations mediator for Palestine, was assassinated there on 17
September 1948.

*Early in October Mamaine returned to England and went to Wales to clear
up Bwlch Ocyn. She then went to Paris, where Arthur soon joined her.
They had decided to live in the country within reach of the capital, and
while looking for a suitable house they moved into a small one in the park of
a château near Fontainebleau.*

Monday 8.11.48   Pavillon du Pré,
                                                 Chartrettes

Dear Celia,

We had a lovely day yesterday. We walked from here across the
Forest to Samois, had a very good and huge lunch there in the hotel
we[1] stayed in, or rather sitting outside it, and came back on a big
commercial barge which was also carrying 230 tons of sugar-beet
pulp. We got on to the barge at the lock at Samois and got off it at the
lock at Chartrettes. It was a lovely day with some black clouds to give
the landscape that air of 'sinistrosity' which K declares essential to his
enjoyment of nature. The Forest is really beautiful now, as you can
imagine. It is $7\frac{1}{2}$ km. to Samois across the forest, 9 along the river.

No time for more.

Love
Mamaine

[1] I.e. Mamaine and Celia.

Nov. 14th [1948], Saturday   Pavillon du Pré

Dear Twinnie,

Thanks for your letter. Obviously my first letter never reached you,
and that is why you don't know where I live or what I did in Paris.

Perhaps you have got it by now? In case you haven't, the answer is we live in a couple of small houses in a big park (30 hectares). We have two rooms in one, the Ripkas (Czech ex-minister of economics, I think) live in the other, they have two children and we share the dining-room with them and the sitting-room too, though they never use that really, so we sometimes have meals with them, and sometimes – when R. is in Paris, for instance – by ourselves. They are extremely nice, so that even K is able to get on with them. We have a cook who does all the cooking and shopping for all, and a *femme de ménage* (Polish) who does the rooms. We are ¼ mile from the Seine, over which our rooms look. They are very pleasant and comfortable and our bedroom, which is also my working room when I am not working with K, has a wood fire which one can keep going all day, as there is plenty of wood. The park is simply lovely, mostly woods and alleys of different kinds of trees – limes, chestnuts, etc. One can easily walk about in it for half an hour or more without going out of it. Chartrettes is quite a pretty little village, probably rather touristy in summer but not now; it has several restaurants. The other side of the Seine is the Forest of Fontainebleau. The country is lovely, and apart from being rather damp the climate is good: very little rainfall, apparently. Altogether it is an ideal place to live and work. Incidentally, don't mention to anyone that we live with the Ripkas as they are recent émigrés and rather want to keep their whereabouts fairly dark. The Winklers[1] come down for weekends with their two children, a girl aged 17 and a boy of 22. The Ws are terribly nice and awfully generous and sweet; nevertheless we rather dread weekends because the huge family meals, with the two children and the Ws, are a bit much.

As I told you, I took K to see the Garys in Paris, and from his point of view it was a success – he liked them both very much.[2] We had lunch with the Camus, but I have seen no more of them as I haven't had a chance yet – I didn't see C. at his play as he was in the *coulisses*. It has had unanimously bad reviews; but at least it is an honourable failure.[3] Romain's book will be out some time in December: he is on tenterhooks.

Love,
Twin

[1] Paul Winkler, head of the Opera Mundi press syndicate, and his wife.

[2] Romain Gary, novelist and diplomat, was then working at the Quai d'Orsay. His second novel, *Le Grand vestiaire*, published in 1948, won wide acclaim. He was married to the writer Lesley Blanch.

[3] *L'État de Siège* opened at the Marigny Theatre on 27 October 1948, but closed after only seventeen performances.

Wednesday [25 November 1948]   Pavillon du Pré

Dear Twinnie,

We have been looking for a house. Even if we only get a horrible fishing bungalow on the Seine, it will at least be good enough for a holiday house – we would only live there for three months in the summer, the chief aim of buying one anyway is to spend K's francs in such a way as to ensure against inflation, which we feel is bound to come. Houses always go up in value, never down. I expect we will buy something hideous fairly soon, so that we can move our furniture over at Christmas and possibly live in it for a couple of months after that until we go to the States, which alas! we intend to do in the spring.

We are toiling away hard at the book [*Promise and Fulfilment*], which is simply a book about Palestine (or rather Israel) – background, history and present-day close-up. It is rather tedious and we are both anxious to finish it; but there is no other book of the kind written by an outsider, and I think it really is fairly impartial, at any rate it tries to be and especially I try hard to keep it so – I constantly press for the exclusion of too vehement or propagandistic arguments. Although it is sometimes rather torture sitting all day plugging away at it, the same can be said of most work; and in spite of that, a life of work is much more enjoyable than a life of idleness. I have quite got back into my Bwlch Ocyn mood of peaceful and un-neurotic content. And we have only had one major row since we've been here, and that was before we started working properly: which proves, if proof were needed, that K's neurosis when not working is the basic cause of the rows. I think the life here is very healthy too, though it is too damp – but where isn't? I could do with just a little more free time in which to read or walk in the country, and an occasional couple of days in Paris in which to do my shopping and see pals. Food is jolly good, though our cook is not good by French standards; but we have masses of lovely *escarole* salad from the garden, meat, *charcuterie* and butter at 9–1200 frs. a kilo.

My question re Vallon referred to one in a letter which you apparently never got. In this I said that we had been out once or twice with M. Vallon, head of the Mint (Directeur de la Monnaie) and a henchman of de Gaulle, who said he knew you but couldn't remember where he'd met you. In case you can't remember him either, he is middle-aged, dark, very French looking, married to a doctor, drinks a lot but is very amusing and *sympathique*. Do try and think.

Love,
Twin

Monday Dec. 6th 1948   Pavillon du Pré

Dearest Twinnie,

Have you tried Tom Hop[kinson] in your search for jobs?[1] He must have contacts in the Hulton Press, which is a big thing, and there might be something there for one with your great experience. I advise writing to him either at *Picture Post* or at 26 Cheyne Row. Also I advise getting hold of his book of short stories, *The Transitory Venus*, just out, which contains some marvellous stories. They really are almost all frightfully good. I don't know whether you know Tom, or whether you would like me to write to him about you? He is very nice and easy to get on with.

I will order the books you suggest and send you in due course my notes on the Ruth Fischer, which is interesting but takes a hell of a time to read.[2] Have you read Auden's *The Age of Anxiety*? Twin, it is WONDERFUL, and gave me more pleasure than any book I've read for years.

Have you read about Garry Davis's activities in the Palais de Chaillot and the Salle Pleyel? It seems Camus is in with him and that he made a very good speech at the Salle Pleyel. I don't know exactly what it's all about, though I do trust anything that C. does; but it does seem to K and me rather like having a meeting and saying 'The people of the world want happiness and the governments don't give it to them'. That is not the question, nor that they want peace and world government. The question is how, and that is more difficult. However, the whole thing probably has some utility and I admire G. Davis anyway.[3]

I made a beautiful strike notice for K, in cardboard covered with blue paper and with the following slogan stuck on in large letters of pink and white paper: more CARROT less STICK. I hope it will do him good. As a matter of fact I think his irritability lately has been due to his flu.

No time for more: I am working even harder these days, to make good, and am putting in a bit of after-dinner work on my own (besides writing to you). The Palestine book will be good, I think.

Love,
Mamaine

[1] Celia had recently returned to live in England.
[2] *Stalin and German Communism* (1948).
[3] On 3 September 1948 a former American bomber pilot, Garry Davis, staged a sit-in at the Palais de Chaillot, the temporary headquarters of the United Nations, and publicly renounced his American citizenship and pronounced himself a citizen of the world. Camus was among a group of French intellectuals who supported his quixotic stand: he spoke in defence of Davis at two large rallies early in December.

Thursday Dec. 30, 1948   Pavillon du Pré

Dear Twin,

Sorry I haven't been able to write for so long, owing to pressure of work. We were very keen to finish at least the first part of the book by Christmas and worked 11–12 hours a day to do so, starting at 9 and often finishing after midnight, sometimes at 2 a.m. So you can imagine not much time or energy was available for anything else; and while we have now slowed down the pace a bit, we are still hard at it. The book should be finished by about Jan 20th. It is turning out quite well. It is extremely damning about the English.

I am happy and well in my vegetable life. We did go to Paris for half a day and saw the Crossmans on their way through to Palestine. I bought some woolly slippers and a coat for the dog, and we returned here in the evening.

In haste,
Twin

Thursday 26.1.49   Pavillon du Pré

Dearest Twinnie,

Is not Mr Bevin an unspeakable swine? To come out now with the statement that if fighting should break out again in Palestine Britain wouldn't be able to stand aside. What have we come to when that maniac can make England go to war against the Jews without anybody being able to stop him? When we heard his iniquitous statement, and the bunch of lies which preceded it, K nearly hit the ceiling with rage. This morning he said to me: 'I always resented your dragging me to Palestine, but now I see you were quite right – I couldn't have gone on writing during the summer if we'd stayed in Wales.'

We have had a very nice American woman called Agnes Knickerbocker to stay for the weekend. She is the wife of H. R. Knickerbocker the American journalist. It is the second time she has come down. She is really terrifically attractive: I like her no end.

My health is very bad these days – I would like to do something about it in London if I can – it is impossible to go on like this.

Well dear Twinnie, we shall, I hope, arrive in London on Thursday next, Feb 3rd; I will let you know more details early next week. How I long to see you. We shall go to Paris on Monday, and shall be at the Hôtel Montalembert (Littré 68.11) for a couple of days, if you want to write, wire or ring.

                                                   Love,
                                                   Twin

Saturday 26.2.49   Hôtel Montalembert

Dear Celia,

K has gone to dine with the Sperbers and other old-time German pals.

We have had a lovely day buying carpets, and have finished up with two Moroccan rugs and one Algerian carpet: the former, which are those lovely orange, brown and white rugs, we got from an Arab stall in the exhibition of *arts ménagers*, and by bargaining with the Arab got each reduced by 15,000 fra.! K is on fine form, though he says everything is going very badly and that Thorez's speech proves that the peace offensive has been abandoned.[1] He is unbelievably sweet and easy to get on with, tried to get me to go along to the Sperbers, and when I refused begged me to ring up during the evening to 'report on my health'.

I had a funny time on the Golden Arrow, because when the French customs officer came along I declared my 3 metres of stuff and was made to pay a vast sum on it; whereupon the man who was sitting opposite me, a good-looking Frenchman, protested violently, and finally got both customs men and gave them a drink and tried desperately to persuade them to reimburse me. When this failed, he ragged them so much by saying 'aren't you ashamed to make this innocent and honest *jeune fille* pay?' and so on that they positively blushed and I am sure rushed off to confession. Afterwards he told me that the chief customs officer had told him he would have given me back my money if the sergeant hadn't been there. I thanked him for taking so much trouble on my behalf, but he said it was only because 'j'ai honte pour la France' that I had been treated with such lack of gallantry by the customs officers.

Sartre and Simone have broken off relations with us, because 'someone who is a friend of Malraux can't be a friend of theirs'! (since they say M. threatened to leave Gallimard[2] if they went on publishing *Les Temps Modernes*). Simone made a great speech to K in which she said how awful the Americans were and how Russia was really the country of a great proletarian revolution and God knows what. Can you beat it? K had lunch with Camus, apparently, and says he was nice but woolly-headed; C. said he is only 10 per cent pro Garry Davis, and seemed uninterested in it. If so why does he make speeches for him? *Je n'y comprends plus rien*, except that all French intellectuals are crazy. K has discovered, what he always suspected, that Malraux is terribly jealous of his (K's) fame. He thinks Malraux is raving mad, and hasn't seen him because M. always asks K to go to his office in the

Gaullist set-up, and K doesn't see why he should. I have hopes that he is becoming less Gaullist; he says he thinks very few of the Gaullists are honest; Palewski is one who is.[3]

K has taken to Sperber's a woman called Frau Buber who was married first to the son of Martin Buber the Zionist philosopher or whatever he was, and then to Heinz Neumann, the genial German Communist leader of the twenties, who subsequently disappeared in Russia and was liquidated: it was he who invented the slogan 'schlagt die Faschisten, wo ihr sie trefft'[4] which is why he didn't get on with the Russians after 1939. This woman, whom I met yesterday, is the daughter of a Potsdam officer and the sister of Babette Gross, who was married to Willi Muenzenberg, former head of the western bureau of the Comintern, since liquidated by the Communists in France. She (Frau Buber) has apparently been the best witness in the Kravchenko trial:[5] she was several years in Siberia, and then five years in Ravensbrueck.

Love
Twin

---

[1] Maurice Thorez was then leader of the French Communist Party.

[2] His publisher.

[3] Gaston Palewski, a Cabinet Minister under General de Gaulle, was one of the creators of the RPF and a member of its policy-making committee.

[4] 'Strike the fascists wherever you meet them.'

[5] A former Soviet official named Viktor Andreevich Kravchenko had recently defected to the West and had published a book called *I Chose Freedom*. The Communist weekly *Les Lettres Françaises* immediately accused him of being in the pay of the CIA. Kravchenko took out a libel suit against the paper, which he won.

Shortly after this Arthur and Mamaine moved to a villa at Fontaine le Port 100 km. south of Paris. It stood on the bank of the Seine opposite the Forest of Fontainebleau and was called Verte Rive.

March 2nd 1949

Verte Rive,
Fontaine le Port,
Seine-et-Marne

Dear Twin,

I didn't send the first part of this letter because new facts came to light concerning the Malraux-Sartre-Koestler row. K saw Malraux and Madeleine that night at the Sperbers and bearded Malraux about whether it was true, as Sartre had apparently said, that M. had told Gallimard that he (Gallimard) hadn't a very brilliant war record, and that M. had something on him about Gallimard having collaborated, which beans he would spill if Gallimard didn't turn out *Les Temps Modernes*. At first when K asked him about this Malraux made evasive replies, but finally he more or less admitted that it was true. K was very taken aback by this and felt his universe crumbling around him. Though the evening continued fairly amicably, K told Madeleine to tell Malraux that he found the whole thing sickening. In these circs, K feels that his great faith in and friendship with Malraux is at an end – it really was a stinking thing to do, don't you think?, in fact, simply blackmail. As K says, even if Malraux had said 'either you give up *Les Temps Modernes* or I leave you' it would have been bad enough, if one pretends one is fighting for freedom, because after all *Les Temps Modernes* is not a communist magazine and even if it were, so long as Gallimard is not in communist pay it is no business of Malraux's what else he publishes; but to add to this that filthy blackmail does really seem a bit much. I believe that K's faith in the Gaullists is rapidly dwindling: Vallon told him that there were only three honest men among them – Vallon himself, Malraux and Palewski. Now as K says Palewski is a dubious asset, Malraux problematical to say the least and Vallon nice no doubt but a complete *farfelu*.

We had Greta Buber to stay for two days, which was absolutely fascinating. She was for several years in Karaganda and several more in Ravensbrueck – seven years in all – and told us the most fantastic stories you can imagine about her experiences. She has, fortunately for herself, a kind of manic desire to talk about them, and does so with complete lack of self-consciousness and extraordinarily vividly and convincingly; she told it all in German, which, to my surprise, I perfectly understood. She says most people can't bear to talk about their experiences in concentration camps, and often forget nearly everything that happens to them there, and these people usually break down afterwards under the strain, whereas she gets it off her chest by talking about it, writing a book, dreaming about it – and she really is apparently quite normal, and very nice and intelligent. She says Karaganda is classed as a light labour camp, but when she first arrived at Ravensbrueck from there she thought she had come to paradise. I wish I could tell you more of what she told us, it was so very interesting. She has gone back to Sweden where she lives. She says Kravchenko is a frightful man and everybody hates him.

Love
Twin

March 7 1949   Verte Rive

Dear Twinnie,

Life is just a bit difficult for me because the house has, as could have been foreseen, several major snags: the *fosse septique* leaks, emitting a pungent odour; the water pump makes a hell of a noise; the house is as sonorous as can be. The consequence of these snags, and particularly of the last one, is that K has been filled with misgivings, and keeps telling me he made a frightful mistake in buying the house, because it isn't at all nice and he'll never be able to work in it. He worries, understandably, about the thought of all the money he will have put into it, not to mention time, only to find that it's a flop and we have to resell it. Poor chap, I feel sorry for him and try to tell him all will be well when we get some carpets, but I am not sure that it will. He has also had a bad cold in his head and chest for three weeks, which is quite unique for him. Also, his New York publishers are being difficult about the Palestine book. But although the New York critics seem to have made a concerted attack on *Insight and Outlook*, provincial reviews have almost without exception been good in the States; and the most violent reviewer, a man called Edman, who wrote in the *New York Times Book Review*, turns out to have written a theory of the comic himself, which isn't mentioned in K's book, so that probably accounts for his venom. So far he has only had one professional reaction, from a very good woman neuro-physiologist – very favourable.

Well, as I say, life is difficult because K is madly irritable, but it's not too bad and won't last once he gets settled down to some work. I am not doing much – yesterday I actually went for a walk in the Forest. It is terrible to find that I am so unused to being able to walk for pleasure that I feel positively guilty when I'm doing it.

The furniture is due to arrive next week. I am longing for it as the stuff here is *so* awful.

Hoping for an early reply, I remain

Yours
Twin

Friday 11.3.49   Verte Rive

Dear Twin,

Cy and Marina's party for Harriman[1] was much as their parties always are: very well arranged but lacking in atmosphere. There was an incredible French *vicomte* there who at the end of the evening (slightly tight no doubt) started *telling Harriman* about the Politburo and what would happen if Stalin died; everybody's hair stood on end, but Harriman took it all right. Then he (the *vicomte*) went on for a long time about a ball which Jacques Fath was giving that night, and which he said *le tout Paris* was going to because they thought the King of the Belgians was going to be there, because J. Fath had said he was; but he was sure the King wouldn't go, because it would be politically most unwise for him to go to a ball given by a *couturier*; so the *vicomte* was going to rush off and have a look to see how many people had been fooled into going, or perhaps he wouldn't, thus being able to say that he hadn't been fooled by this story about the King . . . and so he went on for at least half an hour. It was too comic; but that is how French people *dans le monde* apparently are, and Marina, who knows lots, wasn't at all surprised, since she'd heard some woman say that she didn't want to marry a certain industrialist because it would be annoying to have to sit below her sisters at table, as they were princesses!

I can't remember whether I told you that Cy and the Sperbers came down last Sunday and we had a most enjoyable day, during which Cy and I went fishing in a boat without success, and Cy and Munjo sang Serbian and other songs. Now James Putnam of Macmillans, New

York, is staying here, he is a friend of Arthur's and seems very nice. Everything is going well except one thing, but that is the most important: Arthur is having a really serious crisis about his writing, he has quite lost confidence in himself. It is too awful for him and I don't know what to do – and the silly thing is, it was brought on by Jim Putnam, because Jim has terrific faith in Arthur and keeps on saying so, and it has given Arthur a frightful complex about being unworthy of it. They have both gone off to Paris to have drinks with the Sulzbergers, as we'd specially asked Cy to get some nice Americans for Putnam to meet. I am happily sitting here in bed reading Henry James' *The Americans* and the new Marquand. Oh, I forgot to tell you, I have read Romain's new book [*Le Grand vestiaire*] and think it awfully good. It has a few rather dull passages and some which don't quite come off but I think as a whole it comes off very well and that it is full of excellent things. I will send you a copy as soon as I am up and about. I intend to ask Romain and Lesley down here soon.

I am longing to see your house when it's finished. Also for you to see this one. It is really a sunny warm house, ideal for the summer: all the rooms seem to get the sun all day. Unfortunately our cook has turned out to be a mixed blessing: she is not in the least efficient, loses her head twenty times a day, and looks all the time as if she were at a funeral, which gets terribly on our nerves. Even her cooking is not so good as I had at first supposed. Nevertheless it is a relief to be able to ask people to meals and get almost anything one likes to give them to eat.

I see that *Caligula* was a flop in London – what a shame. Of course the English would never see the point, even if it were well done, which I bet it wasn't.

Love,
Twin

[1] Averell Harriman had been special envoy to Churchill and Stalin, 1941–46, and US Ambassador to the USSR, 1943–6.

Mamaine's health had been deteriorating for some time, and a few days after writing the preceding letter she developed a serious illness. It originated in a cold, which led to a bad attack of asthma. The local doctor tried to cure this by giving her an injection of a drug to which she was allergic, and which therefore almost proved fatal. Mamaine believed that she was about to die, and she suffered acute anguish about the form her death would take, because she was unable to move or speak. As soon as she recovered sufficiently to write, she described this experience in a letter to Celia, dated 18 March 1949, and commented:

It was so surprising – to catch a mild cold one day, and the next suddenly to find one is probably dying. I was also interested to see how *very* clear my mind remained in spite of this curious vertigo, which made me feel as if either I, or the room, or both were swaying, or as if I were flying out first to one side and then to the other, and that if I flew too far I'd go for good; and an endless series of thoughts, most of which I still remember, passed through my brain. For instance, it occurred to me that I would like to say some friendly word to Arthur before dying, such as that I loved him, but I supposed that if he were there I shouldn't be able to say it, because I didn't seem able to speak. The frustration of having one's dying words all ready and not being able to say them!

Arthur has been wonderful as usual and has rushed about getting things from various chemists in Fontainebleau and ringing up doctors – a frightful nuisance, as we have no telephone.

Love
Twin

Monday 21st March 49   Verte Rive

Dear Twinnie,

I am still in bed and beginning to feel that I shall never be out of it – having apparently got into one of those states when one never seems to make any progress. I still don't really feel well enough to get up, though I am not suffering in the least. It is too annoying, because poor Arthur has been left to do all the unpacking and arranging of the furniture by himself, including all the books, of which we have over 2,000: it is nearly killing him. Simultaneously the proofs of the

Palestine book have started to arrive, so he is in a real flap. Thirdly, Jim Putnam has also retired to bed with gastric flu or something; and the cook is quite off her head and is driving us all off ours. But it is wonderful having the furniture. The sitting-room now looks much smaller, which is a good thing, and quite human. It has a bright turkey-red coconut carpet which is dazzling indeed, partly covered by an orange-and-black-on-white Moroccan rug! Arthur now has a blue carpet and bookshelves in his room, and the corridor and landing have been covered with my old brown carpet, so the sound question has considerably improved. Altogether the house is becoming most prepossessing. It is lovely to be able to lie in bed and look out on the river with its barges and tugs gliding past.

I am longing for you to come and stay; in the meanwhile, I shall probably be coming to England fairly soon, to do some research for the Palestine book – when we have got all the proofs.

We've just been having a conference with Jim, who wants Arthur to cut and change his Palestine book radically: I think I have found a good compromise solution. *Insight and Outlook* won't be out in England till the end of May now – they are incredibly slow, it's most annoying.

If you have any sugar to spare (not otherwise) it would be a great help to have some – but not if it's an awful nuisance to send it.

No more now, owing to the difficulty of writing in bed. I must try to do some of K's mail today too. Oh how I wish I was up and about.

Love,
Twin

PS. It is evening now and I am feeling much better: I shall definitely start getting up tomorrow. Oh the river is so lovely, I wish you could see it, it's so quiet and the chaffinches sing away in the forest opposite, herons rise up from the reeds and the motor barges chug along, leaving a trail behind them in the glassy water. From my window I can see down to the bend of the river: just round it is Samois.

Soon after this Mamaine had a relapse and again became very ill. She was moved to a Paris hospital, and Celia went over to visit her there. She recovered slowly, and by the beginning of May was well enough to return to Fontaine le Port.

Monday May 9, 1949   Verte Rive

Dear Celia,

    sorry I haven't written for so long, but the change from the hospital to here, which I did on Friday, made me rather worse for a couple of days. However, I am much better now and getting on fine in my desperately slow way.

    Arthur and the Winklers together have bought a wonderful canoe with sails which is now Arthur's passion – he thinks of nothing else. Yesterday he capsized it with two young people in it! But they salvaged everything.

    Do tell me how Donkey George was.[1]

    Arthur is as angelic as ever, but his life is very difficult, I'm afraid. He says he got on much better than usual with you when you were in Paris this time, and he expressed great approval and admiration of you. I mention this as he so rarely does like or appreciate women, so it really is a compliment.

Love,
Mamaine

[1] Celia had written that she was about to visit George Orwell in the sanatorium in Cranham, Gloucestershire, where he had been since January of that year. He was extremely ill.

Thursday 12.5.49   Verte Rive

Dearest Twinnie,

    I really am making progress. Now I have been out of hospital nearly a week and have recovered from the change, and can do much more on my good days. I stay up most of the day. Yes definitely I am getting better, though I could wish for a speed-up of the process. K is as angelic as ever under terrible difficulties. I think all the time how lucky I am to have him – it is lovely to go to sleep at night (I sleep in the room next to the sitting room) seeing his head through the half-open door, and he plays music on the radio to me and is really wonderful.

Since my illness we have sometimes been able to talk to each other in a new, much deeper way, saying things one can't usually say to anybody at all and with a wonderful understanding between us. He is longing for me to be well and so am I – the house is *such* a pigsty I can hardly bear it, and old Grandin [their daily woman] is *so* hopeless, and there's so much to be done, yet I can't do it. Well, it won't be long now. In the meantime I am still reading *Anna Karenina*, rationing it carefully to a few pages a day, and it seems to me it is one of the greatest joys one can have, to re-read these Tolstoy novels. I do wish you hadn't done it so recently, and that you had the time to do it at the same time as me, so that we could discuss them as we went along. I am simply obsessed by them.

I *am* sorry about Donkey George – how very sad.

Love,
M.

There are *millions* of nightingales here.

Mamaine's condition again deteriorated and she became seriously ill. Arthur flew her over to England, accompanied by a nurse, and put her into a nursing-home in Hampstead under the care of a specialist. She slowly recovered, but was not strong enough to return to France until early in August.

13.8.49. Saturday   Verte Rive

Dear Twinnie,

Home at last, and it's wonderful. I arrived on Wednesday evening. On Thursday evening the Crossmans turned up for dinner with Venice[1] and a boy friend of hers, on their way to Switzerland and Germany. They spent the night here and yesterday, after morning champagne in the sun and a huge lunch, we all set out in two cars for Vézelay, where we arrived about 6.30 and spent the night. Have you ever been there? It is really such a lovely town, on a hill, and the church one of the most beautiful romanesque churches I've ever seen, if not the most beautiful.

This morning the Crossmans left, and Arthur and I drove through Avallon to Chablis. It was most enjoyable wandering about Vézelay and Avallon and Chablis in the sun; there is a very good restaurant in Chablis where we ate *pâté en croûte, écrevisses à la chablisienne, quennelles de brochet, jambon mode d'ici* – all swimming in cream, butter and wine – and drank some delicious Chablis 47. Then we drove slowly back across country.

I am terribly disappointed that Peg and Lu[2] can't come on their way to England to visit us; I do hope they will be able to come in October. If they do they might perhaps coincide with our marriage, which will take place then, I think – K's divorce is supposed to be through by that time.[3]

He is in fine form and working on a novel,[4] the theme of which, as everything else about it, is a secret so far. In order not to interrupt it he has put off his intended visit to America in the autumn – much to my relief, as I didn't really want to go there.

Sunday. Have just been sailing in our canoe. It really is lovely on the river now. The house is in a mess, I'm going to get busy finding wall papers and so on next week.

Imagine, we spend 15,000 fr. *a week* on food here (including entertaining). Isn't it awful? In Wales we spent about £3![5]

Love,
Mamaine

[1] Zita Crossman's daughter by a previous marriage.
[2] The Prince and Princess of Hesse and the Rhine.
[3] Arthur was still married to his first wife, Dorothy Ascher, although they had been separated since 1936.
[4] *The Age of Longing* (1951).
[5] 1,000 francs were worth about £1 in the currency of that time.

Thursday September 1, 49   Verte Rive

Dear Twinnie,

We have had a very hectic few days owing to (a) our great drive to get the house finally furnished, which involved driving round Paris in search of wallpapers, chintzes, etc. and (b) our servant crisis. We put an ad. in a local paper for a married couple, and I interviewed about seven yesterday, while at the same time coping with a new woman from the village who comes at other times, and with the TEN puppies to which Sabby's wife gave birth the day before. The birth of these puppies was most exciting, Arthur and I watched them popping out and it was most fascinating: now they look awfully sweet and glossy, with their little bullet boxer-heads and fast shut eyes. The result of the procession of would-be *ménages* was that we picked a Polish couple, who will come as soon as we have had them okayed by our pal the Melun police chief, in case they are desperate communists or something. The man is a racing cyclist and knows nothing about gardening or anything else, and his wife is very shy and looks nice, but God knows whether they'll be able to do anything.

The result of all these activities is, alas, that I have lost all the weight (about 4 lbs) which I had put on since my return.

Love,
M.

[?] September 1949   Verte Rive

Dear Twinnie,

I think the news about Sonia and George is splendid, and am most impressed by Sonia's courage in making what must have been a very difficult decision.[1] It will of course be wonderful for George, and may save him; in any case I think it can only be good for Sonia to be released from the crushing difficulties of life as a single woman, of finance, or dreary work and solitude. Though she always says she doesn't want children she is awfully good with them and I can't help thinking that having Richard will transform her life. Above all, George is such a very worth while person that anything one does for him is worth while and full of meaning. I'm longing to hear more, especially about his health and chances of recovery.

Love,
Twin

[1] Sonia Brownell had recently become engaged to George Orwell, whom she married on 13 December 1949. His adopted son Richard was then five years old.

Sept. 13, 1949   Verte Rive

Dear Celia,

I haven't had much time to write to you lately owing to the domestic situation. We now have one woman who comes from 8–10 a.m. and another who arrives at 12.30 and stays all afternoon. The latter is kept busy sewing curtains for us, and they both put everything in different places so that the other one can't find it; however, it is not too bad as a temporary arrangement. I have discovered that for the time being I have to spend most of my working hours coping with them and other household problems, and that the only thing to do is not to imagine that one is ever going to have any time for anything else. Like this it is a pleasant surprise if one does. Actually I rest quite a lot, but this climate has got me back to where I was before my illness, there is no doubt that it is a lousy climate for me, but equally nothing can now be done about this except to take things easy and periodically go away for a while.

We've been beautifying the house to some extent with paper and curtains, which has been hard work and has reduced K to a near breakdown with exasperation. He always gets like this when painters and workmen are around, and always thinks he will never be able to lead a quiet life and work again. Considering how he loathes it he has been most good-tempered, and we have had no major rows, except for one yesterday which was my fault, because C . . . B . . . rang up and said could he drop in in the afternoon, and owing to my usual pathological inability to think of excuses for putting people off whom one doesn't in the least want to see (I don't like C . . . B . . . and know that Arthur loathes him) I said okay. When I told K he went quite mad with fury and struck me a stunning blow on the head.* I didn't hit him back as (a) violence seems undignified and (b) because to hit someone much stronger than oneself is obviously useless and highly dangerous; but vowed to myself to take strong measures against him. However, half an hour later he had quite recovered and apologized, and I had put C . . . B . . . off, so all was well.

I am reading *The Naked and the Dead*,[1] which seems excellent. K thinks it is simply wonderful.

I have asked Macmillan to send you K's Palestine book – I *do* think it is awfully good – an example of how history should be written.

Love,
M.

* This is only the third time in our life together that he has done this –
3 times too many, of course, but considering how beserk he goes,
surprisingly few!

[1] Novel by Norman Mailer.

Thursday 22.9.49   Verte Rive

Dear Twinnie,

I'm most relieved that you are in good form these days. I've been
having a moderately hellish time myself, but it looks as though it is
going to improve. The Poles have now moved in and seem nice and
industrious and clean, which is the chief thing. They are simple souls
and I don't think the woman is much of a cook, nor the man much of a
gardener, but he is good at doing odd jobs, of which we have plenty.
Once I get these folks organized I do believe that at last K and I will
have some peace: up to now he has been interrupted twenty times a
day because the water pump isn't working or the lights have all gone
out or something, while I have to stay in all morning because of
visiting tradesmen, and altogether in every way life was difficult to
keep under control. Nor could we both go away for a night, as we
didn't want to leave the house empty. I hope that a satisfactory routine
will be established by Oct. 6th when I come to London, thus I won't
have to worry about leaving K at the mercy of events. I do simply pine
to get away and have some time off from thinking about housekeeping
and servants, I must say. Sometimes now I pop over to the forest in the
late afternoon, it is very quiet and green and one never meets a soul
there now that the summer is over – indeed even during the holiday
season one never did, except along the banks of the Seine.

K has decided to put off visiting America indefinitely so as not to
have any dates hanging over his head. He says when he has finished
the novel on which he is now engaged he will fly over for a brief visit to
contact his psychological and neurological buddies, but won't stay. I
am all in favour of this as I so much don't look forward to visiting the

States with K, for a variety of reasons, the chief of which is the intense boredom of travelling around with somebody famous. In a few years I suppose K no longer will be famous in the States, and then we can go there and have fun. At least that is my idea.

Now the object of this letter is to say, will Adam [Watson] send K full reports of the Hungarian trials, about which I imagine you know all.[1] K takes a lively interest in the subject, as apart from everything else he knows a lot of people who might be involved. Indeed I know one man who has been arrested – a chap called Paul Ignotus who was Press Attaché in London, a misguided liberal. His father was a writer whose *nom de plume* was Ignotus (anon.) and that is now his (Paul I's) name – funny, isn't it? Did you see Kingsley[2] in the New Statesman saying 'a year ago Hungary was still really a People's Democracy' or some such thing? He really is incredible. I do wish we could fix a weekend in Woodbridge when I am in England.

Did I tell you we had a Dominican monk called le Père Piprot staying for the weekend, and he said mass to a congregation consisting of Arthur and no one else.

Yrs.

Twin

[1] In September 1949 Laszlo Rajk, a former Minister of the Interior and Foreign Minister, and several other high-ranking Hungarian Communists were tried on charges of espionage and subversion. Rajk confessed to having been a police spy for the Horthy regime, an agent of the US intelligence service since the war and an active plotter with Tito for an overthrow of the Hungarian government. He was sentenced to death. As Minister of the Interior he had organized many similar trials himself. The present ones were designed to crush any latent Titoism in Eastern Europe.

Adam Watson was at that time Assistant in a research department of the Foreign Office.

[2] Kingsley Martin was editor of the *New Statesman & Nation*, 1930–60.

28.9.49   Verte Rive

Dear Twinnie,

We had a most enjoyable weekend here with the Sperbers and Alex Weissberg. The latter is an old friend of K's (he was married to K's first 'wife') and Sperber's who spent some years in prison in Russia (he was an Austrian Communist at the time), was handed over to the Gestapo, put in a German concentration camp, got out, took part in the Jewish uprising in Warsaw and so on. He is now a successful business man in Sweden. He is really one of the most extraordinary men I've ever met, and certainly has had the most extraordinary life of anybody. Aged 47 and very Jewish-looking, rather fat, rather bald, with a curly smile showing several gold teeth, he is nevertheless awfully attractive and I got on with him like a house on fire, in spite of the fact that we had to speak German together. The amazing thing about Alex is that he can do anything: he used to be a physicist working on *Kältetechnik*, he is a business man of genius, an economist and above all a political man with an inborn sense of politics (so he says). He has been living in Stockholm and working on a book about his experiences, helped by Greta Neumann, but hasn't got very far with it; K is reading the MS and says it is simply WONDERFUL. Alex is married to a Polish aristocrat[1] who saved his life in Warsaw, she is extremely charming and they are both coming here for a couple of days on Friday, I think.

Love,
Mamaine

[1] Sophia Cybulska.

Mamaine now spent a fortnight in London, returning to France in the middle of October.

Thursday Oct. 20, 1949   Verte Rive

Dear Twin,

God was the sea rough! I groaned when I saw it at Dover. However, I managed not to be ill.

Yesterday a great catastrophe befell us: our Pole, Nicholas, suddenly announced that he and his wife are leaving because he has found a job in a restaurant in Fontainebleau where he will be better paid. The fact is, of course, that he doesn't like living here in the wilderness, and they have a flat in Fontainebleau.[1] He is leaving on Saturday, which we think very swinish, as we'd agreed when they came on a month's notice if they left or we sacked them. Sophie is staying till Saturday week. Oh Twin, the whole bloody business of looking for a *ménage* now starts again, just when I thought it was over for good and we'd found the ideal couple. I can hardly bear it, neither can K. It is true that all people who live in the country have servant problems, unless they are terrifically rich. K was so got down by it that he said he thought we probably shouldn't try to go against nature by living here in the winter, but should move to Paris. I pointed out that this would only create servant problems of a different kind, and that we can't keep moving his library about, consisting as it does of some 2000 books. Another annoying aspect of the Poles leaving is that K and I had decided that I should try to go to Haus Hirth[2] as soon as possible, and of course I can't go till we find some new people and they are properly installed and know the ways of the house and the tradesmen, which may take months. And oh I am *so* fed up with spending my waking hours coping with servants. Luckily K is sympathetic and as sorrowful as I, so we drank a bottle of champagne to console ourselves last night.

The divorce will be through in a week or so, I don't know how long after that it will take to get married, or what we shall do in the way of a wedding feast.

Another thing contributed to making my first night here a bad one: that review of *Promise and Fulfilment* in the *Observer*. Poor K is most depressed about having had such bitchy reviews in English papers, it seems to him they are full of venom, which indeed they mostly are, because the English have such a bad conscience about Palestine and simply won't admit it. As a result K is more violently anti-English than ever. I fully sympathize with him, but at the same time am terribly irritated by his going on about it and inclined to accuse him of exaggerating, which up to a point he probably does. I suppose if one were French and one's husband kept on day and night telling one how dishonest and cowardly the French were, and how shamelessly they had capitulated to the Germans whenever they got a chance, one would feel the more irritated because one couldn't very easily defend them.

Incidentally this book *L'Enracinement*[3] is simply wonderful. It is really the most stimulating and astonishing, brilliantly written, original and profound book imaginable, or so it seems to me. K has finally read the Trilling,[4] and now says it *is* rather a good book, though he still doesn't like it.

Alex and Sophia Cybulski have left and are now living in Paris, Alex having been told that it really would be dangerous for him to return to Sweden now. He wants to give you as a reference for a visit to England (visa). So if they ask you about him, his name is Alexander Weissberg-Cybulski and he is okay! You know all about him anyway.

Yrs,

Twin

[1] It is possible that the real cause of the Poles' departure was an article that had just appeared in one of the Communist Sunday papers denouncing Arthur as a leader of the cold war and giving a map of the region round Fontaine le Port, with an arrow pointing to Verte Rive.

[2] A guest house in the Bavarian Alps: see p. 124.

[3] By Simone Weil (1949).

[4] Lionel Trilling's novel *The Middle of the Journey* (1947).

29.X.49   Verte Rive

Dear Twinnie,

The visit of Peg and Lu [of Hesse] was a great success. K found them both very endearing, especially Peg, whom he liked no end. Indeed I simply couldn't get over Peg's niceness, she really is absolutely charming and such fun to be with. I took them to visit the Château de Fontainebleau, as they are great sightseers, and we lunched at Samois with K and in the afternoon all went for a very enjoyable drive, returning here for dinner. The next day they had to go, so I took them to Paris and we went to the Louvre and to a modern art museum or two, and lunched at the Vieux Paris behind the Panthéon, which they liked.

Yesterday, it being a fine autumn day, K and I spent the morning driving and walking in the forest and making a large collection of fungi with a view to looking up which were edible when we got home. I am working studying neurology, but have a long way to go before I learn anything at all.

Love,

Twin

30 October 1949. Bertaux and Denise [Bertaux][1] to lunch. B. told us about his experience with the lie detector in the States; he and K discussed possible experiments in interrogating *à la russe*, but without any physical violence or even drugs. Bertaux said in 3 months (he believed) he could get K to declare himself, with sincerity, the most ardent Stalinist. But said he couldn't do the opposite, i.e. make a Stalinist declare himself an ardent capitalist, because there's nothing solid to convert him to. First time I've seen Bertaux since February 1948 in Lyon. Denise was rather beautiful.

[1] Pierre Bertaux, formerly Professor at the Universities of Rennes and Toulouse, was Directeur de la Sûreté Nationale, 1948–51, and his wife, Denise, daughter of the poet Jules Supervielle.

During her recent illness a London specialist had advised Mamaine to undergo a bronchoscopy. She now decided to do so, and flew to London for the operation early in November, returning to Paris at the end of the month.

29 [November 1949]. Back to Paris with Arthur's Ma, by train. Oysters and white wine outside a café on the Place St Michel. New dismal *ménage* at home, otherwise nice homecoming.

December 2 [1949]. Last night K drew his Ma out on the subject of his childhood. He said he didn't seem to remember ever playing with any other children till he was about 14; she said, no, the other children he knew weren't well-brought-up enough, so she didn't want him to go about with them; and besides, she was afraid he might catch some infection from them. As he continued to pursue the subject she went on the defensive and (according to K) greatly falsified the facts – which he remembers only too well – in an attempt to make out that after all he *did* have some playmates. K's face during this conversation was worth seeing, but fortunately she didn't seem to notice – sparks of hatred flashed from his eyes, he grinned fiendishly. Afterwards in bed he talked about his childhood till late. I loathe K's Ma as much as he does and feel singularly little pity for her. Typically, she handed K a cutting of a poem in which a woman tells her son that when she's dead he will realize how much he loved her. This did not have the desired effect on K.

Nanny Michelmore, King and the twins, August 1924

A studio portrait of Mamaine by Harlip, 1937

Mamaine in Bavaria, by Celia, 1950

Celia, by Mamaine, 1949

Bwlch Ocyn

Arthur and Mamaine at Bwlch Ocyn

Arthur in Wales with Joe and Dina

Mamaine with Nellie, by Arthur

Verte Rive

Mark and Irene Sontag

Albert Camus

Richard Crossman and
Emily

Dick Wyndham, 1948

Arthur and Mamaine at the Berlin
Congress for Cultural Freedom,
1950 (*Der Tag*, Berlin)

Arthur at Island Farm

Island Farm

Saturday December 10, 49   Verte Rive

Dear Twinnie,

We have been to Paris a couple of times since I last wrote; we had lunch with Romain [Gary] and a girl friend of his, which was great fun. Romain was at his nicest and I got on with him very well, as one does when he is like that. I think his slightly fellow-travellerish political statements are due simply to confusion in his mind – indeed he says so – and all I can say is, if confusion still reigns there about that particular problem he can't be very bright. Then we had dinner with the Venards[1] and the William Phillips (editor of Partisan Review). The latter are very nice. We also went to a terrifying but nice dinner at the Vallons, terrifying because everybody there was about sixty except me, and because Vallon insisted on our bringing Sabby up after dinner, and there was a huge Alsatian there, whom Sabby instantly attacked. A terrible fight ensued, everybody fell, very ineffectively, on the dogs to try and separate them, and soon K, the only effective one, was lying on the ground hanging on to Sabby's collar, while somebody else was holding Sabby's legs in the air and I was trying to disengage the Alsatian's jaws from Sabby's ear and Sabby's jaws from the Alsatian's throat. The end was that K was rather bitten and bruised and got a bad shock, from which he suffered only when we got home, about 3 a.m., after going on to a dinner-party.

K and I went round to look at Venard's latest pictures. They are rather different from his former ones, and I thought most of them very good, though not all. K wanted to buy one, but Venard now charges about 100,000 francs[2] for a picture, and K thought this too much. Jacqueline is still working hard on her hideous old men and women.

We had a new crisis with the servants, who threatened to leave because the Winklers' gardener said (which he made up) that the Winklers' cook had said that our servants were being starved by us and only paid 1,200 francs a month. Of course not a word of this is true, the servants eat the same as we do and get 15,000 a month and would never have said anything else, and we didn't for a second believe this crazy story, but it was enough for them to give notice; however, K did his usual act, which he is so good at, of having a long talk with them and by dint of repeating everything 25 times getting it into their heads that they were being idiotic. However, this couple obviously won't last for ever, and indeed in view of their cooking and general level of efficiency we don't wish that they should, so the problem is still with us.

Love,
Twin.

[1] Claude Venard, the painter, and his wife Jacqueline, also an artist. Jacqueline Venard was at that time working principally on drawings of scraggy old men and women in the nude.
[2] Then worth about £100.

December 16th 1949. K rather bad-tempered for the first time for months, says he is always disturbed, never gets a chance to work, and that we spend too much money, which we do. All this year he has been disturbed a good deal by my being ill (4 months) and away (3 trips to England), servants changing, Ma to stay, etc. However, he is working well and getting on fine with his novel [*The Age of Longing*]. I have lots to do, but don't feel very well, which annoys me; perhaps Germany will improve me, if only temporarily; apart from that I've no desire to go away again. K's divorce through at last yesterday.

December 28th, 1949 (Wednesday)   Verte Rive

Dear Celia,

We had a rather exciting Christmas, as follows.

K had gone to Paris on Friday night to see the Weisweillers,[1] who are perhaps going to let him a room in their house while I am away. He said he might not come back till Saturday morning, so I was not unduly alarmed when he still wasn't back by midday on Saturday; but by lunch time I was getting rather apprehensive, since I felt sure he would have rung up if he had intended to stay in Paris for lunch, or even to be late for it. The afternoon wore on, as they say, and still no sign of K, and by 5 o'clock I was pretty well resigned to widowhood, and impatient to know the worst. The telephone rang; I rushed to it, and a gruff and unfriendly voice said 'Votre mari m'a demandé de vous prévenir de ne pas vous inquiéter à son sujet.' 'Mais d'où téléphonez-vous?', I said, 'et où est-il?' 'Je ne peux pas vous dire,' replied the voice. I tried a few more questions, but the chap would only say 'C'est tout ce que je peux vous dire, Madame.' At this moment the Vallons turned up, and I talked to them for an hour while waiting to see whether K would return (I forgot to say the mysterious man said he would come back that evening), but by 6 still no K, so I rang up Bertaux to see if he had any news, and Vallon rang a friend of his at the Préfecture in Paris: the latter knew already that K was lying in jail.

It turned out that he was driving back from the evening with the Weisweillers, which had become rather a blind, at 4 a.m. and finding himself at Charenton, which isn't at all on the way here, he realized that he was in no fit state to drive, so stopped the car and went to sleep. He was found there by some policemen, who took him to the local Commissariat; there he awoke at 11. Taken before the Commissaire – still fairly *alcoholisé* – K asked for permission to ring me; and when they refused it, he socked the Commissaire.

The end was that (after, I think, the intervention of the chap at the Préfecture and Bertaux) he was released, and came back in time for a late dinner. But this rather terrible story – terrible because now K has to appear before the *correctionnelle* and may get a prison sentence, though probably suspended – was really a blessing in disguise, because the tyre of one of the front wheels of the car was about to puncture, and would certainly have done so on the way back, which if he'd been going fast, and as it has a front-wheel drive, would most likely have killed him.

The Vallons were most sympathetic; nobody could have been more so, since Louis Vallon is always getting into that sort of scrape himself. But K was most shaken and has resolved in dead earnest to give up drink and ration himself to 3 brandies an evening at most. I really do think this has done the trick, so I am glad it happened, because he has been drinking much too much again lately and I doubt if anything less than a major shock of this kind could have provided the necessary incentive for him to take a firm line with himself. It was really *wonderful* when he did turn up none the worse except for a few bruises inflicted on him by the police, because knowing how reliable he is about ringing up I had been imagining all sorts of ghastly things:

I thought that he must have got into a drunken *bagarre* with some toughs, who had probably turned out to be Communists as well and had beaten him up or something – otherwise I couldn't explain why he should have have been unable to ring me up himself. Of course I thought of the police station theory, but supposed that they would ring me and say they'd got him; in fact, as I now know, they are not allowed to, because they are frightened somebody will pull some sort of wire before they have time to get the *correctionnelle* aspect fixed up.

The story appeared in various forms in various papers, and God knows what will happen next, and K is most unhappy. But it might be worse.

We spent yesterday in Paris – we went to a movie by ourselves and had a nice evening. Today I feverishly put in a lot of plants for next summer – it's a bit late, but I hope some will survive.

Arthur nearly DIED laughing at *The Young Visiters*[2] – it really is too funny and delightful for words.

Longing to hear more from you. I'm off to Munich on Monday night. I can't help feeling excited, though I don't at all want to leave home and K, and K terribly doesn't want me to go away either.

Love,
Mamaine

[1] M. Weisweiller, banker and financier, was adviser to the French government on the authenticity of paintings.

[2] The novel by the nine-year-old Daisy Ashford, which Celia had sent Arthur and Mamaine for Christmas.

29 [December 1949]. Very embarrassing lunch with the Vallons, Raoul, Torres, to try and rescue K from the *correctionnelle*.[1] Raoul wanted him to get a doctor's certificate (which Suzanne [Vallon] could have given him) that he'd been slightly beaten up, so as to have means of dissuading the Commissaire from pursuing the affair, but K refused to as he said the police were quite decent, hardly did anything to him.

K remembers that after he'd slapped the Commissaire and was being led off back to his cell he was *convinced* they were going to shoot him *at once*. Funnily enough he'd quite forgotten, till I reminded him, that he socked a policeman in Tel-Aviv – at least he thought it was a policeman but it turned out to be the Head of the Israeli Air Force. Journalists rang up all day, as the story has appeared in several papers.

[1] M. Raoul was Louis Vallon's friend in the Préfecture. Maître Torres was Arthur's defence lawyer.

•1950•

In order to get some mountain air, Mamaine went to stay with her old friends Walther and Johanna Hirth, who kept a guest-house in Untergrainau, near Garmisch-Partenkirchen, in the Bavarian Alps.

Jan 2 [1950]. By Orient Express to Munich, then up to Grainau. Snow all along the line: had a sleeper to myself. Lovely room in the small Haus Hirth, under the roof, canary yellow walls and ceiling. Onkel Walther and Tante Johanna just the same and very sweet: nobody else here yet.

7 [January 1950]. After dinner two sweet old men called Gutmann and Zimmermann (a writer and a playwright) came, they used to be very rich but lived in the Russian zone and had a house with lots of other people. Also a nice young doctor named May. He was three years on the Eastern front, says young Russians to whom he talked in his hospitals seemed to think Communism was fine. At Leningrad they ate each other, thus holding out when the Germans thought it impossible.

12 [January 1950]. Talk with Onkel Walther and Tante Johanna. Hartenberg shot himself 4 times through the chest without killing himself. The Nazis tried to cure him in order to hang him, but he was liberated in time.[1]

---

[1] Count Carl Hans von Hartenberg was one of the German officers implicated in the plot of 20 July 1944 to assassinate Hitler. On being arrested by the Gestapo shortly after the failure of the attempt he immediately shot himself twice in the chest, but did not succeed in killing himself. He then contrived to persuade his local doctor to give him, under the guise of an anti-tetanus injection, 'enough morphia to kill a bull', but it did not kill him. Finally he cut his veins with scissors, but survived this also. He spent the rest of the war in detention, at first in a Gestapo hospital and subsequently in Sachsenhausen. He was liberated by the Russians and returned to his estate in East Prussia, where he lived for another twenty years. (See Fabian von Schlabrendorff, *Begegnungen in fünf Jahrzehnten*, 1979, pp. 239 ff.)

16 [January 1950]. Tante Johanna's story. A woman whose husband was reported dead in Russia married again and lived happily with her new husband, by whom she had a child. One day she received a card from her first husband announcing his return the next day. She went to meet him, but he had died in the train on the way. Returning home, she found her second husband had hanged himself.

Last night Burgi's [the cook's] niece's husband was dying in hospital in Heidelberg after an operation for t.b. but she couldn't leave for Heidelberg till this morning at 9 because the earlier trains were for Americans only. Suggested taking her by one of them, but it turned out to be impossible.

21 [January 1950]. Furtwängler's assistant Frl. von Tibermann came to dinner and told some very interesting stories about her visit to the Russian zone with Furtwängler, who gave two concerts there. She said the people are all starving, as their wages are so low and food so expensive; they feel they are abandoned by the West because nobody from the West Zone ever goes there: Furtwängler is the first well-known artist to have done so. The orchestra was so undernourished that it took them twice as long as usual to rehearse, as they had to keep stopping for a rest. In Leipzig, where *only* Russian-trained teachers are in the schools, the former professors, at great risk, have the students to their houses so that they can learn at least something besides what they're told by the Russians. Frl. v. T. said the terror is much worse than under the Nazis.

February 1 [1950]. Gusti Oesterreicher came yesterday, and today I gave her Arthur's and my handwriting to look at.[1] She took one look at K's and said as much as I have found out about him in 6 years. About K, that he used to be rather materialistic but is now becoming more religious, though not belonging to any denomination; that he will go on getting more so, and that this is *der richtige Weg* for him. That he's terribly sensitive to weather and climate, especially to snow, *Vorschneewetter*, foehn, etc. She said that K will write lots more good books. He is *gutmütig*, warm-hearted, *anständig*, *treu*, *aufrichtig aber verschlossen*; though not at all cowardly he has a certain *Angst vor dem Leben und vor gewissen Leuten*. Said, he's very difficult but very worth while; has a rather *weibisch* (not *weiblich*) handwriting, like all artists, because very sensitive.[2]

About me, she said that I am very artistic indeed and must keep up the piano, go to concerts, etc; she said, very good handwriting; great self-control, very *aufrichtig*;[3] egocentric in the sense that I have my own inner life and want to get on with it, which she said I must do. Said, do you write? I said no, I can't; she said, well you probably will write poetry; never, I said, I couldn't possibly. Well you will, she said. Said, my tendency is to give in to K too much and I shouldn't do this, both from his point of view and mine twould be bad. Also, that though I am to some extent torn by conflicting desires, I am much less *unharmonisch* in my inner self than K.

[1] Augusta ('Gusti') Oesterreicher was a graphologist of some renown. Her assessment of character through handwriting was considered so reliable that the police occasionally sought her estimate of the criminal potential of suspects.

[2] He is kind, warm-hearted, decent, loyal, sincere but reserved; though not at all cowardly he has a certain fear of life and of certain people; . . . [he] has a rather feminine (not effeminate) handwriting . . .

[3] Sincere.

February 4 [1950]. Went by train to visit the von Scherpenbergs at Hohenpeisenberg (the Crossmans had told me to do this). Lunch in Weilheim in a sort of Weinstube. Very hot day for Feb., sweated up the hill from the station to the farmhouse where the Ss. live, nearly at the top. Sat with them on the balcony, facing south and looking over the whole chain of the Alps from the Bodensee to Salzburg, and ate apple cake and cheese cake. A meteorologist turned up who said that this is the warmest winter for 500 years, due to sunspots. Von. Sch. is head of foreign trade with the sterling bloc at the Wirtschafts-ministerium. Told me that real wages are not too bad in Germany now, and that unemployment (now at 1.5 m.) will be considerably reduced in the spring by certain plans now on foot, but not enough to get below the danger level of 500,000 or so. Said, the Germans were definitely fed up with planned economy, direction of labour, etc., and chose freely a free economy; remains to be seen if they'll think its drawbacks too great. Frau v. Sch. is Schacht's daughter[1] – tall, thin, English-looking; liked them both a lot and thought how easy Germans are to get on with compared with the French (of this particular class), and especially women, because Germans obviously do not share the French attitude to women, which makes French women themselves so frivolous. Frau v. S. had to go and meet one of her children at the station, so Herr v. S. took me up to the top of the hill and showed me the church, which has lovely Renaissance panelling and a very beautiful rococo Kapella, about 1740. He spent some time in prison at the end of the war, but said he wouldn't have missed it for anything. Most people who have been in prison seem to say this (ex. Leo [Valiani], K). – Wire from Celia to say she's coming to stay here.

[1] Dr Hjalmar Schacht was President of the Reichsbank during the Nazi period and Hitler's adviser on economics.

On 16 February Mamaine left Untergrainau and moved on to Heidelberg, then to Mainz, where carnival was being celebrated, and finally, on the 22nd, she arrived in Schloss Wolfsgarten, near Darmstadt, to stay with the Prince and Princess of Hesse.

February 22 [1950]. Lu read me *Patmos* from his original MS book. Hölderlin's friend Sinclair was at a conference in Regensburg with the Landgraf of Homburg. The L. of H. was very religious, and had, a couple of months before, written to Klopstock – then an old man – saying how much he admired his writing on Christian themes and asking him to write a crowning poem on the subject. Klopstock wrote back saying he'd written so much religious poetry he had nothing to add to it, and therefore refused. Sinclair asked Hölderlin to go to Regensburg on his return from Bordeaux (1801 – his health was already failing). Obviously the Landgraf repeated his request to Hölderlin, and *Patmos* was the result.

Heard a strange bird while walking at Wolfsgarten, it sounded rather woodpecker-like but not quite. Lu told me he saw it when riding, it was a *black woodpecker* – not very common here, he says.

27–8 [February 1950]. Paris. K met me.

March 1 [1950]. K's *correctionnelle*: he was very agitated, and worried about false position of not being able to give real reasons for socking the police officer, i.e. former prison experiences; however, Torres did this for him. The hearing only lasted a few minutes and Torres made a frightful speech in K's defence about his having been buying toys for orphans – we were furious. Sentence: 10,000 francs fine. Afterwards bought a pair of shoes for K, amid great groans from him.

Very nice evening at home, as K human again. He says, war probably autumn 1951 or soon after, so he would rather go to the States as he couldn't do anything here anyway – said he thought California perhaps best, if not too cut off there. Felt more or less resigned – though it's a gloomy prospect. Bertaux told K 3 more Communist arms caches just discovered. Fuchs got 14 years – British intelligence always knew he was a Communist, but okayed him to the Americans all the same.[1]

[1] Dr Klaus Fuchs, who had worked on the Manhattan Project, transmitted information about the manufacture of the atomic bomb to the USSR.

7.3.50   Verte Rive

Dear Twinnie,

Thanks for your interesting letter from Haus Hirth. Yes, aren't Rosa Luxemburg's letters quite wonderful? They really are incredible.[1]

We spent the last three days motoring to Bourges and the Loire with Paul Willert and the Winklers. First Arthur and Paul and I went to Bourges, where we met the Winklers and stayed the night (Saturday). The next day Paul went back to Paris after lunch and the rest of us stayed at Amboise on the Loire; yesterday we visited the castle there, and the one at Chaumont, and then returned slowly for dinner in Fontainebleau. It was all most enjoyable, and I bought a pair of bullfinches from a man in St Aiglan who owned the restaurant where we had lunch and which had a large aviary behind it. These bullfinches are (he says) from last year, they were taken young from the nest and certainly seem quite happy in a cage. I don't suppose I can teach the cock to sing like Peg's, as I believe they don't do that unless they are alone, and have to be taught very young. I was so fascinated by her bullfinch's song, I can't get it out of my head.[2]

The most enjoyable thing about our excursion was seeing Bourges cathedral: it has the finest stained glass in France, after Chartres. It is so beautiful, Twinnie, you can't imagine: really when I was there I thought it was the most beautiful thing I'd ever seen, one could hardly bear it.

I haven't got your edition of Mörike and would be grateful if you could get me one; mine is very small, it contains *Gesang zu zweien in der Nacht* but not *Weht o Wehet, liebe Morgenwinde*.

Please write which Mozart sonatas you like best – which was the one you played the other day?

It is boiling hot spring weather which is nice, but I rather think that it is from now onwards that Paris really starts being bad for one – trees or something. As the servants are out today and I am busy boiling a rather old hen and making a *sauce velouté* to go with it, I had better stop. The bullfinches are sitting on the window sill munching lettuce and cheeping away.

The Gladiators has just been re-issued and is having brilliant reviews.

Love,
Twin

¹ This refers to Rosa Luxemburg's letters to Sonja Liebknecht from prison.
² This bullfinch continually practised a traditional air which it had been taught by its former owner, a peasant.

14.3.50   Verte Rive

Dear Twinnie,

I had a sweet letter from Tante Johanna today, she says at the end '. . . it was so good to have had you here for such a long time and I feel that there was such perfect understanding, so much so that we did not need any words.' This is very pleasing, is it not?

K wrote an article in the *New York Times* Sunday Mag about Hiss and Chambers, saying public opinion was on Hiss's side because people can't bear renegades, whether from the church or party or whatever organized body it is: they don't mind people becoming converts, but don't approve of a defrocked priest taking a girl out dancing. This article provoked a flood of letters, of which the *NY*

Times printed lots, and nearly ALL of them were quite beside the point. This proves I think that complete confusion still reigns everywhere about the problems of ex-Communism, to an extent that very few people are capable of seeing what it is about. It is a parallel to, e.g., the French still not seeing what Freud is about; in 10 years of course everybody will think it elementary, but now they don't, and indeed problems of loyalty *are* jolly complicated.

Hoping to see you before too long,

M. K.

25th [March 1950]. Sperbers and von Weisls for weekend.[1] Von W. defended Negeb front against the Egyptians with 2 cannons; told us stories of the war, all typical, i.e. incredible flukes helping the Jews, inefficiency of the Egyptians. When the Yemenite and South Arabian Jewish tribes – many of the latter really quite unknown and coming from places not on the map, who'd never seen cars or railways – saw the planes which were to transport them to Israel they were not at all surprised; pointed out that Moses said several times in the Bible that God would collect His people on the wings of eagles, and their feet should touch no stones.

[1] Wolfgang von Weisl, former Ullstein correspondent in the Middle East. He was responsible for Arthur's appointment to the Ullstein Press.

March 28th, 1950   Verte Rive

Dear Twinnie,

I can't say with any certainty if or when I'll come to England, but unless the franc position improves even further a visit will I think be necessary. However, I don't like to talk of it much to K at the moment, as he would feel that I'd only just come back and already wanted to be off again. If I do come, we MUST go to Suffolk, quite definitely.

The following birds have arrived here: chiffchaff, redstart, willow-warbler – the latter only yesterday. I do pity you missing the spring in the country. It is too tough, really. I have been pottering about a certain amount in the garden and am wondering what will happen as a result.

There is a very funny piece by Freddie [Ayer] in this month's *Partisan Review* in the series about intellectuals and Religion: you can imagine what it says, but I think it very witty. Wouldn't it be a good idea if somebody wrote a sort of Compton-Burnett novel in which all the characters talked exactly as if they were quoting an article by Fred?

Oh life is wonderful these days.

Love,
Twin

April 2nd 1950   Verte Rive

Dear Twin,

I have fixed for us to be married at the British Consulate in Paris today fortnight, April 15, in the morning. So I think we really have made it at last; but please do not tell anybody about this until it has happened, as I am really getting almost superstitious after all the set-backs and delays we have had. We have given up the idea of having a party, and personally I feel no urge to do so, *au contraire*. I would suggest your popping over for the weekend, if twere not for the expense. Also I know you haven't got much leave going.

Yesterday a film producer called Graetz and a script-writer called Jean Aurenche, who produced and wrote respectively *Le Diable au Corps*, came for dinner and the night with their wives. Graetz had asked K's advice about how to make a psychoanalytical film, and yesterday in his bath K had an idea for a film about a typical case of a frigid woman, which he outlined after dinner to these people. I thought it an excellent idea, though K somewhat spoiled the effect of it by telling it awfully badly in the most frightful French, in which nearly every word was a direct translation from the English, e.g. *engagement* for *fiançailles*, so that it was all the (very bright) script-writer could do to understand it. However, I think they all thought it good, and presumably they must pay K something for this, which will further improve our franc position.

Have you got the monograph on the Yellow Wagtail? It is a lovely book: that series is really awfully good.[1]

I do wish you could come here for a few days later on, say in May when all the birds are back, and see how lovely it is – how different from when you last came. Do you think you could?

Cynthia[2] is here for the weekend. She is awfully sweet.

Love,
Twin

[1] Collins' New Naturalist Series.
[2] Cynthia Jefferies first began to work for Arthur as his secretary in 1949. She was living in Paris at the time. They married in 1965.

April 6th [1950]. Dinner party at Mac Goodman's for Chipman, Sperbers and us.[1] Violent political argument during dinner between K on one side, and Chipman and Sperber on the other, re whether to collaborate with de Gaulle. K said, the French will only consider the Communists as criminal when they are officially declared to be so; de G. is the only man who would imprison them, and thus the only hope of establishing clearly their allegiance to a foreign power. Chip. said, is de G. strong enough to cope, if in power? Munjo said, war will take place anyway, so no point now thinking how to prevent it as it's too late; must consider questions of principle. K lost his temper completely and shouted that he really couldn't stand the unreal and frivolous attitude of the Left any longer. Said, if you think everything's lost then for God's sake tell people either to collaborate with the Russians or clear out, for the sake of their children, but don't arm them and look as though you were going to help them effectively if you're not. This extremely violent outburst of K's seems to have had a slight effect on Chipman's complacency; at any rate he listened to K's arguments for the rest of the evening. Afterwards K and I went to a café opposite, and he said how unbearably irresponsible he found all the sentimental leftists: they are just as unable to bear hearing the truth about the Left as the Jews are unable to face their own problems: witness their loathing of K and his Palestine book.

[1] Mac Goodman was one of the organizers of the International Rescue and Relief Committee; Norris Chipman was then First Secretary at the American Embassy in Paris. He was an expert on Soviet affairs, and Arthur considered him very clear-sighted about Russia.

Monday April 10th 1950   Verte Rive

Dear Celia,

No news since I last wrote, except that the film deal is off because the script-writer turned out to be a sort of second degree fellow-traveller – like all French intellectuals, as far as I can make out – and said he didn't want to make a film which would be either pro-communist or anti-communist – he said this in connection with filming *Arrival and Departure*, which the producer wanted to do. As K said, you might as well say you don't want to make one which is either pro or anti bubonic plague, and even though the film wasn't to have been a political one at all obviously K and this chap could never work together. It is really remarkable how one never can find a Frenchman who isn't a fellow-traveller; apparently the whole film industry is entirely riddled with them in every branch. K is very bitter these days about this and also about the idiotically unreal attitude of leftists and idealists such as Sperber and Chipman. I am all on his side, as I do think it makes one sick to see those leftists trying to keep a virgin conscience by e.g. not having anything to do with the Gaullists, or the Americans or whoever it may be, and watching France, and indeed all Europe, go to the dogs with a complacent grin, or with the hope that they'll after all be saved in spite of themselves by the Americans. I am explaining myself badly, but I mean, the present French government is incapable of preventing the Communists from sabotaging the unloading of military supplies everywhere except in Cherbourg (where the Force Ouvrière has a hold) and I do think this is an inadmissable degree of weakness, and that however awful de Gaulle may be he couldn't help being more effective than that.

Yesterday evening we had dinner with an ex-Gaullist who turned up called Cardin, a wild adventurer à la Barbereau, who got drunk and made a few passes at me, rather to my amusement, especially as he kept saying 'tu es farfelue, toi' (I may explain that this was while K and Cardin's girl friend had gone to fetch Sabby from the Winklers'). Most Gaullists are very disillusioned, it seems. This one has left the RPF altogether and runs a factory.

I have got Julian Symons' biography of AJ[1] – did I tell you? It is *extremely* good. I have just been reading *The Cocktail Party*, have you read it? I think it's terrific, K says he thinks the end falls off, but I don't agree.

Love,

Twin

Birds seen or heard for the first time this year (migrants)
March 18 chiff-chaff   March 22 redstart   March 27 willow-warbler
            April 8 blackcap   April 8 cuckoo   April 9 swallow
I think all these dates are very early compared with England – about a week earlier, I imagine.

[1] A. J. A. Symons, author of *A Quest for Corvo*.

11 [April 1950]. K depressed: decided to try and sell the house this summer and move to the States, leaving everything here (selling it) except his books.

14 [April 1950]. Stephen Spender for lunch; both got on well with him; haven't seen him for six or seven years.

April 18th 1950   Verte Rive

Dear Twinnie,

The marriage went off all right on Saturday, British Consulate, 11 a.m. I thought it a very simple and dignified ceremony; the Winklers were our witnesses. Afterwards we went and and drank some champagne and then went for lunch to a wonderful restaurant called Le Cochon d'Or. We stayed in Paris for the afternoon and had a rather peculiar evening with Stephen Spender and a married couple called Berlier (?)[1]: Madame Berlier is American and an ex-girl-friend of Stephen's – she was very nice. We all had dinner together at the Canette. K was fairly plastered (he had been drinking at the Flore with these people, Arthur Calder-Marshall,[1] an American woman and a frightfully *louche* German Communist, ex-comrade of K's, whom for some reason he got very sentimental about, much to everybody else's embarrassment and boredom). I enjoyed the evening because I do like Spender (he had been to lunch with us the day before, and even K thought him very nice), but a typical incident occurred at the end of dinner, which was, that M. Berlier took offence at one of K's drunken remarks and walked out in a huff, dragging his wife with him, and

[1] M. and Mme Bernier.

134

leaving K staring wide-eyed, as he had simply no idea what the whole thing was about. The fact was that he had been teasing the nice Mrs Berlier about something and wanted to say to her husband 'Vous n'y êtes pour rien' but instead of this he had said 'quant à vous, vous ne comptez pas', which of course infuriated Monsieur Berlier.

We then went on to the Saint Yves, which is now a *boîte chantante*, as Cynthia, who was with us, said it was fun; but K didn't like it and wanted to go to the Lapin Agile. Here the second typical incident occurred, for I knew full well that if we did this K would insist on driving there and back, and felt that drunk as he was I simply couldn't face such a long drive with him at the wheel, so I started to procrastinate, at which K walked off himself. Stephen, Cynthia and I followed soon after and saw K sitting in his car. He said, I'm going home; are you coming? I said, Yes, if you let me drive; and at this, as foreseen, he drove off, so Cynthia and I spent the night with Stephen in a flat which had been lent to him. It was lucky Cynthia was there as otherwise I would have had to go to a hotel, which is a bore after midnight if one hasn't got a room. Sunday morning Cynthia went off early and I had breakfast in a café on the quais with Stephen and went with him to see an exhibition of German primitives at the Orangerie (He said: I've always wanted to spend a night with you, it's too bad it was your wedding night.) For some reason this was quite extraordinarily nice: Stephen is so easy to talk to and one can talk to him about anything.

The fact is that unfortunatley K is at present having one of his 'mad fits', and has been for some time; it is the first one since we were in Palestine. This is the reason why whenever we go to Paris he gets drunk and behaves abominably. I got back on Sunday to find him very remorseful and full of self-loathing; as he said, it is very rare that we go out in the evening and he doesn't get drunk, in spite of his firm resolution never to do so after the Charenton incident. He is in an awful state of nerves, and we have decided that as soon as he finishes his novel, which will be in about a month, he will go to the Pyrenees by himself for a month. He needs solitude and a change of atmosphere: he hasn't been away from here really since October 1948.

I am reading a new Simone Weil book which has just come out. It is called *L'Attente de Dieu* and consists of letters to a priest about her attitude to God and the Church, and some articles on this and similar subjects. It is extraordinarily interesting, for it turns out that Simone Weil was really a mystic, also it is fantastically well written and good. I'll buy it (this copy belongs to the *doctoresse*) and send it to you. There is a very interesting account of her spiritual development; I will copy you out a bit:

> 'À quatorze ans je suis tombée dans un de ces désespoirs sans fond de l'adolescence, et j'ai sérieusement pensé à mourir, à cause de la médiocrité de mes facultés naturelles. Les dons extraordinaires de mon frère, qui a eu une enfance et une jeunesse comparables à celles de Pascal (her brother is a mathematical genius who now teaches at Chicago University) me forçaient à en avoir conscience. Je ne regrettais pas les succès extérieurs, mais de ne pouvoir espérer aucun accès à ce royaume transcendant où les hommes authentiquement grands sont seuls à entrer et où habite la vérité. J'aimais mieux mourir que de vivre sans elle. Après des mois de ténèbres intérieures j'ai eu soudain et pour toujours la certitude que n'importe quel être humain, même si ses facultés naturelles sont presque nulles, pénètre dans ce royaume de la vérité réservée au génie, si seulement il désire la vérité et fait perpetuellement un effort d'attention pour l'atteindre. Il devient ainsi lui aussi un génie, même si faute de talent ce génie ne peut pas être visible à l'extérieur.'[2]

Then there is a description of the effect on her of her time in the factory, of certain isolated experiences, of her reasons for not wanting to be baptized, etc., etc.

The first nightingale was heard by me last Saturday 15th; there have been occasional ones since, but not many so far. The redstarts are building a nest in a corner under the roof, on a drain-pipe on the terrace, just by the dining-room door. My bullfinches are bathing themselves madly; they do this a great deal. At lunch today K pointed out a great spotted woodpecker climbing up the tree just outside the dining-room window.

Imagine the expense of life here: in the last few weeks – having had quite a lot of guests – we have been spending an average of 30,000 frs. (£30) a week on housekeeping alone, excluding heating, telephone, light and all extras; yet we don't live luxuriously by French standards, eat only rice or macaroni or eggs, etc., for lunch, don't buy much fruit, and hardly ever any *charcuterie*, and I haven't been drinking at all during this period. It really is awful, isn't it?

Love,
Mamaine.

PS. Gardening is the greatest pleasure in life, if one doesn't do too much.

[1] Arthur Calder-Marshall, novelist, biographer and editor of several of the English classics.

[2] At fourteen I fell into one of those fits of bottomless despair which come with adolescence, and I seriously thought of dying because of the mediocrity of my natural faculties. The exceptional gifts of my brother, who had a childhood and youth comparable to those of Pascal, brought my own inferiority home to me. I did not mind having no visible successes, but what did grieve me was the idea of being excluded from that transcendent kingdom to which only the truly great have access and wherein truth abides. I preferred to die rather than live without that truth. After months of inward darkness, I suddenly had the everlasting conviction that no matter what human being, even though practically devoid of natural faculties, can penetrate to the kingdom of truth reserved for genius, if only he longs for truth and perpetually concentrates all his attention upon its attainment. He thus becomes a genius too, even though for lack of talent his genius cannot be visible from outside.

Translation by Emma Crauford, from *Waiting on God* (1951), p. 17.

May 4th [1950]. James Burnham and Raymond Aron for dinner.[1] Discussed project for the Kulturelle Freiheit Congress in Berlin at the end of June. K set to work to reorganize it. Burnham explained how in the event of war the USA could render Russia impotent in a day or a few days by dropping bombs on all major Russian cities. He looked quite pleased at the idea: K and I were horrified. Burnham looks very sweet and gentle – and obviously is – but he is much less scrupulous about means than K, who doesn't look sweet and gentle and isn't. Since Acheson's recent speeches have been cribbed almost word for word from James's new book, he seems to be rather influential.[2] K has given up drinks except at weekends.

[1] James Burnham, political philosopher, author of *The Managerial Revolution* (1941), etc. His book *The Coming Defeat of Communism* was published in 1950.
[2] Dean Acheson was then US Secretary of State for Foreign Affairs.

5 [May 1950]. Took James to dinner with the Bertaux to meet Yehudi Menuhin (who is now married to Diana Gould). Liked Y. M. very much and found him very easy to get on with. He is a serious, gentle-looking young man with considerable charm.

Bertaux, K and Burnham had a long discussion of a thesis of K's, viz., that when faced with a dilemma men had to look for moral guidance of one sort or another. Bertaux denied this, said cool calculation was enough. Burnham suggested writing a sequel to *The God that Failed*[1] about 'What I would not do', i.e. which means one categorically rejects. K was very good on this, said, with everything it is a matter of degree, but one can draw arbitrary lines, e.g. I will tell the truth but not the whole truth. Burnham again much less scrupulous than K, said he wouldn't necessarily reject torture in certain cases, K said he would in all cases. Burnham: What about black propaganda? K: rejected. Burnham: What about putting covers on leaflets for Eastern Germany making them look as though they originated there? K: Okay, because simply a move to get them past the censor, which is legitimate if one rejects censorship in principle.

[1] *The God that Failed* (1950), edited by Richard Crossman, was a collection of essays by various writers, most of whom were ex-Communists, about their disillusionment with the Communist Party. The contributors were Arthur Koestler, Ignazio Silone, André Gide (presented by Enid Starkie), Richard Wright, Louis Fischer and Stephen Spender.

15 [May 1950]. Have been thinking about Anthony Chaplin[1] the last 2 or 3 days and wondering whether to write to him or ring him up at Jouy. Today had a letter from Celia saying she'd run into him the other day in London – been seeing him a lot over the weekend. Think this must be telepathy.

[1] The Hon. Anthony Chaplin, later Viscount Chaplin, zoologist and composer, Hon. Secretary of the Zoological Society of London 1952–5. He was then living near Paris at Jouy-en-Josas.

6 [May 1950]. Went into the forest; brought back 2 eggs from similar yellow-hammer nests, one in broom about 4 ft, the other in bramble about 2 ft.

27 [May 1950]. K just finished (yesterday) his book *The Age of Longing*, 1st draft.

I go into the forest nearly every day for an hour or two now. Yesterday, instead, rowed up the creek behind the reeds opposite the house to look at the reed- and sledge-warblers. Got from Betty

Winkler, and planted, enough annuals to fill in gaps in my beds: *oeillets d'Inde*, snapdragons, asters, etc.

June 1st 1950   Verte Rive

Dear Twinnie,

Many thanks for your interesting letter from Corsham. I have hardly had time to read it properly yet, but am writing nevertheless to say, how WONDERFUL if you could come over. Oh I do so hope you can.

We had a very exhausting but enjoyable weekend in Alsace with the Vallons, visiting Strasbourg (which is lovely), Riquewihr, the Vosges, Colmar (Grünewald's Isenheim Altar is there), Mulhouse, Belfort and lots of small places. Alsace is very beautiful and the villages are mostly lovely, full of 16th century half-timbered houses, with wood piled up in the streets and an almost Bavarian atmosphere; it is just like visiting Germany to go there, except for the wonderful French food. The weather was very bad for most of our trip, however (we left Paris on Friday night and returned on Tuesday evening). Vallon always insisted on our going to the best and most *coup de fusil* restaurants and hotels if he possibly could, even if nobody was in the least hungry. However, I do so love motoring, especially in a region one doesn't know and which is so beautiful, that I greatly enjoyed it. Besides, K is now on good form and he and I at least didn't quarrel and always wanted to do the same things. The wild flowers everywhere are very lovely now – deep purple clover and scarlet poppies, poppies and cornflowers, mustard and cornflowers and poppies, and so on, all mixed in different ways in great patches in the fields.

I am trying desperately hard to get my bullfinches to breed and they did get as far as laying two eggs, but as they had in the meantime flung the nesting materials out they broke them (this was while I was away). Then I gave them a greenfinch's nest, which they seem to like, and play about with, but they haven't started laying again. Yesterday K and I tried to fool them with a reed-warbler's egg, but they only broke it; however I haven't given up hope, it's a question of perseverance, I'm sure.

Tw.

*During the first half of 1950 Arthur had become increasingly involved in
planning the forthcoming Congress of Cultural Freedom, an international
meeting of writers, scholars and scientists which was to be held in Berlin in
June of that year under the patronage of Bertrand Russell, Benedetto
Croce, John Dewey, Karl Jaspers and Jacques Maritain. In Arthur's
words: 'Its opening session coincided with the beginning of the Korean war.
It served a double purpose: as a kind of intellectual airlift, a demonstration
of Western solidarity with the brave and battered outpost of Berlin, a
hundred miles behind the Iron Curtain; and an attempt to dispel the
intellectual confusion created by the totalitarian campaigns under the
slogan of peace. Out of the deliberations of the Berlin Congress arose an
international movement with branches and publications in a number of
European, American and Asiatic countries, among them* Encounter,
London, *and* Preuves, Paris' (The Trail of the Dinosaur, *1955, p. 179).
Mamaine accompanied Arthur to Berlin.*

Friday June 23rd 1950. Left from the Gare de l'Est 8.30 in a sleeper for
Frankfurt. Found to our surprise that Bertaux had provided us with a
bodyguard to the frontier. Further found that Sartre had the next
sleeper – he was going to a dramatic congress in Frankfurt. There
being no restaurant-car on the train, the police *commissaire* at the
station had ordered for us boxes containing food and wine from the
station buffet, so we invited Sartre, the bodyguard and two Poles
(Czapski[1] and another), who like us were *en route* for Berlin, to join us
in our compartment and eat them. Our first meeting with Sartre since
'diplomatic relations' were broken off about 18 months ago. S. now
doesn't drink at all but lives on Corydrane[2] and was looking rather ill.
However, he was as gay as ever, though he said he hardly ever goes out
now in the evening as it's so difficult to find anyone he agrees with
about politics.

[1] Josef Czapski, painter and editor of the émigré Polish journal *Kultura*. One of the officers who
prepared the first report on the Katyn massacre.
[2] A benzedrine-type stimulant drug.

Saturday 24th [June 1950]. On arrival in Frankfurt we were seized upon by an American schoolgirl or college girl who'd been detailed to find us and the Poles and shepherd us to the plane for Berlin. It rapidly became obvious that she would never be able to do this, for a complete muddle reigned as to our reservations and tickets and most of the planes were full of people going to Berlin to watch a football match. On K's initiative we made our escape from the American girl – who'd been joined by another one – and got on to a plane which arrived in Berlin at 12.30. The less resourceful Poles arrived some nine hours later.

Found Burnham already in Berlin, and I went out with Marcia [Burnham] to view the Kurfürstendamm while K, Burnham and Lasky planned the congress.[1] Dinner with Silone and Darina and an Indian whom they had collected in Florence and brought along, nobody knows why. Silone at first very surly, later rather more expansive but disagreed with K about most things, especially the question of an alliance with the Right. Silone said (1) you can't tell Italian schoolteachers whose own local fight is against the Church for lay schools to drop it and fight Stalinism; (2) if half the Abruzzi peasants are Communists and the other half not, but both halves are fighting against Prince Torlonia, you can't ask the non-Communist half to fight instead against the Communist Abruzzi peasants. (Silone always comes back sooner or later to the Abruzzi peasants and Prince Torlonia); (3) he repeated his story about his resistance movement during the war and how he sacked anybody from it if they turned out to be British or American intelligence agents, because he wanted to fight 'ma guerre à moi' with a clean conscience; (4) he thinks the strength of the anti-Stalinist front lies in its internal difference. K agreed, but said in a war one must have a co-ordinated strategy between allies. He finally got a very grudging admission from Silone that he was on the whole in favour of the Atlantic Pact.

[1] Melvin J. Lasky, American writer, journalist and editor who founded and edits two leading monthly reviews, *Der Monat* (Berlin) and *Encounter* (London). He was executive secretary of the Congress for Cultural Freedom.

Sunday [25th June 1950]. K, I and our bodyguard Hermann took a car and toured Berlin. Very few people in the streets and few cars; in the place we went to for a beer there was nobody else at all. Typical Berlin driver who explained everything to us with great conviction and thoroughness and assured us that Berlin had the most beautiful surroundings of any town in Europe. K tried to find his old haunts and the houses where he lived years ago, succeeded with one or two, but most have been destroyed.

Monday 26th June [1950]. Frantic work all morning on K's speech, which he largely rewrote and had to get typed in German and English. Just got through in time for a quick lunch before the meeting at 3 in the Titania Palast. Took along Herbert Read, who'd just arrived from England and had lost his ticket for the meeting. Speakers: Reuter, Silone, Romains, K, Hook, Czapski, Kanellopoulos, Alfred Weber, Haakon Lie.[1] Orchestra behind the speakers played Egmont at the beginning and Leonora No. 3 at the end. In spite of the great heat, the audience listened attentively even to a long, rather academic speech, largely about German guilt, by old Weber,[2] and to all the other speeches, of which some (especially Romains' and Silone's) were very poor. Great enthusiasm for K's speech; he and Silone seem to be the popular heroes so far. K, got down by the heat, took off his jacket and spoke in his shirt sleeves. Great applause when he said 'Let thy communication be yea yea, nay nay'; the words 'ja ja, nein nein' subsequently became a kind of slogan for the congress.

Dinner at the Schwarze Ferkel with the Burnhams; reception Wannsee [given by] Reuter, in the garden. Met Hildebrandt, leader of the *Kampfgruppe Gegen Unmenschlichkeit*[3] – a good-looking young man with a rather soft face, very dark eyes, greying hair. The Russians have made one or two attempts to kidnap him, and once kidnapped a man who had the same name as one of Hildebrandt's men, whom they kept for a time and treated rough but released when they discovered they had got the wrong man. The *Kampfgruppe* is the best known of the various groups which work in the East Zone, help people to get out, etc., but it is criticized on the ground that there is too little control on recruits and it has Communist spies in its ranks and other politically unreliable elements; also that Hildebrandt is not a big enough man for the job, which is obviously true. At the reception K got together for his nightly planning meeting with Irving Brown, Burnham, Hook and Lasky.[4] Said afterwards he had never drunk so much in his life, but was not at all drunk.

[1] Ernst Reuter, a former Communist and subsequently a leading Social Democrat, was then Mayor of Berlin; Jules Romains, the French novelist; Sidney Hook, the American philosopher and political thinker, was a chief organizer of the American Committee of the Congress; Panayotes Kanellopoulos, prominent Greek politician and intellectual who later became Prime Minister; Haakon Lie, then General Secretary of the Norwegian Labour Party.

[2] Alfred Weber, German sociologist.

[3] Fighting Force against Inhumanity. Arthur visited its HQ and was much impressed by its activities. He found that it already had detailed information on the fate of 27,000 people who had been arrested in the Eastern Zone.

[4] Irving Brown, European representative of the AFL and one of the founders of the international free trade union movement (ICFTU) in Western Europe.

Tuesday 27 [June 1950]. After lunch Carlo Schmid took Jakobsen (a Dane) and me and Rousset[1] in his car to the Potsdamer Platz, where Jakobsen and I walked into the Eastern Sector down the Leipziger Strasse; we walked about for an hour or so, then took a U-Bahn out. Great contrast between East and West Sectors: the former is incomparably more dreary-looking and the shops – of which there seem to be very few – mostly contain very poor quality goods. Even the shops for unrationed food (HQ food shops), which are too expensive for most people, have very little in them; virtually no vegetables or fruit, very little fish (and a queue of people for it), but a certain amount of *charcuterie*, which, however, is obviously too expensive for almost everybody. The windows look very poor, with just a few packets of *pâtes alimentaires* and margarine and tinned herrings – worse than a London grocer during the war. There are a lot of women police and '*Trümmerfrauen*' demolishing the ruins (*Trümmerfrauen* also exist in the West Sector, but not nearly as many). No cars except outside ministries. A certain amount of propaganda posters. Street names in German and Russian. A few *Volksschütz-polizei* about but no Russians. Population of East Sector 1.1 million, of West Sector now 2.2 million. Bookshops contain books by Thomas Mann, Anna Seghers, Carlo Bondoni and Arnold Zweig, but nothing much else except a few cheap-looking booklets or pamphlets. Clothes in HQ shops did not seem terribly expensive, but looked of very poor quality indeed. People look tired, and the feeling of vitality which is so striking in West Berlin is absent.

Went to bed early because of bad laryngitis, my voice almost completely gone and didn't feel too good. K working with his team of self-appointed organizers, as usual.

[1] Carlo Schmid, German politician, writer and professor, leading member of the SPD; Frøde Jakobsen, Danish diplomat and Member of Parliament; David Rousset, author of *L'Univers concentrationnaire* (in English, *A World Apart*, 1951).

Wednesday [28th June 1950]. Interesting political panel meeting in the afternoon. Speakers: André Philip,[1] Haakon Lie, Burnham and K. Afterwards several people made speeches, which chairman Reuter tried to keep down to 5 minutes; most attacked K, some defended him. Borkenau[2] created a sensation by saying he was glad the Americans had sent troops to South Korea and thus avoided another Munich. At this Rousset protested loudly and there were cries of 'hear hear!', and table thumping from Freddie Ayer and Trevor-Roper. After some commotion the meeting went on with good speeches by Schlesinger, Kogon and Lasky.[3] Julian Amery,[4] who arrived in the middle, also made a speech, which was not very good. K's speech on the meaninglessness of left and right, withering away of dilemmas, etc., was the best, and was the focal point of the meeting. Sat next to Herbert Read and at the same table as Silone, who passed me a note saying 'Arthur serait un bon député socialiste italien.' Me: 'Pourquoi?' Silone: 'Nous disons toujours: a) le vieux socialisme est moribond, b) le Labour a trahi le socialisme.'

Saw Rousset later at *Fidelio*, he laughed about his eruption at the meeting and said 'We can't after all be the ones to declare war in Korea.' K says the only people with political experience in their caucus meetings are Irving Brown and himself. Hook and Lasky are also good and nice, though Lasky is lacking in political passion.

[1] André Philip, formerly a prominent figure in the French Resistance, was one of the leaders of the French Socialist Party.
[2] Franz Borkenau, historian of Communism.
[3] Arthur J. Schlesinger Jr, American contemporary historian, writer and academic; Eugen Kogon, German writer, author of *Der SS-Staat*.
[4] Julian Amery, Conservative MP.

Thursday [29th June 1950]. Lunch English General Bourne,[1] with Reuter and other English delegates, who now include three MPs: Julian Amery, Christopher Hollis and Harold Davis. Big public meeting in the Funkturm gardens, 15,000 people. Speakers: Rousset,

Carlo Schmid, Amery, Silone, Kogon, a South American who kicked up a fuss because he'd come 4000 miles to speak and nobody had taken any notice of him, Irving Brown, Nicolaevsky.[2] All boring demagogic speeches, Rousset's very disappointing, kind of 1936 Popular Front speech about what an anti-fascist he was and how many camps he'd been in, etc. At the end K read the Manifesto and finished up by saying 'Die Freiheit hat die Offensive ergriffen'.[3] This Manifesto has really been almost entirely written by K and pushed through by him, Burnham, Brown, Hook and Lasky by forceful offensive tactics, so that virtually no opposition was encountered, though Silone had obviously come prepared to make some.

Party in the evening at a hotel on the Wannsee. The whole of this congress is in a way like one long party, at which one is always having drinks and meals with various groups of people, mostly old friends, with real parties thrown in at intervals.

[1] Lieutenant-General G. K. (later General Lord) Bourne was Commandant of the British Sector.

[2] Boris I. Nicolaevsky, former Director of the Marx-Engels Archives in Moscow (now in the Hoover Institution, Stanford, USA) and historian of slave labour in the USSR.

[3] Freedom has seized the offensive.

Friday [30 June 1950]. Slept late and went to the Zoo with Greta Neumann and K and our two bodyguards. There is a Tiergarten for baby animals, very sweet. Very hot day. Lunch with Vlasovite called Yakovlev[1] and the following people: Arthur Schlesinger, Sidney Hook, Solomon Schwarz, Sheba Strunsky, K.[2] Yakovlev is a big blond neanderthaler. He told his story in short sentences, which were then translated by a young American from the School of Slavonic Studies somewhere or other who is tagging about with him. As Yakovlev talked his face remained quite expressionless and he did not look at any of us. Example: Y. speaks for a while in Russian, looking round the room or down at the table; Translator: 'I was then taken prisoner by the Germans. Out of 30,000 Russian prisoners 28,000 died of starvation.' Another short Russian statement by Y.; Tr.: 'Death from starvation is better than death by the NKVD.' More Russian, delivered with the same lack of expression; Tr.: 'Contrary to the common belief, death from starvation is quite a pleasant death.' And so on. I stared fascinated at Yakovlev as if at an animal in the zoo, and was very surprised when he suddenly looked at me and smiled.

He lives in Munich, says he always walks in the middle of the street. K said, If you want people to help you, keep your politics to yourself, so that as many people as possible can join you in negative alliance against the common enemy. In fact Yakovlev's politics remained a mystery, though for some reason he kept talking about the monarchy and it was clear that he was against this.

Drinks Greta and James. Greta said some groups in Berlin who are doing political work in the East Zone put out very sectarian papers, e.g. anti-Stalinist anti-American neo-socialist, and expect people to risk their lives to distribute these tracts. She and Burnham discussed a possible film about the camps, which should be a feature film on a high artistic level.

K visited Free University. Very impressed. Drinks Suhrkamp,[3] who suggested K should meet Bert Brecht, but K refused, saying he had no basic values in common with somebody who still sticks by the Party though his wife disappeared in Russia and is presumably dead. After dinner sat with Jim Farrell,[4] whose impressions of Berlin are exactly the same as K's, namely that the former academic spirit in the tradition of Kant, Hegel and Schopenhauer has been replaced by a much closer fusion of theory with reality.

[1] Boris Yakovlev, though anti-fascist, had served under General Vlasov, founder of the independent Russian army which fought against the USSR during the war. He was editor of an émigré Russian monthly magazine, *Literaturny Sovremennik*, subsidized by the Fund for Intellectual Freedom.

[2] Solomon Schwarz, distinguished Russian economist who lived in exile in New York. Together with David Dallin and Boris Nicolaevsky he published the first study of Soviet slave labour. Sheba Strunsky was the founder of the International Rescue and Relief Committee.

[3] Bertolt Brecht's publisher.

[4] James T. Farrell, American novelist, author of *Studs Lonigan*, etc.

Saturday July 1st [1950]. Visited the Eastern Sector again in the morning with Jakobsen and a very nice Danish general. Moscow-like feeling about the astonishing Trepto monument to the Red Army, with sculptures done to the design of a Stalin-prize-winning sculptor in a style reminiscent of Nazi art, except that the figures wear beards, Russian-type shirts, etc., and are obviously supposed to be workers. At the end of the gardens – which are very beautifully kept and watered by several women gardeners – we went up to the kind of chapel on which is a Red Army soldier 12 metres high; a Volkschütz-polizist reeled off figures about the dimensions and how many thousands of different colours are in the mosaic round the walls. Russian Sector includes Unter den Linden, Alexanderplatz, ends at Potsdamer Platz and Brandenburg Tor.

Everybody greatly amused by yesterday's meeting with the two professors from the East Sector, Havemann and Holitscher (see K's Diary).[1]

Drinks with Peter Tennant, now political adviser to General Bourne, and members of his staff. Just as K was talking about the situation in Korea, which now looks rather bad, a typical upper-class woman with a white face, a string of pearls and a small hat came in saying 'I'm sorry I'm late but Alan has been playing cricket!' We laughed, but she obviously did not see the joke. Dinner at Lasky's house with the Silones, Burnhams and Bondys[2]; not a very gay party, though K did his best to make it so by drinking a considerable amount of wine. He spent a good part of the evening repeating over and over again to Silone that though he had a great fraternal feeling for him, Silone had made things rather difficult a) by reading a newspaper all through the first meal we had with him, in Rome, and b) by always behaving as if he were a broad-bottomed Abruzzi peasant and K were a cosmopolitan gigolo. Silone was obviously very bored by this but made some kind of friendly answer, which, however, did not satisfy K as he was too drunk to understand it, so he went on repeating his accusations – with some effect, apparently, for we were told that after we left Silone said 'He seems to think I think he's a gigolo.' K very unhappy because he thought real fraternal feeling missing with Silone, Burnham and Lasky; kept me awake till 3.30 talking about this.

[1] Several members of the Congress had been invited to meet Professor Havemann, a scientist, and Professor Holitscher, the philosopher, before the press. Arthur described this meeting in his diary: 'We arrived at the Hotel am Zoo about a quarter to 8 and found a host of journalists, photographers and radio people. After some fuss we sat down at a round table surrounded by this press crowd – on the one side Havemann and Holitscher, on the other Lasky, Hook, Nicolas Nabokov, Irving Brown and I. Havemann objected that we were "four against two", so Irving and I got up grinning and sat in a corner. Next Havemann read a statement to the Press to the effect that they had never issued an invitation and first thing he had learned about this alleged invitation was through the press, and that we were meeting by pure chance as he happened to be having tea with friends in the Hotel am Zoo. Lasky and Sidney [Hook] tried to pin them down as to whether they considered Stalin to be the greatest living geneticist, philologist, etc. Havemann tried to evade [the question and] to bring in the hydrogen bomb. But as Hook and Lasky, with their dynamic temperaments, prevailed at the microphone Havemann declared he must have dinner first and proposed continuing at 11 p.m. Hook offered sandwiches, but to no avail.

Holitscher declared 'You are not a Professor of Philosophy because a) you have bad manners, as you hit the table, and b) you have lied about the invitation' – and left the table. Havemann said he would turn up at 11 but did not, so Lasky had the empty chairs photographed. As they didn't turn up Lasky rang up Havemann and found that he was at Eisler's.'

[2] François Bondy, Swiss journalist and intellectual, editor of the monthly review *Preuves* (Paris).

Sunday [2 July 1950]. K (with hangover) made a very good speech at a meeting of Hildebrandt's Kampfgruppe; told the story of the two East Sector professors as an example of *Selbstentmenschlichung*[1] and the story of the little Communist boy who came yesterday with a bunch of flowers for me, saying to K 'I've read *Spanish Testament* and I feel sure you can't be a police spy as they say you are, but must still be on our side really' – an example of the way people are brought up under the Russians. He spoke well and was a great success.

Left by military plane for Frankfurt.

[1] Self-dehumanization.

On his return from Berlin Arthur, in collaboration with certain other members of the Congress, immediately began working hard to implement the various projects that had been agreed there, while at the same time trying to find a permanent organizer for them. He conferred almost daily with James Burnham, Raymond Aron, Irving Brown, Melvin Lasky, David Rousset and Georges Altman, editor of the anti-Stalinist paper Franc-Tireur, *either in Paris or at Verte Rive, to which all of these came for meals or for the night. During this period Mamaine had no time to write letters. Her next one to Celia is dated 21 July 1950 and begins with a brief mention, omitted here, of their visits. It continues:*

It was too wonderful seeing you[1] and I am pining for our next meeting, which I expect will be in the early autumn, since I intend to come over to England then to stock up for the winter and try to put on a little weight – I simply can't do it here however hard I try. Also we don't look like going away to the Pyrenees: K says it's no holiday for him if he has no secretary. What a fool he is, damn him. There is to be another meeting *here* at the beginning of August: Silone, Carlo Schmid, Irving, Mel Lasky and probably Rousset. But the difficulty in the way of concrete accomplishments is the lack of suitable

Frenchmen for the organizing work (the problem we discussed when you were here).

I spent two evenings in Paris on July 13th and 14th, on the former dancing in the streets (with the Sperbers), on the second we watched fireworks from the roof of the Monnaie, which is just opposite the Vert Galant, from which they set them off: it was wonderful. Now [Arthur's] Ma is staying here for ten days. But K and I are snooping off this evening to dine with the Burnhams and Servan-Schreiber,[2] the *Monde* journalist, and (perhaps) Bertaux.

I have started reading K's novel [*The Age of Longing*] and am in a stew till I finish it about whether I shall like it. At any rate I am NOT jealous of the heroine, as K thinks all writers' wives always must be!

Tw.

[1] Celia had spent the weekend of 7 July at Verte Rive.
[2] Jean-Jacques Servan-Schreiber, journalist, politician and author, was foreign affairs editor of *Le Monde* 1948–53.

26 [July 1950]. K spoke on the Congress at an Anglo-American Press Association lunch. About 40 journalists turned up. Things going very badly in Korea; K less worried about immediate war than I. Would like to get us both back to England, but K still feels he'd hate to live there as the English don't like his books, besides he thinks they live in the moon. The other day he suggested that we should go and spend 6 months in Berlin. At other times talks of going soon for a fortnight to the US to fix about visas for us to go [and live] there.

Ma as awful as ever, doesn't listen to or understand a word one says and it's awfully hard to be nice to her. K very tired but good-tempered.

27 [July 1950]. James Farrell came down with two American trade unionists from the Auto Workers' Union, very nice, intelligent men. Also a Dutch journalist. Discussed K's project to take significant numbers (say 400,000 in a year) of Frenchmen from various jobs and professions to America for a visit, so that they should get a chance of comparing American standards of living with their own. Farrell is very sweet and endearing – I do like him more and more. Talked also about Silone, and of disappointment when one meets writers. At the end of the evening the nicer of the two Americans, whose name is Woodcock and who apparently, like Farrell, is of working class origin, said to K 'Well anyway, *you're* not a disappointment.'

30 [July 1950]. Aron for lunch, with his wife: he seems to me virtually the only French intellectual I know who is really intelligent and clear-headed without being at all mad. In the afternoon Collinet, Gorkin, Ferra and his wife, all together: they obviously have a plot to get their magazine *Paru* financed by the Congress while retaining jobs on it and changing it hardly at all; but they wouldn't come clean about this, saying only that the Congress Magazine could take over their subscribers.[1] Aron said he thought the only possible hope death of No. 1.

Korea going worse than ever. Churchill said he felt less hopeful than in 1940, that Western Europe is less prepared for defence than South Korea.

A French Force Ouvrière man named Lafond came down in the evening and K and I dined with him in the Clos de Béricy. He seemed more possible to work with than most people we've seen; he is a railway inspector.

[1] Collinet, Gorkin and Ferra were members of a Trotskyist-anarchist splinter group.

August 2nd [1950]. Took Ma to Paris for her last day and night. Lunch with Polanyis at the Bouteille d'Or. Misi [Polanyi] seemed at a loose end for his holiday, so K characteristically sought to fix things up for him by wiring Eric Strauss, who doesn't know Misi but had invited us to Anacapri, describing Misi's situation and giving his address. We afterwards heard that this worked and Misi is going there. The Polanyis are wondering whether to go to Chicago, where Misi has twice been offered a chair of social economy.[1]

Took Ma to dinner in the Eiffel Tower restaurant, went shopping with her, drove her to the Bois, gave her some champagne in the Rue de la Paix and took her up to Montmartre after dinner for drinks on the Place du Tertre. But K very 'nervous' owing to his meeting with Aron, who should have taken some action on Congress lines (mag) but has done nothing. K is now quite obsessed with the Congress and thinks of nothing else. He therefore talked to me about it during dinner, and Ma kept butting in with idiotic questions like 'Do they want you to make a politic you don't agree with?' and 'It's not worth it unless you get lots of money for it'. K's efforts to make her understand that no money is involved were in vain.

[1] He did not accept it.

4th [August 1950]. Have been correcting K's novel, working very hard since Ma left.

Monday 7 [August 1950]. Sidney Kingsley[1] and his wife came down for dinner and the night. Had been dreading what I supposed would be a high-powered American theatre man, but they both turned out to be very nice, and after dinner at Samois we sat up till 1.30 playing Russian and German Communist records which have been sent to K from Berlin. In bed, K insisted on going on singing, with me (as alone he can't hit the right notes) the Volga Boatmen and other Russian songs till about 3.30.

[1] American playwright, author of *Front Page*, etc. He was about to adapt *Darkness at Noon* for the stage.

8th [August 1950]. K still on very good form because of having finished his book, which we sent off yesterday. Sat on the terrace and Kingsley explained his project for the stage version of *Darkness at Noon*: it sounded quite good.

L'Action[1] accused K of planning terrorist militia (!) from here with Burnham and Brown.

K has been in a great state about the Congress ever since Berlin, i.e. for six weeks or so. He hardly sleeps at night and thinks about the work all the time. It is an obsession with him. For one thing he feels he alone is really capable of running it; but of course nobody believes K's willingness to work at it is not dictated by some ulterior motive.

Told K he must go away for a holiday next week, that it is ridiculous to stay here in order to help an organization which is incapable of standing on its own feet without him, and which at the same time doesn't want him to do the work, because (I suppose) they're all leftists and consider K too right-wing. K now says he'll try to get himself off the Executive Committee and on to the International Committee only.

¹ A Communist weekly.

10 [August 1950]. K went to Paris for a meeting with Altman, Silone, Aron and Irving. Returned for a late dinner, bringing Altman. At today's meeting K exercised his *droit de veto* against three people: (a) Nicola Chiaromonte,¹ whom Silone proposed as his substitute on the Executive Committee when he's not here. K objected on the ground that as late as 1949 Nicola Chiaromonte, whom he doesn't know, in an article in *Politics*, professed the belief that socialists should fight against their own governments and not fight the latter's war; (b) secretary proposed by [François] Bondy. K: 'Is she efficient and can she write good French?' Bondy: 'I don't know if she's efficient, but she's politically okay – *speaks* French well, although a foreigner; (c) Marillescan, whom Irving proposed for work in the Paris bureau. M's first suggestion on what the Congress and *Les Amis de la Liberté*² should do was 'publish a cheap edition of the classics', as only when the workers were educated, etc., etc.! K says Silone is quite hopeless, makes a speech for 10 minutes before saying anything, and his only comment on K's 10-page pamphlet explaining the Congress and [*Les*] *Amis de la Liberté* was 'It must contain a paragraph stating that we are opposed to the *Reader's Digest* and Coca-Cola.' Wouldn't even read the pamphlet.

K kept me up till 1.30, though I was very exhausted and am not well now. Said, Everything done by the Congress has been done by me so far (Manifesto, letter to 500, pamphlet, etc.) and nothing will come of it; to this day not 1 word has gone out from the Berlin office to supporters telling them what's been happening. First they lost the English text of the Manifesto, then the French text, so no text has been sent out yet.

¹ Nicola Chiaromonte, political essayist and drama critic, became co-editor with Silone, and later editor, of a journal founded by the Congress, *Tempo Presente*.
² *Les Amis de la Liberté* was an organization founded by Arthur to promote discussion groups among prominent intellectuals throughout France. It continued to operate for some time but eventually petered out.

14 [August 1950]. [Sidney] Kingsley and Graetzes down yesterday, but I stayed in bed. K had written a scene of his play, which he (and I) thought much better than Kingsley's, but Kingsley didn't like it, or rather, doesn't want to have K as co-author, and doesn't want the play to be too highbrow. K disappointed, as he feels Kingsley can't get the right atmosphere of Communists talking, etc., and will spoil it. He sat on my bed till I pushed him out at 1, talking about whether to try and stop Kingsley doing it and tell him K will publicly disown it if he does or to let him go ahead. K said: It's right for me to be uncompromising, my only trouble is that I am not sure enough of myself to avoid a guilty conscience at my outbursts, and thus become apologetic afterwards, which spoils the effect. I said I thought that in view of the extreme difficulty of getting intellectuals to work together one should *not* be too uncompromising and that it would be better if he left the Executive Committee on more general grounds. K said he thought I was perhaps right, but uncompromisingness on Kingsley was the right line.

17 *[August 1950]*. The day before yesterday K went to Paris in the evening to take the Kingsleys out. I had to stay here, as I am not allowed out by the doctor. Yesterday morning about 8 K rang up and said he'd had a burst tyre and had to get a new inner tube as the spare was no good. Cynthia was coming out; she turned up at lunch time. K had rung again to say that owing to the holidays all the garages in Paris were closed and he'd had to drive round for hours in a taxi before he could find his inner tube; so as he had to be in Paris in the evening he'd decided to stay there. At about 6, or maybe 7, Raymond Aron rang and said he'd found Arthur outside his flat and that Arthur had a kind of 'nervous breakdown' and was in bed. Me: 'Do you mean he's got an awful hangover?' Aron: 'Well no, 'e says it's not exactly that.' About half an hour later K rang and said he was going to stay and dine with Aron. I reminded him that he had a date with Bertaux to dine at the Sûreté; K said he'd quite forgotten, but he'd fix it. At 8.30 he rang again and said would I ring Bertaux and make up some excuse for him. Did so. Cynthia and I cooked our dinner (the servants were out) and I went to bed and we started a game of cards. At 11 suddenly I heard a car, so Cynthia made off to her room and I ran downstairs to find Aron and K. They said they'd had nothing to eat, so I gave them

eggs and bacon, fruit, etc., and sat with them while they ate it. K said
to Aron, 'How do you feel about this Congress work we are doing – is
it worth it?' Aron said he couldn't decide, thought the work should
have been done five years ago, but that one could never say it's too
late, since we don't know whether war will come next year or in two
years or five years. K said, I can't go on any longer telling Frenchmen
with wives and children to do things which will inevitably put them in
the MVD's black books while I know that I myself, not being French,
can clear out before the next occupation comes.

This morning K and I took the following decisions: (I) to go off for a
holiday next week, as soon as the car (which K smashed up yesterday)
is repaired; (II) to donate all K's profits from Kingsley's dramatization
of *Darkness at Noon* to the IRRC or some similar organization to help
intellectual refugees from Eastern Europe. K very pleased with this
idea, which he intends as an example to other writers to renounce part
of their royalties for the same ends, as a gesture of international
solidarity: it also frees him of all responsibility for Kingsley's version,
which he hates; (III) to resign at once from the Executive Committee
of the Congress, giving grounds of health and (IV) to go and live in
England – first in London for a bit and then perhaps get a house in the
country. As this last idea has been my dearest wish for some time I am
very pleased about it indeed. K says he thinks an incident like this and
the Charenton one are warnings of fate which one must take and get
something good out of. He believes his 'pattern' is to be saved time
and again by such warnings, in the form of apparent disasters. K is full
of faith in a kind of guardian angel who looks after him and points out
the right path, which he (K) is then particularly good at taking. As a
matter of fact I share this faith with regard to K. He says his pattern
when drunk is one of self-annihilation: he has fantasies about hanging
himself, and tends to do suicidal things like hitting police *commissaires*
or (in this case) having a car accident.

17.8.50   Verte Rive

My dear Twinski,

This brings wonderful news: we have decided to go and live in
England. The way in which this decision came about is too long to tell

in a letter, but it's definite, I think. I am coming over in September, and will be followed shortly by K (he may have to go to the States for a fortnight first). We will then spend the winter in London while looking for a permanent abode. Of course I shall look around in case the ideal small country house turns up in England; but I don't know whether, even in the unlikely event of one existing and being within our means, K would fancy the idea, as he is very strongly opposed to life in the country in England. Anyway he simply does not want to get a house in which to live for the rest of his days; the idea of doing this is anathema to him. However, *au jour le jour*, and personally I do not at all mind the idea of six months in a town for a change during the winter, provided K can be kept off the bottle, which he can and will be.

Love,
Twin

Friday August 25th [1950]. HOLIDAY. Left 9 a.m. and drove hard all day, through Gien, Issoudun, Limoges (where we visited K's haunts in 1940, when he lived there a couple of weeks while joining the Foreign Legion – chiefly a riverside pub where he used to walk alone every day for a drink, but which he could no longer identify with certainty), Brive, and finally to Beynac on the Dordogne, a very lovely place with a castle on a high rock above the village. Bad hotel whose patron wouldn't even taste the wine when we told him it was corked, but just replaced it by another equally bad bottle. This was the beginning of a constant series of incidents demonstrating the decay in French cooking and hotel-keeping. Bliss to have got away from Fontaine and sleep in fresh air, with full moon above the Dordogne.

Saturday 26 [August 1950]. Lovely drive in blazing sun to Sarlat, where I went to see the local doctor to get a prescription for opium pills, as am suffering from mild dysentery. Sarlat turned out to be very beautiful, and there was a lively market, consisting largely of hens, ducks and rabbits, in the little square between the Renaissance houses. K bought a pair of blue trousers. Lunch Montignac and visited caves at Lascaux, though was again feeling very ill and had to keep rushing up from oxygen-less air to avoid fainting or being sick. K evinced a wish to see the Grottes at Les Eyzies, and was very cross with me for being ill, because he said he couldn't bear me to miss the splendours of Les Eyzies and refused to see them without me. Said, all right I'd go too; but withdrew this on seeing thousands of steps leading up to the caves. So K went alone and hated it; afterwards he recovered his temper, and we stopped finally in a little hotel at Montflanquin, on a hill. All the country round Sarlat, Montignac and Les Eyzies is incredibly beautiful, and would be an excellent place to stay with a car or a bicycle.

Monday 27 August [1950]. Rather less beautiful country from Montflanquin to Pau, but very pretty farms with separate white towers for grain(?). On to the foothills of the Pyrenees – not quite so lovely now as in November. Through Oloron to Mauléon and back via Sus and Susmiou, where K spent some time in 1940 as a *soldat isolé*, with others, in the hayloft of a farmhouse. He used to walk from Susmiou to Sus every evening and drink 2 litres of the white wine of the region in the dark little room of the only café there . . . Found the same café, room, patronne and wine, and in Susmiou the same hayloft and the farm opposite where the *soldats isolés*, including K, used to steal apples by raking them out with a stick. Both tiny, sleepy villages. Then to Navarreux, and up through Oloron again to Lescun, where we dined in our pub. A lovely evening: *Drum da gehäuft sind rings / Die Gipfel der Zeit . . .*[1] Lescun is over 1000 metres high.

[1] Hölderlin, *Patmos.*

Monday 28 [August 1950]. Bad weather, so decided to leave Lescun and go north. Over the Col d'Aubisque and down to Arrens and Argelès. Then to Lourdes. Both appalled by the whole sordid mummery, and K said, when we'd watched the miserable pilgrims wheeled into and out of the bathing places on stretchers and wheelchairs, amid prayers and chanting – a woman with a chalk-white face, a deformed cripple, a child, etc., etc. – that he couldn't even feel pity for them, for it seemed to him that none of the people had faces, that they weren't really human. This made me rather cross, as I was feeling desperately sorry for these poor deluded victims of so much phoney mummery, whose sufferings thus deprived of all sense and dignity do not appear tragic, but still infinitely pitiful. But inclined to agree about the faces of the patients, priests and crowd; and nauseated by it all and by the whole town with the rows of cheap souvenir shops, bottles for holy water, etc. I felt the same as last time (1933).

Went on via Tarbes through violent rain, turning into lovely golden light on trees, farms and fields against a black sky as we drove into Montauban in the evening.

Tuesday [29 August 1950]. Drove along the Tarn to Gaillac, where we had lunch in a very poor café. Wandered through the old streets with my camera while K bought some *réchappé* tyres (new ones unobtainable). Dinner in Moissac, where K had been when covering the flood of the Garonne for Ullstein, 1929 (?). K suffering post-book depression, but enjoying himself.

Wednesday [30 August 1950]. Lovely drive on blazing hot day through Bruniquel, Aveyron valley, Penne, St Antonin and back via Najac. Visited the Montauban Natural History Museum.

Thursday [31 August 1950]. Drove up to the Massif Central. A stretch of *very beautiful* country just before going down to St Enimie, and extraordinary Gorge du Tarn (seen from above). This country would be excellent to paint, as crumbling white and grey stones and deep red earth combine in every shade and form, sometimes with black rocks, sometimes with yellow-green grass growing sparsely on chalk. In Mende we found the Cirque Amar and spent the evening at it. Nice little mountain town with a good hotel and lovely air (though raining).

Friday [1 September 1950]. Lunch by a mountain lake, in a garage, with a couple of 'gardiens' who gave us bread, sprats, sausage and cheese and charged a vast sum. Night at Royat. K resisted the appeal of the bar, says he has a terrible fear of alcohol – didn't dare to go out without me.

September 2 [1950]. Up the Puy de Dôme, as K had to go up the highest mountain for miles around though we could see that the summit was concealed in a thick cloud. Then on to Pouilly s/Loire, decided to stay at the hotel where K remembered having had a lovely drink in 1939 when he heard war was declared, returning from the South with Daphne. Walked to the next village in search of Pouilly Fumé without success, but it was a nice walk, sunny at last. Hotel turned out to be a *maison de passe* full of business men with tarts, and horrible.

Sunday 3 [September 1950]. Left Pouilly, where the patronne charged a huge sum, including 250 fr. for ironing the counterpanes on which we'd put our suitcases. K thought this symbolic of the decay of France. He with difficulty restrained himself and me from making a scene, said if he had he would have gone the whole hog and got the police, which is boring and takes up time. He said nevertheless that moderation and restraint did not suit him and were not as a rule, he felt, the right course for him. On to Sancerre.

As the weather was very bad and I felt suddenly desperately tired we decided to go home.

We found Misi [Polanyi] still there, and spent a pleasant evening discussing his and others' religious beliefs, the papal encyclical, etc. K's view: the chief function of religion (apart from the contemplative one) is to provide moral guidance in cases of real moral dilemma, and to give a reason for believing that there is a right way to behave which is ethically preferable to a wrong way. He attacked Catholicism and Catholics with violence, said that the Pope's arch-reactionary encyclical (about Adam being the first man, and dogmas not to be taken symbolically) is important in view of the present political situation in Italy.

Wednesday September 6 [1950]. To London by Golden Arrow. Dinner Celia. Left K in Paris.

September 7–15 [1950]. Very enjoyable week in London. Hope I can stay here some time. Everybody seems very nice compared with the French (this always strikes me at Dover) and meals, though bad, can be had for 2/6 in a pub as compared with 200–250 fr. in comparable French bistro (=5/-). The air is bracing after Paris and Fontainebleau;

there seem to be an awful lot of people I'd forgotten about whom I've known for years and like very much. I have concluded that (unlike K) I really like people, and after 5 years of almost solid country life wouldn't mind 6 months in a town. Can stay with Celia indefinitely.

16–17 [September, 1950]. Orford with Celia. Rowed to Havergate Island to see if any avocets were about, left the dinghy on the shore for quarter of an hour, returned to find it floating out into the estuary, as the tide had come up. Saved by the lucky appearance of two men in a sailing boat, just as I was attempting to stop Celia from flinging herself into the icy sea to retrieve the dinghy. Sunday night K arrived, late after a frightful gale in the Channel (and at Orford).

18 [September 1950]. Dinner in the House of Commons (private room) with the Crossmans. Other guests: John Strachey (now Secretary of State for War), Arthur Schlesinger Jr and his wife and Raymond Aron. Very lively discussion about the isolationist line of the Labour Government, and of the British in general. John and Dick defended this against everybody else; their line is that they'd be delighted to see France, Germany, Italy and Benelux getting together so long as Britain doesn't have to be in, submitting to the authority of shady foreigners and having the welfare state corrupted by immoral inhabitants of non-socialist countries. They believe enough integration on a functional level can be achieved for defence purposes (to which Aron and K objected that only a new idea can make Frenchmen and Germans fight, a new flag or myth – united Europe). Dick now believes the Americans should 'look after' Europe, the British after Asia, as we're 'better at it'. John said the Chinese Communist regime was probably the best regime the Chinese had had for 2000 years, and that a split between China and Russia seemed to him probable within a decade.

All this was most entertaining and amusing until Dick became rather bloody towards K, who was (Dick alleged – untruthfully) mixing up the Saragat breakaway with the Lombardi breakaway a year later.[1] He said 'It's just a bloody anti-British lie'. K: 'It's what?' Dick: 'A bloody anti-British lie'. At this K walked out, followed by me, and refused to be moved by Dick's rather belated withdrawal and the pleas of Aron and Schlesinger. Got K a room at the Grosvenor Hotel and fetched his luggage from the Commons. K said the real reason for his walk-out was that he couldn't stand Dick's frivolous attitude to politics, his irresponsible articles in the *New Statesman*, and his support of what K considers a suicidal line of isolation. Felt rather unhappy, chiefly because I have witnessed so many outbursts from K that I couldn't help feeling that the real reason was neither Dick's abuse nor his frivolous attitude (much as this always maddens K) but some sort of sub-conscious urge not to have any friends. Apart from the old stories – our walk-out on Sartre re Kaplan, K giving Camus a black eye, walking out on the Crawshay-Williams because Elizabeth would knit – he has had several outbursts of rage at dinner-parties: 2 in the presence of Altman and me against Sperber and Chipman (subject: frivolity about politics). However, it seems Aron and Schlesinger were on K's side and let Dick have it when we'd gone; John disappeared as quickly as possible.

[1] In February 1947 a section of the Italian Socialist Party led by Saragat had broken away from the main party because its leader, Pietro Nenni, insisted on cooperating with the Communists. A year later Lombardi, an Italian trade unionist, left the Stalinist trade union to which he belonged and formed his own along social-democratic lines.

20 [September 1950]. K and Schlesinger visited [Bertrand] Russell to get him to withdraw his resignation from the Congress, which he'd made after (apparently) receiving a report from Freddie [Ayer]. They succeeded, though Russell was cold to K, who was seeing him for the first time since Peter's [Peter Russell's] walk-out on *me* in 1946 or 7.

Lunch Graham Greene. K outlined his scheme for writers to evolve a system of self-taxation for the benefit of refugees from Eastern Europe. Graham agreed and expressed his readiness to make over 10% of his continental royalties. K typically said that he felt the need to make a real financial sacrifice and thus, by hurting himself, to appease his conscience. G. said he also felt the need to appease his conscience, but he had other ways of hurting himself, e.g. in personal relations; that K couldn't expect all other writers' neuroses to coincide with his own. K agreed. They decided to approach a few more top-income-class writers to form a core. Cases to receive help would be selected (via IRRC) irrespective of political opinion, religion, etc., and subsidies limited to 2 or 3 years.[1]

K is nice and easy, for him; nevertheless, separation of a week or so and freedom of life alone makes me realize what a strain it almost always is being with him, because of his violent and often unpredictable behaviour, constant changes of mood and never-failing desire to make people do something different from what they want to do, e.g. if one says one wants to eat spaghetti for lunch, K says have ravioli, it's better, you say all right and he says, no, have risotto. This is the anti-live-and-let-live aspect of his character, and is sometimes very nice if one doesn't feel like making decisions.

[1] Aldous Huxley, Stephen Spender and Arthur were the only British writers to contribute to the fund. The money was used to subsidize a Russian literary magazine published in Munich and other similar émigré journals; to pay for translations, typewriters and the rent of rooms or offices; and – in the case of Ivan Bunin, later a Nobel Prize winner – to pay for an operation.

23 September [1950]. Lunch Geoffrey Crowther, Barbara Ward, Arthur Schlesinger, K at Brown's[1]. Geoffrey remarked, re Korea (where the UN troops now seem to be winning rapidly): if you reject the old colonial exploitation type of regime, and the communist type, it implies that there is a third alternative. But is there, and if so what is it? If e.g. we win in Korea soon, what form of government should a liberal want for the Koreans? He said this seemed to him a good example of the disadvantage of having no secular religion on our side, and to show the necessity of trying unceasingly to work out what to do. K: Even if on the logical plane, and taking a historical perspective, one is convinced that catastrophe is inevitable, one should on the plane of *action* behave *as if* this were not so, because one can't be sure (e.g. German victory in 1940 seemed certain, but wasn't). One's duty (K said) is to act *as if*, while remaining logically aware of the perspective in which one does so.

[1] Geoffrey Crowther (later Baron), editor of *The Economist* 1938–56; Barbara Ward (Lady Jackson), economist, author and assistant editor of *The Economist* 1939–76.

For some time Arthur had been considering the idea of spending half of every year in the United States, as he felt he needed a wider view of world affairs and a deeper knowledge of American culture. Accordingly in September 1950 he went there to look for somewhere to live. He found a house he liked in Pennsylvania, on an island in the Delaware River, and was able to buy it. Mamaine spent that autumn and early winter in London. She stayed with Celia and took regular piano lessons from Joseph Cooper. At the end of December she joined Arthur in New York.

·1951·

Island Farm, Stockton, New Jersey. 6 [sic] February 1951. No time or inclination to write about my life in London from the date of my last entry to the date of my arrival in New York, 27 December. These 3 months were among the most pleasant I have ever spent. Worked hard (average 4 hours a day) at the piano and made some progress, but not nearly enough. Played Barcarolle and some pieces by Lennox Berkeley which Joe said are good for technique, and the Mozart sonata. Interesting fact: anxiety which haunted me ever since my illness ending August'49, and which was quite bad recently, disappeared for good the day I started playing. Short visit to Paris, where I stayed with Sperber, saw Greta Neumann, spent 1 day at home collecting papers for K.

4.1.51

Island Farm,
Stockton,
New Jersey

Dear Twinnie,

Here is an account of my doings since I left.

The first day in New York was almost too cold to bear, with a temperature of about 14 below freezing, icy winds but bright sunlight. We went in the evening, with Agnes Knickerbocker,[1] to a very smart and dreadful party, at which, however, we didn't stay long. The second day we ourselves gave a drinks party, to which came the Max Eastmans, Bertram Wolfes,[2] Mary McCarthy and her husband (whom Arthur introduced to everybody as Mr Bone, though that is not his name[3]), some people from Macmillans and the head of the Voice of America, a rather nice man called Kohler;[4] also Agnes and Erich Maria Remarque.[5] Afterwards we went out with the two latter and spent a night on the tiles, which was far from enjoyable, because Remarque had just been jilted by his girl-friend and soon got very drunk (as apparently he always does) and was dreadfully boring about it, also somewhat pitiful – he is a rather charming old boy of about 54, I should think. Agnes was very tired, so was I, and besides I got very worried because I saw K was drinking quite a lot and thought damn he is no better after all, and this made me quite desperate, so finally, at El Morocco, I started drinking heavily myself and got very tight. We were drinking pink champagne, which Remarque insisted on our having. At the end of the evening we somehow landed up in the apartment of an American columnist and his Japanese mistress, all more or less staggering and not enjoying it at all. Apparently my fears about K were unfounded, as it seems he really does not get drunk, and indeed he wasn't particularly drunk that night really, and certainly behaved admirably.

The Max Eastmans and the Bertram Wolfes are extraordinarily nice, and the former are off to Europe, so you may run into them later on in London. Edmund [Wilson] is due to come to New York next week, so I will be seeing him.

On Saturday we moved out here. Twin, this is a really lovely house, all white weather-boarding and very prettily shaped, and extremely comfortable and roomy inside. The island is heavenly. There is a road that runs down the middle between rows of fruit trees, and on either side of this road are fields, at present containing maize. At the end and all round the island are woods and undergrowth, teeming with birds of quite unknown species (I saw about six or seven kinds in my one walk round) and grey squirrels. Around the house are a few big trees, I'm not sure of what kind, and fields or lawns. It is on the tip of the island so the river runs round quite close to it on two sides. On the third there is a drive leading down to the bridge. Then there are big barns and vast chicken houses; there are even two cocks and two curious looking Muscovy ducks. Most of the way round the house is a covered veranda. The living room is on the ground floor, and is very nice indeed, long and low-ceilinged with a fireplace at one end, white walls and ceiling, a light grey carpet, and stairs leading up from it to the upper floors. On the next floor up are three bedrooms and a bathroom and shower; on the top floor our bedroom and bathroom and K's working room, which is lovely. On the *sous-sol*, which is actually the ground floor too because the ground slopes down (and in fact the sitting-room is rather above ground level, there are steps leading down from the veranda either side) – on the *sous-sol*-ground floor, as I was saying, is the dining room, which is potentially pleasant but needs working on; next to this on one side are various cellars, etc., on the other the kitchen, which is small but very nice indeed and well fitted out. Out of the kitchen another staircase leads to the two servants' rooms and bathroom. Beyond the kitchen is a breakfast room in which we shall eat for the time being, when not eating in the kitchen; beyond that is a room which in the distant future can, I think, be made into a lovely music and sitting room for me. It is right out at the end of the house and as sound-proof as anything could be. The whole house is awfully well heated by a wonderful system which you turn on to whatever temperature you like for day and for night, and it automatically regulates itself to these temperatures at the appropriate time (or is supposed to, actually it's rather erratic).

So much for the house: you see it is really ideal for us, and very comfortable inside, I think incredibly pretty outside and very sunny. The Island is really lovely; and the country all around is absolutely lovely too. It is not at all flat, but hilly and undulating and wooded, with pretty villages and houses everywhere, and awfully nice people. At a mile or so from the house is our local village, Stockton, which is in New Jersey, though actually we are in Pennsylvania. Stockton is very pretty, there is a super inn with a lovely bar, a very good grocery store where shopping is a pleasure, as you just wheel a barrow round and put everything you want on it and pay as you go out. I love all the people I have met so far. Of course I feel very homesick, but I must say I can think of worse places to have to live in – this is really one's dream place if it weren't so far from Europe.

The only insuperable problem is servants. We just can't afford to have one with any regularity, at a dollar an hour. However, we have a char – a great big Polish-American woman – who comes over in her own car three times a week to help with the dirty work. I don't know yet how much work I'll have – I imagine quite a lot. But we are going to eat very simply, as we really have absolutely no money left, and on the contrary owe Macmillans the equivalent of £7000, and have to get a hell of a lot of things for the house. We have been shopping frantically these last two days and today bought most of the glass and china we will need from a glass and a china factory near here – I mean, one factory for each. Here we were able to pick up so-called 'seconds', i.e. imperfect plates and things, which look more or less like the perfect ones but cost half as much. We have got some very pretty things I do think. Antique furniture is hellishly expensive here, but we are determined to get pretty things as far as possible for our sitting room because it really is such a lovely room. I shall go to New York and search round at auctions.

I'm afraid K's Bill may take ages to come through, and it is by no means easy – his is literally only the fourth case of this kind for just one person⁶. I was interrogated by the immigration officer the other day, and so was K; everything seemed to go well so far.

However, it may not have reached a stage where we can go away by the end of March, when we intend to return to Europe; on the other hand, it may. In any case we shall be back in France, DV, by early summer.

It is too soon to say, until we have settled down, in what sort of form K is. He has got much fatter and I find being with him a bit of a strain after these months of freedom (a non sequitur sentence) but I dare say things will turn out all right. Also, I am unhappy at the prospect of having to wait God knows how long before I can get at a piano again. But we can't possibly afford to buy a decent one here, and I think will probably eventually bring out the Blüthner from France, if you agree and will sell me your half – it is in frightful condition but can be reconditioned, I imagine.

We haven't decided what to do about farming our land yet, but I suspect that we'll let it to a farmer and just keep a few hens, a pig, etc., for ourselves, as in this country it is just a waste of time having a small farm of whatever kind unless you do all the work yourself – you could never make enough profit to cover the labour costs. We have acquired from a local SPCA two tiny black puppies, half springer half God knows what; they are about 6 months old. Agnes was out for the weekend and we took her over to a house where we'd heard there were some boxers for sale, as we thought of getting one for her. When we got there it turned out a hunt was on, and a man rushed up brandishing the bloody head of a fox, its tongue hanging out, which they'd just caught! We live in Bucks County, the Hecate County of

Edmund's *Memoirs of Hecate County* – full of intellectuals and smarties and show people and everything else.

K and I both adore Agnes who is awfully nice. I rang up Eleanor[7] and am seeing her next week when I have time to go to New York again. It takes about 2 hours by car, but it is a beastly drive and I can't drive the car yet (we have a big beautiful Cadillac convertible with every conceivable gadget). One can also get up by train in various ways which I have yet to explore; that is obviously the thing to do. Eleanor says she knows this place well: she used to come to this neighbourhood a lot.

We have a super radio, really incredibly good, and a super gramophone which will play long, medium or quick-playing records –long-playing ones, as you know, have a whole concerto on two sides or less; our radio has a new thing called frequency modulation, which makes the tone simply marvellous – we've just been listening to the Tchaikovsky violin concerto played by Heifetz, and it sounded as good as if one were in a concert hall with good acoustics.

It's too soon to say definitely about climate, weather and health here. But I think the latter should be all right – nothing fatal has occurred so far.

Love,
Twin

[1] Agnes Knickerbocker (see letter of 26.1.49) was by then widowed. She was general secretary of the Fund for Intellectual Freedom. She is now Mrs Joseph T. Walker.

[2] Max Eastman, historian of Soviet Russia and biographer of Stalin and Trotsky; leading figure of the anti-Stalin left in America. Bertram D. Wolfe, historian of the Soviet system and author of *Three Who Made a Revolution* (1948), etc. He was at that time Fellow of the Russian Institute, Columbia University.

[3] His name was Bowden Broadwater.

[4] Foy Kohler, diplomat. He was ambassador to the USSR, 1966–7.

[5] Author of *All Quiet on the Western Front*.

[6] A special bill was needed to allow Arthur, as an ex-Communist, to reside in the United States.

[7] Eleanor Perényi, *née* Stone, writer and journalist. She was an old friend of the twins, who had stayed with her in Ruthenia in 1937 during her marriage to Baron Zsigmond Perényi. She was now working on the Magazine *Mademoiselle*.

January 18th 1951   Island Farm

Dear Twinnie,

We are still frightfully busy but things are settling down at last.

This is quite a big house, and it is a hell of a job to keep it moderately clean and do the cooking, washing up, laundry, ironing, mending and all K's correspondence, as well as buying the basic furniture, etc., which we have by no means done yet. It is true that we have a char who comes three times a week for five hours, she is a vast Italian American married to a Hungarian and comes in her car, *peut s'en faut* in a mink coat. She's a good-natured thing and gets through a certain amount of work, but she is only a Learner at driving a car, so if the weather is bad and she suspects icy roads she doesn't turn up. The weather is quite extraordinary here, and completely unpredictable: on the same day you get a snow storm, then a gale, then thaw and rain; the next day it is like spring with a lovely warm sun; but by evening it may be freezing again or doing any of a number of other things – one never knows from one minute to the next what is going to happen. Agnes and one of her daughters, aged 13, were here for the weekend, and they skated on the canal which runs along parallel to the river on the mainland; it is a very pretty canal, with wooden bridges at intervals, and on Sunday there were lots of children skating along it, which looked lovely.

Everything is going well re K's Bill (which, however, is dreadfully complicated, it seems) and we very much hope to be able to come over to England towards the end of March. If K gets stuck here, which I hope for his sake he won't, I will come anyway in the spring to take steps about selling Verte Rive. We don't think there is much point in keeping it if we don't intend to live there, and for my part I don't really want to spend more time than I can help there because of the climate, while K is rather browned off with France altogether. This place seems very good from a chest point of view. Eleanor, with whom I dined at her flat in New York last week, assured me that it is a swamp here in summer and the heat unbearable; no doubt it is, and the fact that all the windows are covered with mosquito netting is rather ominous. Still, perhaps with luck we can get to Europe or somewhere during the hot weather.

As I write I am doing my washing in the washing machine – a marvellous installation which we acquired with the house. Twinnie, I am longing for you to see this house – it really is a civilized place, the sort of house one can imagine living in for quite a time. We have ordered a vast semi-circular couch for the living room, and when we have this and some curtains and a few other things the place will start looking habitable.

K has been in a rotten mood lately, owing to not having been able to work for so long, I suppose, and I keep doing awfully unpractical things for which I curse myself, so life has been a considerable strain; however, I don't mind, because it is fine to be in the country and with plenty to do and lots to look forward to, when I get a chance to go to New York and look around and see Edmund, also I know K will be all right as soon as we are a bit more settled, which will be at any minute now. I spoke to Edmund on the phone the other day and he said he is longing to show me round New York. The only difficulty is that as we have no servants I can't leave K alone very often or for very long. But it may be that we shall eventually get a couple of European refugees – we are trying to, at any rate.

The play of *Darkness at Noon* came on last week in New York with Claud Rains as Rubashov, and it appears to be a success, though I suspect that it is too intellectual even in the Kingsley version to have a very long run. All our earnings from it go to the Fund for Intellectual Freedom, anyway.[1] We have not seen the play yet but intend to go next week. K's novel [*The Age of Longing*] is due to come out here towards the end of February, and some time in March in England, I think.

New York is obviously a fine place to shop in, but I doubt very much whether I shall ever ever ever have the money to buy one single thing.

I'm longing to know whether you are going to Germany – how I shall envy you if you do.

Eleanor did not really get past dropping the brass when I was with her, nevertheless it was awfully nice seeing her because she is really intelligent and owing to her European background easy to get on with. She has a part-time job with the magazine, three days a week, and is writing a novel I think the rest of the time. I stayed talking to her till nearly 1, it was so nice to be with an old friend and somebody who knows Europe and likes talking about it.

Can't think of any more news, and anyway I must stop and take the clothes out of the machine and then cook the dinner before K comes downstairs for our daily highballs or old-fashioneds – I only drink Bourbon here because once one gets used to it it is a good clean drink, better than gin, and one needs a good slug of something strong after the sort of day's work I do, believe me.

Love,
Twin.

[1] The play of *Darkness at Noon* was very successful in New York, where it ran for eighteen months. Arthur gave all his royalties from it to the Fund for Intellectual Freedom: they amounted to $40,000, which, incidentally, was only $1000 less than the sum he had paid for Island Farm.

30.1.51   Island Farm

Dear Twin,

The winter seems to have started here, the temperature is 20 degrees Fahrenheit today. We have acquired a lovely big St Bernard dog from the SPCA, who rescued it from a farm where it had been abandoned and was starving to death. It is only a pup really, but is about the size of a calf and twice as strong; its name is Nellie. It is already very devoted to us and prowls round the house all day and sleeps on the doorstep at night, though it has a stable full of straw where it could go.

Agnes came down for the weekend with a comic Frenchman called Henri de Vilmorin (brother of Louise); he is an incredibly handsome man of 48 and a real *farfelu*, but a very amusing one. Turn-ups on his cuffs, red silk tie and handkerchief, a large moustache, brought his own vodka and Dubonnet as he said he couldn't drink anything else, but managed to down quite a lot of Bourbon as well. We took them over to the Schulbergs and had a funny evening there with nice Budd S. and his wife.[1]

Budd Schulberg has joined K's Fund, the FIF; its members to date are: Aldous Huxley, John Dos Passos, Jim Farrell, Stephen [Spender], K and Schulberg. The paying-out is done so far in Munich, where a magazine and publishing firm are being set up for émigré Russian writers; they are going to publish among other things some works by Russians still in the USSR who write tripe for official publications but good stuff for themselves. There is a woman in Munich at the offices of the International Rescue Committee who is running it for the FIF, she is Markoosha Fischer, wife of Louis, and she writes the most moving accounts of the meetings of these exiled Russian geniuses, who are overjoyed to have a chance at last of seeing their work in print. As soon as funds get more plentiful they are going to help refugee writers from other totalitarian or satellite countries too; but they have reluctantly decided that East Germans exiled to West Germany don't qualify because they are still in their own language territory and therefore relatively favoured, despite individual hardships; and alas one can't help very many people or it wouldn't be effective at all.

We saw the play of *Darkness at Noon* last week and afterwards had a night out at the Twenty-One, in Harlem, etc., quite fun. It ended in the Champagne Room at El Morocco, where there was nobody else – it was about 4 a.m. – and where K and Torberg[2] sang very out of tune Viennese songs with two Viennese musicians who play there. The play was rather awful, but it is quite successful, I think.

I am working fearfully hard here – the char hasn't been at all for over a week, as she says she can't drive when the roads are icy. I should think I have written about thirty letters today for K. I never get through with my work, and K is in a rotten mood as a result of living in such a disturbed environment for so long. The other day when Agnes and he and I were having dinner in the kitchen he suddenly worked himself up into a rage and stampeded about knocking things over (having knocked over the kitchen table and bespattered us all with wine). Agnes and I spent the rest of the evening mopping up wine, whisky, brandy, blood, glass and china; K also broke a couple of chairs and a lamp, and almost broke his foot kicking at things, so he is now limping about. He has hardly spoken to me since, i.e. for two days; I am hoping this state of affairs will not last too long. There was no apparent reason for his outburst nor for his behaviour since; but as I say the cause is not being able to work properly, and I quite understand how this must drive him mad; but it is inevitable in a new house where nothing works properly or is organized smoothly, so that carpenters, plumbers and electricians are always turning up – we've been through it twice before in our previous houses.

I saw Edmund in New York last week and met his wife, who is charming.[3] He wants me to go up and spend a day with them, but God knows when I'll be able to get away, owing to the impossibility of leaving K with nobody to look after him.

Love,
Twin

[1] Budd Schulberg, novelist and film scenario writer. His novels include *The Disenchanted* (1950) and his screenplays include *On the Waterfront*.

[2] Friedrich Torberg, Austrian writer, had emigrated to the US while the Nazis were in power. He returned to Vienna after the war and edited the magazine *Forum*.

[3] Edmund Wilson had recently married Elena Thornton, *née* Mumm.

February 6th [1951]. Am working very hard, as at the moment we have no char or help at all, and what with doing K's letters, correcting the French translation, shopping for the house, etc., and my being ill last week, the house still hasn't been cleaned up properly. Do all the laundry and ironing at home too – this takes a lot of time. Extraordinary how I don't really mind in the least never seeing anybody, though K and I don't talk much as he is too bad-tempered, I too bored and fed up with him. Otherwise cheerful, though usually pretty exhausted. Oh for a piano! K has started an autobiographical novel.

Feb 12, 1951   Island Farm

Dear Twinnie,

Life has been hectic as usual with work of one kind and another and I am exhausted. But thank goodness the char turned up today, the first time in 3 weeks or more. I was beginning to despair of ever getting the house cleared up properly – every time I started washing the floors some other urgent thing intervened. However, K has solved a problem in connection with his work which was worrying him and seems to have become human again and even rather nice – I don't know if it's permanent or only very temporary.

Everybody here takes the war threat very seriously, the papers are full of instructions on what to do in an atomic attack, and every time you buy anything the shop people always say You'd better get it now, they'll be off the market soon, no more material available, prices are rising, etc. Of course there is such incredible plenty here that it would take them six years of hard work to get down to a stage which we would regard as luxury. But it is true that things do vanish off the market to some extent. Prices have been frozen – but at an all-time high level! The Americans really *are* well-meaning, though. But one sees why they set so much store by money. There are so many wonderful things in the shops that all sorts of things one's never dreamt of become 'musts' – I mean gadgets of one sort and another to make life without servants tolerable. And they are all awfully expensive. So one does get to feel one has to have more money.

We have got a large semi-circular couch for our sitting room, and when it arrived we both decided we hated it, but then after pushing it round all afternoon in various arrangements we thought maybe it would be all right after all. We are gradually acquiring more furniture, but antiques are really impossible to get except for *astronomical* prices, and this makes everything very difficult.

I do hope we can go over to Europe in the spring – I shall be miserable if we can't.

Jamie and Yvonne [Hamilton] are coming to New York soon, so let me know if you want me to give them anything for you. But it can't be expensive – our money is going to run out in March at the latest and we won't have one penny then. God knows what we'll live on.

We've been working all day writing a report on the FIF operation I told you of, with extracts from the letters of the Russian émigré writers in Munich. They are an extraordinary collection of sagas, all these men have been repeatedly arrested in Russia and spent years in camps. The magazine is a real big one, like the so-called 'fat' literary mags in Russia in the last century in which all the great Russian novelists' works were first published.

I have been reading Boswell's *London Journal* – it is *wonderful*. Do get hold of it.

Love,
Twin.

PS. Incidentally K doesn't think there'll be a war for another year.

14th Feb[ruary 1951]. K decided to make his book a straight autobiography. He said, if I make it a novel, all the characters like, e.g., Willie Muenzenberg who play important parts in it will lack conviction and half the point of them will be lost; also, it would inevitably become a psychological *Entwicklungsroman*, whereas I want it to be focussed on the political events of my time. I said I saw another objection to the novel form, namely, that K as a character would never be consistent enough to be convincing unless he split himself into ten characters. K said this objection had occurred to him, and he agreed. Having made this decision his temper improved no end and we had a few tolerable days until interruptions of one kind and another caused a relapse.

They included a meeting with Irving Brown to discuss the Congress which is deteriorating fast. Irving obviously doesn't want K to run the Congress in any way, yet is unable to make anything of it without him. This meeting depressed K.

I am not feeling very well and am suffering from a bad fit of depression since about 4 days – the first one of its kind since we left France, or rather since K came to the States in September. I feel empty and can't see why I am alive.

Feb[ruary] 27 [1951]. In bed since a week with slight bronchitis, not bad but I thought at first I had pleurisy; however, it turned out not to be. Cynthia arrived from England on Saturday, thank God,[1] as K grumbles a bit about having to get my dinner, etc. Starting to get up today.

[1] Cynthia Jefferies had come out to Island Farm to work for Arthur.

March 1st [1951]. *The Age of Longing* came out this week: mixed reception. *NY Times* and *Herald Tribune* Sunday reviews very good, daily reviews bad, very bad *Time* and *Newsweek*, good *Saturday Review of Literature*, rave review in *Philadelphia Enquirer*. Many of the bad reviews seem unfair and personally hostile; this is probably the cause of K's outburst of today. Says he's only worried about the sales; this may be so, as we depend on them very much and are broke unless the book sells well.

5 March 51   Island Farm

Dear Celia,

Just a boring line to say that I am much less gloomy than when I last
wrote and things really do seem to be looking up a bit – at least I think
they are about to. We had more snow, but today was a real spring day,
all sorts of bulbs are coming up and all sorts of unknown bird-songs
are heard. Today I saw cardinals, American robins, juncos. Agnes
did finally come, and we had a nice weekend.

Last night when Agnes and I were chatting about English and
American journalism, K suddenly said 'By far the greatest journalist
in the world is Alan Moorehead.' 'Do you really think that?' I said.
'Yes, he's the greatest by miles,' replied K (who knows something
about journalism). K also greatly admired Alan's piece in the *New
Yorker*, he said 'It's wonderful, wonderful, wonderful' (which it is).

I am still rather weak and wobbly, but K is doing his best to force
me to take it easy; he has been very affectionate the last 3 days, except
for occasional sulks.

                                            Love,
                                            Tw.

[? March, 1951]   Hotel Duane,
                                              237 Madison Avenue,
                                              New York 16, N Y

[The first page of this letter is missing.]

We had a really AWFUL and catastrophic evening with the
Schulbergs last week; they came to dinner with us, and Budd said he
wanted to discuss the FIF with Arthur, and everything went as wrong
as it possibly could. It started by K being very aggressive and trying to
bully Budd; Budd refused to be bullied and became rather evasive;
this made K worse; everybody got rather drunk (except me). When
they had left K and I had a really major row in the course of which we
decided to separate, and then decided not to – at least K thought we
had decided not to, but I didn't realize this till the next day. The cause
of the row is not worth telling, as it was one of those things which are

purely subjective on both sides that occur between married people, and no objective account of it can be given. It was a dark night, pouring with rain, and a strong gale blowing – however, I put on a lot of clothes and wandered off down the island and back, but was too worn out to think clearly. Ever since then things seem to have gone all right and K has been affectionate and cheerful. But God, how many more of these scenes will I have to go through, and how will the whole thing end? One thing K agreed about was that he couldn't live with any woman, however perfect, and he agreed with my analysis of his attitude as being a hostility to women derived from his hatred of his mother.

I have a *craving* to go to Italy, and 'twould be wonderful if we could do so together in the autumn: let's scheme and plot for this and perhaps we can.

Sperber's first book[1] has just come out here and had awfully good reviews.

K's book is going well, but we are down to our last dime all the same, as we've had to spend so much on the house. It's too tantalizing to see the shops here and not be able to buy anything; today, however, I broke out and bought a pair of red shoes – shall I ever be able to wear them? They are awfully nice, and cost $15 (£5 – cheap for shoes here).

No servants still except for a *lousy* char whom I had to collect from 5 miles away and take home and who did no work at all. But with Cynthia here it doesn't matter so much.

We all went to see *King Solomon's Mines* [the film] yesterday so that K could see it, and I enjoyed it as much as the 1st time.

Is it spring in England? It's cold here and now pouring with rain; there are no flowers out. I don't really believe there ever is a spring here, I think it must go straight from winter to summer.

Love,
Twin

[1] *Et le Buisson devint cendre* (Paris, 1949), translated under the title *The Burned Bramble* (London and New York, 1951). It was the subject of a short piece by Arthur entitled *The Little Flirts of St Germain des Prés*, first published in *Le Figaro Littéraire* and reprinted in *The Trail of the Dinosaur* (1955), p. 60.

March 24 [1951]. Dinner NY with Bob Morris and Senator and Mrs Brewster.[1] K spoke of the bad impression made in Europe by McCarthy and said a change of emphasis and a formulation on McC's part would be of great value in counteracting this. He suggested that an amnesty should be granted to the former Communists who have made a full avowal, whatever crimes they had committed for the CP (short of murder, which they'd hardly confess anyway). The Senator said he wasn't much interested in Europe but saw K's point, especially where American liberals were concerned. He said, could he bring McC[arthy] down to our island for a talk with K; K said, yes, if we also get some other European intellectuals so as not to leave him as sole spokesman for Europe.

[1] Bob Morris was the lawyer in charge of getting Arthur's Bill through the Senate. Senator Brewster was one of the senators who were to introduce it.

March 25th 1951

Island Farm

Dear Celia,

No particular news since I last wrote, whenever that was. I've been doing a great drive to get some of the house furnished, and with this end have been twice to Philadelphia and also to New York. Arthur and I had dinner with one of the Senators who are introducing his Bill; this one is called Sen. Brewster, and is a very Republican Republican, a dry (anti-drink), obviously quite a nice chap and intelligent as far as they go, but oh how many miles between him and us, we both felt. He remarked that the only member of his household who had read any of K's books was his gardener, who has read *Darkness at Noon*. K spent the dinner and the rest of the evening – during which we went to a movie and had drinks with his nice Republican lawyer, Bob Morris, and a staunch Republican girl whom the latter brought along – trying to persuade all these Republicans that a change of emphasis on their part vis à vis Communists and former Communists here would do them no harm. I was rather interested in this, as I saw that this is what happens to all these 'political men' who, like K, start by being leftists for many years, then in despair at the woolly-mindedness of the leftists swing towards the right, and pin their last hopes on liberalizing the rightists. The same pattern occurred in Malraux, who, as you may remember, was always telling us that it would be possible to strengthen the left wing of the Gaullists, that de Gaulle was really *un homme de gauche*. The difference is that K is fully aware of the hopelessness of this undertaking, though his urge to do *something* makes him take it on without hope of success. It was clear the other evening that most of his arguments fell on deaf ears. He was principally concerned with the repercussions of McCarthy on the Europeans, and this is a problem which American politicians simply are not in the least interested in, busy as they are coping with their political machine and getting themselves reelected.

We tried to find out from Bob Morris when the Bill was likely to come up and whether we could get away to Europe this spring. Unfortunately he didn't seem to know, so it is all still in the air. However, he said that if it was delayed for long we could apply for a return visa for K and might get it, which would enable us to go, though we might have to return at a moment's notice if the Bill comes up. I would be depressed by this, only that I see that K is becoming very impatient to get back to Europe himself, and if he really wants to a way will be found, no doubt. The pressure of this godforsaken country is getting him down, and more particularly such institutions as the best-seller list (which appears in the weekly papers), which makes writers feel like commodities on the stock exchange, also the idiotic reviews with their completely false standards, and in general the externalizing influence of everything, the difficulty of leading anything approaching a simple life, and the impossibility of solitude and contemplation, even when one lives damn it all on an island. K and I feel exactly alike on these things and we also both feel that it is a good thing to live here some of the time because one can't really know what the world is like if one doesn't sometimes face up to the worst aspects of it; but we would like to spend at least six months every year in Europe, without which we would feel trapped and imprisoned by cars and gadgets and washing machines and television.

Talking of TV, has the Crime Investigation Committee (Costello case) been reported at all in England? It has all been televised here, and in any drug store or bar one can sit and watch the most extraordinary underworld characters testifying by the hour. The impact on the country has been considerable; everybody watches it. We went yesterday into a bar in Harlem and the negroes were riveted on the TV screen while one of these gangsters was testifying.

No time for more; my life is very tolerable these days, but I'm impatient for spring, and even more to 'cleanse my soul', as Yvonne [Hamilton] put it, by getting to Europe.

Love,
Mamaine.

March 25th [1951]. Yesterday K said we must do something soon about getting back to Europe: he said he couldn't bear to live here unless he knew he could get there for 6 months every year. I myself am more and more homesick for Europe. I remember standing in the cloisters of St Trophime in Arles and thinking I couldn't bear to live in a country where nothing like that exists. Even the countryside here doesn't look real – it's still yellow and withered-looking, no green grass or purple buds, hardly any sign of spring.

April 2nd [1951]. K says he is simply allergic to American liberals. I asked him if Republicans weren't worse and he said, probably, but it takes me a bit longer to get bored by them because I don't know in advance every single thing they're going to say.

April 5th 1951   Island Farm

Dear Twinnie,

Thanks for your letter. It is not true of course that K is becoming an American citizen. Better scotch that rumour.

We have been rather miserable, as my laryngitis turned into one of those coughs which one can't get rid of and I had to spend two or three days in bed and have some penicillin, but I am all right now and up; while K has been having an attack of ulcer or something which makes him tired and irritable. He now has a phobia against poor Cynthia and all his irritability is directed against her: I try to defend her. I am happy to say that he is getting absolutely fed up with being in America and is pining to come to Europe; we are trying to fix to go some time in May. I guess that once there we shall stay at least until the late autumn, as the trouble is that we can't afford to live here for more than about six months a year, however low a standard of life we maintain – and our standard is *much* lower here than in France. Life is so expensive here that it is just impossible on books alone, K would have to produce a best-seller every year, and the knowledge that he relied on his books to make money would finish him as a writer. Fortunately we don't want to stay here the whole year anyway. We are going to try to sell Fontaine and spend the summers either in a country pub in France or travelling about, for instance K has suddenly decided that he would like to live on the Rhine for a while, perhaps in Johannisberg! He wants to go to Munich too to see his Russian writers. This all sounds extremely promising and I am all agog to see what we will do. Life is more than tolerable here if one knows one can get away for a long spell soon.

It still isn't quite spring weather, but the daffodils are coming out – there are lots in the garden – and the forsythia round the house is out: the spring migrants will be here in a week or so, which I look forward to.

On Wednesday Edmund and Elena are taking us to see the new musical, *The King and I*.

Love
Twin

PS If you see Lu, I want to know a) was the Grand Duchess Sergei really his aunt? and b) what does he know about her – don't forget.[1]

[1] The Grand Duchess Sergei of Russia was the sister of Prince Ludwig of Hesse's father, the Grand Duke of Hesse, and of the Tsarina. She appears as a character in Camus's play *Les Justes*.

April 8th [1951]. Lovely weather since a few days. Although I have done no housework for a week (because in bed) I determined to spend a couple of days out of doors, pottering round the island with field glasses and through the barns and chicken houses and stacks. Picked some daffodils; saw a skunk and a good many birds, with which I am now gradually becoming familiar. They include: bluebirds (wonderfully pretty and sweet), phoebe, flicker, purple grackle, crested tit, song sparrow, chipping sparrow, downy woodpecker, blue jay, turkey vulture, American robin, cardinal – all unknown in Europe.[1] Today K and I walked round the island – it was the first time he had been to some very pretty parts of it, where I often go. K is on good form these days and is very amiable. This and the weather and the prospect of going to Europe soon have cheered me greatly.

He said, If you thought there was going to be a war within the next 3 years, wouldn't you rather it happened now and get it over? Me: Well, I *do* think there's sure to be. K: Yes, but if you knew for certain. Me: No, every day we have before the war comes and either kills us or makes life intolerable is a day of grace. K: Well, I'd rather get it over now. – Re America, K says the question is: is all this crime and corruption a phenomenon of adolescence or of decay? Growing pains or the rot of the moribund? Police corruption is on a scale unimaginable even to people (like us) who've lived in France.

Al and Nancy Hart came for drinks and stayed for dinner.[2] Mrs H[art] remarked that she felt very 'county' about Hunterdon County, where she lives: 'It's not at all like Bucks County, which is full of Jews, God knows'. Al Hart told K that in view of K's present position here, and the ambivalent attitude of the critics and writers to him, it would probably be a good thing for him to write next a novel about an American theme, in which his attitude to 'this country and its problems' would be stated. K retaliated that even if he could or wanted to do this, being by nature a social critic his comments on America might not be to their taste. Was struck dumb by this proposal of Al's, ignoring as it does a) the kind of writer K is (which Al as his editor ought to know) and b) the fact that the Americans are not by a long chalk the only, or even the most important, public for his books. But to Americans the only thing worth aiming for is success (and money) *here* and *now*. K was conciliatory, but got very depressed when the Harts left and said, no wonder there are so many American liberals and fellow-travellers, they just don't feel their way of life is worth defending and if one says you must defend relative freedom against total unfreedom they don't see what you're talking about: if I had been brought up here (said K) I would be a 'liberal' to this day, probably.

[1] This is not true of the crested tit, of which three races are to be found in Europe.
[2] Al Hart was Arthur's editor at Macmillan's, New York.

On 11 April Arthur and Mamaine motored to Washington to spend a weekend with Bob and Jane Joyce: see letter of 25 April.

[April] 16th [1951]. Back via Baltimore, where we went to see a doctor friend of Agnes at the Johns Hopkins hospital, with a view to arranging a check-up, as K is worried about my health, which is very bad these days. He turned out to be a Pavlovian and was only interested in showing K his paper on the effects of alcohol on sexual potency. I was paralysed with fear, as doctors and hospitals have this effect on me these days; however, this doc. was not the right one (being a psychiatrist) so I shall have to go again.

[April] 20th [1951]. By car to NY, lunch S. Fischer,[1] train to Boston for weekend with A. Schlesinger, Jr. Dinner A. MacLeish, Thornton Wilder, Mary McCarthy and her husband, Mollie Brazier,[2] George Fischer (son of Louis) – very nice evening. Discussion on whether writers have to have an audience, present or future; could e.g. Keats have written his letters if he hadn't felt they would reach a wider audience? Later, K was attacked by all for saying that Sen[ator] McCarthy had done some good and that, though K didn't like or approve of him, if he hadn't existed it would have been necessary to invent him, in order to show up Hiss [and certain others]. Opposition argument was that if McC. and his friend got into power no American troops would be sent to Europe.

[1] Samuel Fischer, head of the German publishing firm S. Fischer Verlag.
[2] Dr Mary A. B. Brazier, neurophysiologist, was then working at the Massachusetts General Hospital. She is now Emeritus Professor of Anatomy and Physiology at the University of California.

Sunday [21 April 1951]. Mollie B. and the Broadwaters came back in the morning and the conversation of Saturday evening was resumed. Mollie B. talked of experiments with mescaline and scopolamine for getting people to divulge (a) intellectual, non-affective (b) emotional secrets. Said scopolamine alone is no good with (a) and is only successful with (b) in the case of neurotic subjects with a desire for catharsis; but mescaline is very effective with both.

K has been very nice and companionable for some weeks now, no nagging or rows at all. [He is] very overworked with FIF chores and correspondence.

April 25th 1951   Island Farm

Dear Twinnie,

The last few weeks we have been travelling about a certain amount. After I last wrote to you we went to Washington for a weekend to stay with the Joyces (who have a very pretty house there in Georgetown); then we went up to Boston for a weekend with the Arthur Schlesinger Jrs, in Cambridge; then I went for a few days to Baltimore. In between there were various activities, I forget what, which meant that I have had no time at all.

The weekends in Washington and Cambridge were great fun, especially the latter. In Washington we went for drinks to Adam and Andy's house. Andy looked rather sweet, though it is difficult to imagine her as an ambassadress.[1] Adam was also nice. We attended a couple of jumbo dinner parties, one given by the Joyces, at both of which we encountered Intelligence bigwigs, senators, columnists (including Stewart Alsop of the *Herald Tribune*). We also drifted around Washington looking up old pals of K's in the State Department, meeting various people (including Freda Utley[2]) and in my case going to the Senate; in the course of our social life we had drinks with Senator McCarthy (quite accidentally). He is a hairy-pawed thug of about 40–46 who has, it seems, made a few rather good speeches and shown up several people who would otherwise have remained unnoticed, and most of whom still go on working in important posts anyway. But Republican senators, of which McC. is one, are really awful, and if they came to power no American troops at all would go to Europe; that is why it is such a pity that some of the showing up of infiltrators can't be done by Democrats and liberals, instead of Acheson and Co. covering up for the State Dep[artment] like mad.

Washington is a hotbed of intrigue and one has to watch one's step all the time to see that one is not branded as having pals in the enemy clique from the one one's with, which if you don't know who is who's enemy is rather difficult.

The Cambridge weekend was unmitigatedly enjoyable. We landed in a dinner party consisting of Thornton Wilder (who is *sweet*), Archibald MacLeish, with whom I got on rather well on the subject of Rilke and St John Perse; Mary McCarthy and Bowden Broadwater – a lanky bespectacled young man with short narrow trousers and a bow-tie; a nice young man, former member of the Komsomol, George Fischer, son of Louis; and a very nice and intelligent neuro-physiologist called Mollie Brazier. All these people, with the exception of the first two, remained around all the rest of the weekend – they went off for the night, and most of them reappeared early in the morning, George Fischer later in the day, and all stayed till midnight on Sunday. It was great fun. We took Cynthia, who stayed in a hotel. Mary McC. and Bowden took her and me for a sight-seeing tour of Cambridge and Boston, which are lovely towns, the latter very Henry-Jamesian-looking with street after street of tall narrow eighteenth-century houses. A vast cocktail party was also given in our honour by the Schlesingers. I couldn't say who came to it – nothing but academics, I suppose. We flew back to New York, as we had a lunch date with Sidney Hook on Monday.

Do send me the book you mention about the Greeks. I would love to have it.[3]

K's reviews in England have been remarkably good and intelligent, even old Peter's [Peter Quennell's] might have been worse. Ring Stevie [Miss Stephens at A. D. Peters] and ask her to send you a copy of the book.

I would *love* to go to Aldeburgh[4] with you if only we can come over. As for the Italian project, don't count on me, I think it more than doubtful that I could manage it.

It's too funny Alex Weissberg having cropped up in your life. I warn you you'll never get rid of him for an instant from now on. But, as you say, he is awfully interesting and also I think very charming, so perhaps it doesn't matter, till his maniacal side starts getting you down. Never leave any sweets in his vicinity: he will eat a whole box without stopping or looking up. Please convey to Alex that I am very fond of him, if you can manage this in German: he is always making speeches to me to which I make no response, and I don't want him to think I'm fed up with him.

My chest is rotten these days, but rotten; it is the spring, no doubt. We have had two days of intense heat – about 80 degrees. Now it is lovely, all our pear trees are out and there are violets everywhere. Arthur went to New York today, and Cynthia and I did frenzied housework all day to clean the place up a bit. But it's so big and there's so much to do that at the end of such a day one finds there's still almost as much that needs to be done as at the beginning. However, we enjoyed having the house to ourselves and a chance to get down to some work.

Love,

Twin

[1] Probably because of her youth: later, when her husband was made ambassador to Senegal, she became the youngest ambassadress in the Service.

[2] Freda Utley, author, journalist, lecturer. A former member of the Communist Party, she had worked as a senior scientific researcher in Moscow 1930–6 and had married a Russian Jew. After his arrest and disappearance she published *The Dream we lost: Soviet Russia Then and Now* (1940) and many other books. She became Director of the America-China Policy Association and a member of the Department of Politics advisory council, Princeton University.

[3] Possibly *The Greeks*, by H. D. Kitto (1951).

[4] That is, the Aldeburgh Music Festival.

29 [April 1951]. Lunch von Neumann (Princeton).[1] Bermann Fischer,[2] wife and daughter and v. Neumanns to dinner. Thunderstorm. Saw five deer on the island.

K says v. N[eumann] is a genius, he is also charming and amusing. K was delighted with the evening; he attempted to discuss his favourite subject, viz., is American crisis sign of puberty or of climacterium? V[on] N[eumann] denied the existence of a crisis except as a place on a curve, said one part of the organism can be senescent, another not; said a civilization is successful when it is doing what it sets out to do, whether or not what it is trying to do is desirable. He also said, quoting Veblen, that in a Puritan country where people are denied normal satisfactions and pleasures, they are driven to seek success, whereas in a Catholic country (e.g. France) they can enjoy themselves without being successful so they don't have to bother.

¹ John von Neumann, one of the leading mathematicians of his time and a key figure in the Los Alamos atomic bomb project. He was of Hungarian origin.

² Gottfried Bermann Fischer, son-in-law of Samuel Fischer and Director since 1932 of S. Fischer Verlag, which he contined to run after his emigration to the United States: see his autobiography, *Bedroht, Bewahrt*, 1971.

May 6 [1951]. Von Neumanns to drinks, went with them to the Stockton Inn for dinner. Discussion on free will v. determinism. N. said his position was that he thought one couldn't be sure one's actions were not all determined by one's past history, etc., plus factors which one cannot know now and probably never could know; nor could one be sure that they were: all one could say was that the *feeling* of freedom was a fact, and that it was of great importance even if really an illusion. K said he couldn't bear the thought of 100% determinism, which would deprive him of responsibility for his acts and thus of credit for his good ones; said he has to believe in the intervention of a hidden variable. However, since the latter might simply be a so far unobserved, or unobservable, determining factor, he seemed really to be almost in agreement with v. N., though more inclined to a kind of mystical belief in real freedom (from electrons up). Also discussed emergent vitalism; very nice evening. Neumann, who is 47, is very lucid, not at all dry, academic or pompous and has a good sense of humour. His wife is also nice and gay and rather attractive.

9 [May, 1951]. Bought a power tractor to cut the grass with. K spent the entire day doing this at top speed, which he greatly enjoyed. Cynthia raked the grass up into heaps. I bought electric shears for the hedge, yards of hose, a watering can, weed killer, etc., and played about with them; also raked grass, painted furniture, sunbathed (temperature 75° in the shade). Lovely day.

May 12–14 [1951]. Bob and Jane Joyce for the weekend. Cocktail party at v. Neumanns Saturday, where we met several mathematicians. Sunday lunched out of doors. Arthur, Bob and Jane cut and raked grass. The Neumanns came to dinner. At this Neumann, when pressed to give his opinion on the immediate future of Europe, said he saw only two alternatives: preventive war (which the Americans obviously wouldn't start, he thought) or Russian occupation of Europe. Regarded the latter as the price we'd have to pay for not starting a war, but plainly thought the first alternative preferable, though he did not say so explicitly (except in Hungarian, to K). Bob said 'We believe that in 3 or 4 years' time we shall be able to defend Europe'. Very enjoyable weekend; K very pleased.

A pair of Baltimore orioles have recently arrived, very beautiful. Nests and eggs everywhere. Sunbathed and started clipping the hedge with new electric clippers. Relations K-me excellent these days, thank God – he never says a cross word, is considerate and affectionate.

[May] 19 [1951]. Lunched with Edmund W[ilson] in Princeton and spent the afternoon with him there; drinks with the Berrymans.[1]

[1] The poet John Berryman and his wife. For an account of this evening see *Poets in their Youth* by Eileen Simpson (formerly Eileen Berryman), 1982, p. 220.

24.5.51   Island Farm

Dear Twinnie,

Thanks for your interesting letter (about spoonbills, Monteverdi, etc.), which I have just received.

Our situation is still hanging in the air and we are fed up with never knowing what we can do next. Our present plan is for me to go to Europe at any rate towards the end of June, in order to try to sell the house in France. If K can, he will come of course; but if things haven't got any further here he'll have to stay here, and then I shall have to return in about a month as otherwise things become very complicated, for the dreary reason that K has to have Cynthia to work with, yet she can't live here alone with him, nor will there be anybody at all to look after him when I'm away, so we'll have to park Cynthia out somewhere and K will have to go out for most of his meals, which he'll hate. It will be *most* unsatisfactory if I can only go to Europe for a month and have to spend most of that packing things up at Fontaine (if we succeed in selling it); but there is still a good chance that the Bill will get through in the meantime. The uncertainty is gnawing into us, and frankly I'm absolutely counting on a long stay in London, so that if I don't get it I shall be most unhappy. I'd rather put off coming till later and stay some time. But if we are to sell Verte Rive we must do it soon, because it is a house which people would only buy in the summer, and the *vacances* begin on July 15th so I ought to start before then.

The other night K and I had one of our periodic conversations about what to do and where to live, which I don't take very seriously except that they show which way the wind is blowing. K said, in view of the difficulty of living here as a writer without doing hack work, and of the fact that we already have money in England, what did I think of the idea that we should sell the house (this house) for a large sum, convert the money into pounds, and then either get a house in England where we could live in relative comfort for quite a time, or go and live in Bermuda (where one can live on pounds). I said I was afraid he would not like living in England, as he is always saying so; and as for Bermuda, it seemed to me an utterly pointless place to live in, and I suspected it of being full of rich English people, which would not make for a congenial atmosphere. I also said that everybody knew it was crazy to live in one place when all one's money was somewhere else, but on the other hand I thought it was time we stayed put for a while, especially as we have this lovely house and I can't imagine finding another one so nice and being able to afford it. Also, I said, wouldn't he feel a bit cut off in Bermuda? He replied that he didn't mind if he was, since in the first place he cares less and less about people, and in the second he feels he has written all he can about political issues, and if he's not writing about them it will not be so essential for him to be in the centre of things. Isn't K extraordinary how quickly he can change his whole idea of where and how he wants to live? But I don't worry, for whatever we do we never do it for long, and I really don't care particularly what it is, so long as it keeps him happy and isn't bad for his work.

K has finished writing his introduction to Alex [Weissberg]'s darn book[1] and I've been reading it. It is a fascinating book, though strictly *entre nous* we have our doubts as to its complete veracity, if one can judge by the passage on K, which is full of staggering inaccuracies in spite of the ready availability of material. For example Alex states that K was the first European to cross the Arabian desert and visit King

Abdullah, which is not only mad but also silly when you think that as Transjordan was already at that time a British protectorate or mandated territory it was plainly teeming with Europeans. But as a matter of fact it doesn't terribly matter whether there is a good deal of romancing in the book or not; it would only concern trivial incidents, and the main lines are of course true. It sheds a good deal of light on Alex's really extraordinary character. He sat through his harrowing experiences with thick-skinned imperviousness and insensitivity (the book is not at all harrowing to read), and hardly even worried when he was handed over to the Gestapo in 1940, though of the 100 people handed over at the same time Greta Buber is the only other one to have survived, so far as is known, and Alex, being a Jew, had far less chance than she. Alex was clearly very brave and dignified in his encounters with his interrogators. His survival is mainly due to his character and to his mixture of *débrouillardise*, physical toughness and almost superhuman optimism.

I wish I had Mozart's letters. I never seem to have anything really good to read; I mostly just vegetate, working in the house and garden. Soon it will get too hot for this to be much fun, I suppose.

Love,
Mamaine

¹ *Conspiracy of Silence* (1952).

June 3 [1951]. Nice party at the Neumanns last night – the usual collection of mathematicians, physicists, meteorologists, etc. Discussion on the motives of scientists. Von N. said he thought them primarily aesthetic. Said, one might call it a question of taste: Archimedes was virtually as far advanced as Galileo or Kepler, but no progress had been made in between because of the sudden change of 'taste' from science to religion with the rise of Christianity. One strong spiritual force, in becoming dominant, greatly weakens all others, i.e. there can be only one at a time; thus with the resurgence of science in modern times religion has been almost eclipsed. In other words the same force is diverted into different channels and is capable of switching suddenly from one channel to another, though this may not be realized for several centuries.

Excellent article by Sperber in today's *[New York] Times Book Review* about ex-Communists' literary aims (to transmit development of consciousness, not results of experience).

June 16th 1951   Island Farm

Dear Twin,

Many thanks for your letter from Cambridge – what an enjoyable weekend you must have had. I was also fascinated to hear about the Diplomats, who have of course been the subject of lively but uninformed discussion here and in Washington. There I lunched with Adam [Watson] and a man called Jack Davis from the State Department (he is said to be one of the 'China policy clique' here), and Adam said that when Maclean was in Washington he used to go around saying that until he went there he had believed that the Americans really wanted to go to war with Russia anyway, but he now saw that they didn't, and wondered how on earth one could put this across to the Russians, who believed the opposite. This would seem to confirm the theory 'plutôt Hess que Hiss'; but for my part I think Herbert Butterfield's theory sounds more plausible.[1]

Hope you got my last letter saying that I am arriving Sunday 1st in the afternoon and hope to stay with you till the following Wednesday 4th, then to move on to France, and to return to England later for a longer stay. I shan't be able to bring much, as I am simply unable to save any money. We have had so many people to stay and for drinks lately that my funds are more than exhausted: we have spent something like the equivalent of £30 on drinks in the last few days. However, I will try, if Cynthia (who's leaving on the 27th) has underweight luggage, to send via her a bit of ham, which may come in handy if you're having people to dinner. I'm not certain about this, but I think it can be done.

I haven't much news, and will reserve any there may be until I see you, including a story of a drunken bearded former champion wrestler who appeared during dinner when the Kohlers (head of the Voice of America) and the Bertram Wolfes were here, produced a swastika armband from his pocket, and refused to leave though socked good and hard by me.[2]

Various people have been here for the weekend and some still are: nothing exciting. It's a bit too hot for comfort. I work fearfully hard these days, but I like doing it and it makes time go fast until I come to England. Yesterday a bird banding man came over and tried to enlist me as a bird-bander. I agreed. Unfortunately he is an awfully boring man, a positively aggressive bore. Ringing here is done under Government auspices, and on a much bigger scale than in England; and this island is right on the migration route, so is the ideal place.

I *wish* I could go to Aldeburgh. I'm longing to hear about it.

Love,
Mamaine

[1] Celia had written to Mamaine on 12 June *à propos* of the recent defection of Guy Burgess and Donald Maclean to the USSR: 'Herbert had the following ingenious theory: that the Americans have something secret now up their sleeve with which they hope any minute to put an end to the Korean war, as they have frequently talked lately about a Korean peace; and that they would have had to communicate it to the British, and therefore that Maclean and possibly Guy B. would know about it; and that the Russians consider it vital to find out American plans themselves at this crucial moment.'

[2] Mrs Ella Wolfe has given me an account of this incident, which she remembers clearly. Arthur had invited this man, whom he did not really know, over to the island for drinks late one afternoon. By the time he arrived Arthur had already had a good deal to drink. Nevertheless, all went well until the guest announced that he had fought for Franco in the Spanish Civil War. At this Arthur, 'though half his size', flew at him. Ella Wolfe and Mamaine entered the fray to try to separate the two men: neither of them emerged from it without injury. Eventually the unwelcome visitor 'was shown out of the house and disappeared across the bridge'.

June 23–25 [1951]. Weekend with James and Marcia Burnham in Connecticut. Beautiful country and villages, K very sweet and sympathetic when I was ill most of Sunday. Saw a humming-bird feeding on a delphinium from the bathroom window, in the early morning sunlight.

27th [June 1951]. Left for London by air, after 5 hour wait at Idlewild, culminating in a row between K and a BOAC transport man. K was quite justified in his anger, but as usual spoilt his case by completely losing his temper and shouting at the man. When we finally got into the plane there was another hitch and we had to get out again. This was the last straw for K, after his row, and he proposed we go back to New York and start again the following day; dissuaded him from this, and once we got going he cheered up and wouldn't stop talking, though I was dropping with sleep. What a relief to get to Scotland – the cold air, the incredibly bad food, the English-looking fields. Everything wonderful after America.

8th [July 1951] Sunday. Paris, dinner Jenka [Sperber] in a Chinese restaurant off the B[oulevard] St Germain. Jenka said I ought to do something about my clothes; she said: even Munjo says you are *beaucoup trop modeste*. She told me Malraux recently said to her: 'Je ne fais pas de la politique: je fais de l'histoire'.

Friday 12 [July 1951]. To England, taking Ma, who's been with us for a week.

14th [July 1951]. Peg and Lu [of Hesse] to dinner. Peg (wonderful as ever) talked about Rudolf Pechel,[1] said Pechel badly wanted to see K and tell him how great his influence is in Germany, and that he is the one writer to whom the Germans will listen.

[1] Rudolf Pechel, former editor of the *Deutsche Rundschau* and its publisher both before and after the war. Author of *Freedom in Struggle* (1957) and other books. From 1942 until the end of the war he was interned in Sachsenhausen for anti-Nazi activities.

14th [August 1951]. Back to France by train. K met me, took me to Fontaine for dinner.

Postscript

A month later Arthur and Mamaine separated for good. There are, of course, some indications in Mamaine's letters and diaries of that period as to why they did so, but I have omitted them, because the factors that lead to the breakdown of a marriage are usually many and varied and it is not possible for a third person to be sure of having fully understood them. The situation was, naturally, a very painful one for both of them, but fortunately they remained on close and friendly terms. Mamaine came over to London, bought a small house just south of the Brompton Road and found work with a firm of publishers. Arthur remained in France long enough to sell the house there and then also came to London, where he bought another one within walking distance of Mamaine's. They used to meet at least once a week and got on very well together, but from then on they led separate lives.

The following spring Mamaine went to Majorca, taking with her a camera and a list of Balearic birds, and spent a very enjoyable holiday in the small coastal village of Cala Ratjada staying with her old friends from Merionethshire, Mark and Irene Sontag, who had gone to live there.

In the beginning of March 1954 she fell ill with a bad cough which developed into acute asthma. She spent most of April and May in hospital, occasionally being discharged during periods of remission, which she spent with me. At the end of May she was again in hospital and seemed to be recovering, but she had another relapse and died on 2 June 1954, at the age of thirty-seven.

Mamaine never for a moment regretted the years she had spent with Arthur, nor did she ever cease to love him. At the end of her life, when he visited her in hospital, they felt as close to each other as ever, and this made her very happy. She summed up her feeling about her relationship with him in a letter to me dated 8 April 1950:

'In fact I am awfully happy with K simply because I do love him so much, not a day goes by without my thinking what happiness it is for me to be with him. . . . Whatever happens to me from now on – and I have no reason to suppose that anything awful will – I shall consider my life has been well spent since I have spent six years of it with K. For apart from anything else I greatly believe in K as a writer, and I would do anything, even leave him if it were necessary, to help him fulfil what I consider to be his destiny. I should count myself and my life of little importance in such a case.'

Index

Abdullah, King of Jordan, 189
Acheson, Dean, 137 & n2, 183
Action, L' (journal), 151 & n1
Acton, Harold, 74
Agronski (Agron), Gershon, 89 n2
Aldeburgh Music Festival, 184 & n4, 191
Alsace, 139
Alsop, Stewart, 183
Altalena (ship), 87 n1, 88
Altman, Georges, 148, 152, 160
Amery, Julian, 144 & n4, 145
Amis de la Liberté, Les, 152 & n2
Anglo-American Palestine Commission, 1946, 34 n4
Aron, Raymond: Koestlers meet in Paris, 61 & n2; visits Koestlers at Verte Rive, 137, 150; and Berlin Congress, 148, 150, 152–4; in London, 159–60
Aschaffenburg, Professor, 17
Ascher, Dorothy *see* Koestler, Dorothy
Ashford, Daisy: *The Young Visiters*, 122 & n2
Attlee, Clement (*later* Earl), 39
Auckland, Robert Eden, 3rd Baron, 8
Auden, W. H.: *The Age of Anxiety*, 97
Aurenche, Jean, 131
Aury, Dominique, 38 n1
Ayer, (Sir) Alfred J., 24 n7, 29, 33 & n3, 131, 144, 160
Ayrton, Michael, 82 & n1

B., C., 112
Barbereau, 72–4
Beauvoir, Simone de, 40, 43, 59, 62, 73, 100
Begin, Menachem, 93
Beloff, Nora, 73 & n1
Berenson, Bernhard, 75
Bergson, Henri, 58
Bergson, Peter, 92 & n1
Berlin *see* Congress of Cultural Freedom
Bermuda, 188
Bernadotte, Count Folke, 93 & n1
Bernier, M. and Mme., 134–5
Berryman, John, 187 & n1
Bertaux, Denise (*née* Supervielle), 118 & n1
Bertaux, Pierre, 118 & n1, 128, 137–8, 140, 149, 153
Betjeman, (Sir) John: *New Bats in Old Belfries*, 27
Bevan, Aneurin, 34 n5
Blair, Richard (George Orwell's adopted son), 24 n3, 111 & n1
Bevin, Ernest, 54 & n2, 99
Blanch, Lesley (Madame Gary), 96 n1, 105
Bondy, François, 147 & n2, 152
Borkenau, Franz, 144 & n2
Boswell, James: *London Journal*, 173
Bourdan, Pierre, 61 & n2
Bourdet, Claude, 51 n1
Bourne, Gen. G. K. (*later* Baron), 144 & n1
Brazier, Mary A. B. (Mollie), 182

& *n*2, 184
Brecht, Bertolt, 146
Brewster, Senator Owen, 177 & *n*1
Broadwater, Bowden, 163 & *n*3,
   182, 184
Brown, Irving: and Berlin
   Congress, 142 & *n*4, 144–5, 147
   *n*1, 148; post-Congress work,
   151–2, 174
Brownell, Sonia (later Mrs George
   Orwell), 111 & *n*1
Bruckberger, Father Raymond-
   Léopold, 60 & *n*2
Buber-Neumann, Margarete
   ('Greta'), 101–2, 115, 145–6,
   163, 189
Buber, Martin, 101
Bunin, Ivan, 161 *n*1
Burgess, Guy, 190 *n*1
Burnham, James, 62, 137 & *n*1,
   138; and Berlin Congress 141–2,
   144–8, 191; AK meets, 149;
   L'Action accuses, 151
Burnham, Marcia, 141–2, 147, 149,
   191
Butterfield, (Sir) Herbert, 190 & *n*1
Bwlch Ocyn (Merionethshire
   house), 22–3, 36–8
BZ am Mittag (newspaper), 2

Calder-Marshall, Arthur, 134 & *n*1
Calman-Lévy (French publisher),
   61
Camus, Albert: Koestlers meet in
   Paris, 43, 59–60; leaves *Combat*,
   51 & *n*1; anti-Stalinism, 53;
   accompanies MK to London,
   81–2; supports Garry Davis, 97
   & *n*3, 100; AK gives black eye,
   160; *Caligula*, 55, 105; *L'Etat de
   Siège*, 95 & *n*2; *Les Justes*, 180
   *n*1; *La Peste*, 55
Camus, Francine, 43, 81–2
Capa, Robert, 87 & *n*2

Cardin, 133
Carrefour (journal), 53 & *n*1
Cerletti, Aurelio, 78 & *n*3
Chambers, Whittaker, 129
Chaplin, Anthony (*later* Viscount),
   139 & *n*1
Chapman, Guy, 21
Charreyron, Comte, 89
Chartrettes (near Fontainebleau),
   94–9
Chiaromonte, Nicola, 152 & *n*1
Chipman, Morris, 132–3, 160
Churchill, (Sir) Winston, 150
Ciliga, Anton, 56 & *n*5
Collinet (Trotskyist-anarchist), 150
   & *n*1
Combat (French newspaper), 51 &
   *n*1, 82 *n*3
Comité National des Ecrivains
   (France), 60 & *n*3
Communist Party: AK joins, 2–4;
   AK quits, 5; in USA, 176
Congress of Cultural Freedom,
   Berlin, 1950: meeting, 137, 140–8;
   post-meeting committee work,
   149–54, 174
Connolly, Cyril, 19–20
Cooper, Joseph, 18, 162, 163
Crawshay-Williams, Elizabeth, 26
   *n*1, 160
Crawshay-Williams, Rupert, 24 *n*7,
   25 & *n*1, 63, 160
Crime Investigation Committee
   (USA), 1951, 178–9
Croce, Benedetto, 140
Crossman, Richard: visits Bwlch
   Ocyn, 33 & *n*4, 34–6; Koestlers
   meet in London, 39; and AK's
   Thieves in the Night, 46; spends
   Christmas with Koestlers in
   Wales, 70; meets Camus, 82; trip
   to Israel, 98; visits Fontaine le
   Port, 109; and von
   Scherpenbergs, 126; edits *The*

God that Failed, 138 & *n*1;
entertains Koestlers in
Commons, 159–60
Crossman, Zita, 35, 39, 70, 109–10
& *n*1
Crowther, Geoffrey (*later* Baron),
161 & *n*1
Cyprus, 92
Czapski, Josef, 140 & *n*1, 142

Dadelsen, Jean-Paul de, 82 & *n*3
Davis, Garry, 97–8 & *n*3, 100
Davis, Harold, 144
Davis, Jack, 190
Dewey, John, 140
de Zoete, Beryl, 55–6 & *n*1
Dolmetsch Music Festival,
Haslemere, 12
Dos Passos, John, 170

Eastman, Max, 163–4 & *n*2
Edelman, Maurice, 82 & *n*2
Eden, Emily, 8
Edman, Irwin, 103
Edwardes, Alice, 9, 12
Eliot, T. S.: *The Cocktail Party*,
133
Encounter (magazine), 140

Farrell, James T., 146 & *n*4, 149–
50, 170
Fath, Jacques, 104
Ferra (Trotskyist-anarchist), 150 &
*n*1
Figaro, Le (newspaper), 83
Fischer, George, 182, 184
Fischer, Gottfried Bermann, 185 &
*n*2
Fischer, Louis, 138 *n*1, 171
Fischer, Markoosha, 171
Fischer, Ruth: *Stalin and German
Communism*, 97 & *n*2
Fischer, Samuel, 182 & *n*1
Fitzgerald, Edward, 10

Florence (Italy), 74–5, 78–9
Fontaine le Port (near
Fontainebleau): villa (Verte Rive)
at, 101, 103, 105, 107, 110–13,
117 *n*1, 192; sale of, 168, 180,
187–8, 193
Forster (neurophysiologist), 59 &
*n*3
Franco, Gen. Francisco, 3–5
Franc-Tireur (newspaper), 148
Freud, Sigmund, 52–3
Fuchs, Klaus, 128 & *n*1
Fund for Intellectual Freedom, 160
& *n*1, 170–1, 173, 175, 183
Furtwängler, Wilhelm, 125

Gallimard (publisher), 100 & *n*2,
102
Gary, Romain, 95 & *n*1, 119; *The
Grand Vestiaire*, 95 *n*1, 105
Gates, Pauline, 40
Gates, Sylvester, 40 & *n*1
Gaulle, Charles de, 45; Malraux
and, 58, 72, 101 *n*3; AK and, 73;
and French communism, 132–3
Gide, André, 138 *n*1
Gillie, Darsie, 40 & *n*2
Goodman, Celia Mary (*née* Paget;
MK's twin sister): birth and
childhood, 8–11; education, 11–
12, 16–17; life with uncle Jack,
13–15; political beliefs, 15; in
Italy, 17–18; coming out, 18;
lives in London, 19; in war, 20;
stays at Bwlch Ocyn, 24 *n*3;
works on *Polemic*, 24 & *n*7; lives
in Paris, 48 *n*2; visits MK in
Wales, 57; works on *Occident*, 63
*n*1; seeks work, 97; visits MK in
Paris hospital, 107; at Haus
Hirth, 127–8; visits Verte Rive,
137 & *n*1, 148 & *n*1; MK stays
with in England, 168–9, and
Alex Weissberg, 184

Goodman, Mac., 132 & n1
Gorkin (Trotskyist-anarchist), 150 & n1
Graetz, Paul, 131, 152
Greene, Graham, 160
Grenier, Jean, 73
Gross, Babette, 101
Gruener, 54 & n3
Guidotti, Gastone, 81 & n2
Gutmann (writer), 124

Haganah (Jewish force), 83–5
Hahndel, Hans, 17
Hamilton, Hamish (Jamie), 55 & n1, 82, 173
Hamilton, Yvonne, 173, 179
Hardy, Daphne (*later* Henrion), 6–7, 32 & n1
Harriman, Averell, 104 & n1
Hart, Al, 181 & n2
Hart, (Sir) Basil Liddell, 35 & n1
Hart, Nance, 181
Hartenberg, Count Carl Hans von, 124 & n1
Haus Hirth (Bavaria), 116, 124–7
Havemann, Professor, 147 & n1
Hebrew Committee for National Liberation, 93 n1
Henrion, Henri, 32 & n1
Hesse and the Rhine, Prince and Princess of, 110 & n2, 117, 127–8, 180, 192
Hildebrandt (of Kampfgruppe gegen Unmenschlichkeit), 142, 148
Hirth, Johanna, 124–5, 129
Hirth, Walther, 124
Hiss, Alger, 129
Hitler, Adolf, 3
Hölderlin, Friedrich, 127
Holitscher, Professor, 147 & n1
Hollis, Christopher, 144
Homburg, Landgraf of, 127
Hook, Sidney, 142 & n1, 144–5,

147 n1, 184
Hope, Winifred (*née* Paget; MK's cousin), 14
Hopkinson, Tom (*later* Sir Thomas), 23 & n1, 26 n2, 97; *The Transitory Venus*, 97
Horizon (journal), 82
Horthy, Miklos, 114 n1
Hughes, Richard, 38 & n2, 63
Hungary: 1947 crisis, 56 & n4; 1949 trials, 114 & n1
Huxley, Aldous, 161 n1, 170

Ignotus, Paul, 114
International Rescue and Relief Committee (IRRC), 78, 154
Irgun Zvai Leumi, 85, 93
Israel, 83–94; *see also* Palestine
Italy: Koestlers visit, 73–9

Jakobsen, Frøde, 143 & n1, 146
Jameson, Storm (Mrs Guy Chapman), 21
Jaspers, Karl, 140
Jefferies, Cynthia (*later* Koestler): in France, 132 & n2, 135, 153; in USA, 174 & n1, 184–7, 190; AK's irritability with, 179
Jerusalem, 87–9
Jerushalmi, Mr, 85
Johnson, Mr & Mrs (owners of the Oakley), 66
Joliot-Curie, Frédéric, 31 & n1
Joliot-Curie, Irène (*née* Curie), 31 n1
Joyce, Robert P., 67, 78, 182–3, 186–7
Joyce, Jane, 67, 78, 81, 182–3, 186–7

Kaganovich, Lazar M., 5
Kallinikov, Josef: *Women and Monks*, 88 & n1
Kampfgruppe Gegen

Unmenschlichkeit, 142 & *n*3,
148
Kanellopoulos, Panayotes, 142 &
*n*1
Kaplan, Harold, 40 & *n*1, 59–60,
73, 160
Kimche, Jon, 88 & *n*2
King (Suffolk gardener), 10
Kingsley, Sidney, 151 & *n*1, 152–4,
169
Klopstock, Friedrich Gottlieb, 127
Knickerbocker, Agnes (*later* Mrs
Joseph T. Walker), 99, 163 & *n*,
166–8, 171, 175
Knickerbocker, H. R., 99
Koestler, Adela (Arthur's mother),
34; arrives in England, 38 & *n*3;
on Freud, 52–3; in Paris with
MK, 118, 150–1; AK's relations
with, 118, 176; MK takes to
England, 192
Koestler, Arthur: birth and
background, 1–7; Zionism, 2; in
Communist Party, 2–4; first
marriage (to Dorothy Ascher), 3;
in Spanish Civil War, 3–5;
resigns from Communist Party,
5; arrested and imprisoned in
France, 6; escapes to England, 7;
war work, 7; meets Mamaine,
20–1; in Palestine, 21; relations
with Mamaine, 23, 26, 29, 32–3,
48, 65, 67, 70, 77, 94, 96, 100,
109, 161, 171, 175–6, 183, 187,
194; proposes world peace plan
to Bertrand Russell, 29, 31;
temper, 32, 49, 103, 112–13,
135, 160–1, 171, 191; restlessness
with England, 45–6, 50, 116,
149; verses and translations, 46
& *n*3; depressions, 50, 52;
interest in mysticism, 51–2; on
Jewishness, 55–6; on 'Tragic and
Trivial planes', 68–9; 1948 US
lecture tour, 78; covers first

Israeli war (1948), 83–94; and
Mamaine's illness, 106, 108;
canoeing, 108; divorce from
Dorothy and marriage to
Mamaine, 110 & *n*3, 116, 120,
131, 134; strikes Mamaine, 112;
denounced by Communists as
cold war leader, 117 *n*1;
childhood, 118; relations with
mother, 118, 176; prosecuted in
France for assault on police,
121–3, 127–8; handwriting
analysed, 125; at 1950 Berlin
Congress, 143–8; committee
work for Congress on Cultural
Freedom, 149–53, 174; self-
destructiveness, 154; and Fund
for Intellectual Freedom, 160 *n*1,
170 *n*1, 183; lives in USA, 163–
91; US special residency bill, 166
& *n*6, 168, 177–8; irritability at
Cynthia Jefferies, 179;
disenchantment with USA, 179–
80; marriage breakdown, 193
WORKS: *The Age of Longing*,
110 & *n*4, 120, 138, 149, 169,
174; *Arrival and Departure*, 7,
133; *Darkness at Noon*, 5, 31, 35
& *n*4; German text, 43 *n*2;
dramatisation, 151, 154, 169 &
*n*1, 171; *The Gladiators*, 129 *n*2;
The God that Failed (contributes
to), 138 *n*1; *Insight and Outlook*,
28 *n*1, 51, 62, 103, 107; *The
Little Flirts of St Germain des Prés*
(article), 176 *n*1; *Promise and
Fulfilment*, 87 *n*1, 96, 98, 103,
107, 116; *Scum of the Earth*, 6–7;
Spanish Testament, 148; 'Les
Temps Héroïques' (*article*), 66 *n*1;
Thieves in the Night, 46 & *n*2; *The
Trail of the Dinosaur*, 140, 176
*n*1; *Twilight Bar*, 24 & *n*5; *The
Yogi and the Commissar*, 7, 20

Koestler, Cynthia *see* Jefferies, Cynthia

Koestler, Dorothy (*née* Ascher; AK's first wife), 3, 110 *n*3

Koestler, Mamaine (*née* Paget; AK's second wife): death, 1, 193; origins and background, 7–11; education, 11–12, 16–17; life with uncle Jack, 13–15; political beliefs, 15; reading and interests, 16–17; in Italy, 17–18, 74–8; coming out, 18; lives in London, 19; in war, 20; meets AK, 20–1; childlessness, 21; 1946 visit to Switzerland, 25–8; painting, 30–1, 33; verses on Bwlch Ocyn, 36–8; 1946 Paris visit, 39–44; studies psychology, 45 *n*1, 48; piano playing, 50, 162, 163; in Trieste, 78–81; loses suitcase in Dunkirk, 82–3; in Israel, 83–94; homes near Fontainebleau, 94–9, 101–13; ill health, 105–9, 120, 182, 185; marriage to AK, 110, 131, 134; servants leave, 115–16, 119–20; studies neurology, 117; bronchoscopy operation, 118; handwriting analysed, 126; interest in birds, 127–30, 132, 134, 136, 138, 180–1, 187, 191, 193; French holiday tour, 155–8; in USA, 163–91; returns to UK, 192; marriage breakdown, 193; on feelings for AK, 194

Kogon, Eugen, 144 & *n*3, 145

Kohler, Foy, 163 & *n*4, 190

Kollek, Theodore (Teddy), 33 & *n*5, 39–40, 48

Korean War, 140, 144, 149–50, 161, 191 *n*1

Kravchenko, Viktor Andreevich, 101 & *n*5, 103

Labiche, Suzanne (*later* Agnély), 59 & *n*1

Ladas, Alexis, 84 & *n*1, 90, 92

Lafond (of Force Ouvrière), 150

Laleine-Laprade, Odile de (Mrs Michael Tweedie), 82

La Malfa, Ugo, 75 & *n*1

Lambert, Constant, 19

Lasky, Melvin J., 141 & *n*1, 142, 144–5, 147 & *n*1, 148

Lawrence, T. E., 58–9, 68

League of Zionist Activists, 2

Lettres Françaises, Les (journal), 101 *n*5

Levi, Carlo, 75 & *n*1

Leyden, Wolfgang von, 17

Lie, Haakon, 142 & *n*1, 144

Lippmann, Walter, 61 & *n*3

Lloyd, Seton, 19

Lloyd George, Frances, Countess (*née* Stevenson), 35

Lombardi (Italian trade unionist), 159 & *n*1

Lombardo, Ivan Matteo, 76 *n*3, 77 & *n*2

Lutyens, Elizabeth, 49

Luxemburg, Rosa, 128 & *n*1

Mabel (Suffolk cook), 10

McCarthy, Senator Joseph, 177–8, 183

McCarthy, Mary, 163, 182, 184

Maclean, Donald, 190 & *n*1

MacLeish, Archibald, 182, 184

Macmillan, Harold (*later* Earl), 34 *n*5

Mailer, Norman: *The Naked and the Dead*, 112 & *n*1

Majorca, 193

Malraux, André: Koestlers meet in Paris, 41–2, 58, 72; anti-Stalinism, 53; as Gaullist *chef de propagande*, 72–3, 178; in Sartre-Gallimard dispute, 100, 102; claims to make history, 192;

Index

Royaume-Farfelu, 67 *n*3
Malraux, Madeleine, 41–2, 59, 102
Manchester Guardian, 83
Mangeot, Sylvain, 40 & *n*2
Mann, Thomas, 5
Maritain, Jacques, 140
Martin, Kingsley, 114 & *n*2
Mauriac, François, 60
May, Dr, 124
Melbourne, William Lamb, 2nd
 Viscount, 16
Menuhin, Diana (*née* Gould), 137
Menuhin, Yehudi, 137–8
Merleau-Ponty, Maurice, 59
Michelmore, Ellen (nanny), 9
Moorehead, Alan, 175
Mörike, Eduard, 129
Morris, Bob, 177 & *n*1, 178
Mouvement Républicain Populaire
 (MRP, France), 31 & *n*2
Muenzenberg, Willi, 101, 174

Nabokov, Nicolas, 147 *n*1
Nagy, Ferenc, 57 *n*4
Nenni, Pietro, 26 & *n*1, 78 *n*2, 160
 *n*1
Neumann, Greta, *see under* Buber-
 Neumann
Neumann, Heinz, 101
Neumann, John von, 185 & *n*1,
 186, 189
New York Herald Tribune, 83
New York Times, 53, 129; *Book
 Review*, 190
News Chronicle (newspaper), 3–4
Nicholas (Polish gardener at Verte
 Rive), 111, 113, 115–16
Nicolaevsky, Boris I., 145 & *n*2
Norton, (Sir) Clifford, 27

Observer (newspaper), 67, 69, 116
Occident (journal), 63 *n*1, 66
Oesterreicher, Augusta ('Gusti'),
 125 & *n*1

Ogden, C. K. & I. A. Richards:
 The Meaning of Meaning, 59 & *n*2
Orwell, George, 24 & *nn* 3, 7, 26
 *n*2, 108 & *n*1, 109, 111 & *n*1

Paget, Eric Morton, (father of
 MK), 7–12; death, 13
Paget, Georgina Byng (MK's
 mother), 7–8
Paget, Germaine ('Mamaine'; uncle
 Jack's wife), 14
Paget, Jack (MK's uncle), 12–15
Paget, Meg (MK's aunt), 9
Palestine: AK first visits, 2, 21;
 AK's views on, 34; Crossman
 and Attlee discuss, 39; Bevin
 and, 54; UN and, 64, 66, 69; *see
 also* Israel
Palewski, Gaston, 101 & *n*3, 102
Paris: Koestlers in, 39–44, 57–61,
 72–4
Partisan Review, 40 & *n*1, 51, 131
Paru (magazine), 150
Pavelitch, Ivan, 62
Pechel, Rudolf, 192 & *n*1
Perényi, Eleanor, 167 & *n*7, 168
Perényi, Baron Zsigmond, 167 *n*7
Peters, A. D. (AK's agent), 48, 55
Petitjean, Armand, 60 & *n*1, 67 &
 *n*3
Philip, André, 144 & *n*1
Phillips, William, 119
Pietra, Italo, 77 & *n*1
Piprot, Father, 114
Pitt, William, the Younger, 15
Polanyi, Michael ('Misi'), 23 & *n*2,
 25, 51, 150, 158
Polemic (journal), 24 *n*7
Preuves (journal), 140
Putnam, James, 104–5, 107

Quasimodo, Salvatore, 81 *n*1
Queipo de Llano, General Gonzalo,
 4

Quennell, Peter, 19, 184

Rains, Claud, 169
Rajk, Laszlo, 114 n1
Raoul, M. (of Préfecture), 122 & n1
Rassemblement du Peuple Français, 72 n1
Read, Herbert, 142, 144
Reid, Anne (*née* Paget; MK's cousin), 14–15
Remarque, Agnes, 163–4
Remarque, Erich Maria, 163–4 & n5
Reuter, Ernst, 142 & n1, 144
Rhine, Dr (of Duke University), 51
Ripka, Hubert, 95
Roberts, Mary, 55–6 & n2
Romains, Jules, 142 & n1
Rome, 75–8
Rothschild, Baroness Alix de, 29 & n1, 72
Rothschild, Baron Guy de, 29 & n1, 61, 72
Rothschild, Dr Miriam, 29 n1
Rousset, David, 143 & n1, 144–5, 148
Ruffini, Attilio, 75 & n3, 77
Russell, Bertrand, 3rd Earl: friendship with Koestlers, 24 n7, 25 & n2, 29–30, 33; and AK's world-saving plan, 29, 31; makes advances to MK, 35; and Congress of Cultural Freedom, 140, 160
Russell, Conrad (BR's son), 26 n2, 33
Russell, Lord Odo, 30
Russell, Patricia ('Peter'; BR's 3rd wife), 26 n2, 30 & n1, 33, 160

St Denis, Michel, 82 & n1
Saragat, Giuseppe, 78 n2, 159 & n1
Sartre, Jean-Paul: Koestlers meet in Paris, 40, 43–4, 59–60, 75;

disagreements with AK, 60, 74, 100, 102, 160; Koestlers meet on train, 140; health, 140; *L'Etre et le Néant*, 73; *Huis Clos (In Camera)*, 40 & n4
Schacht, Hjalmar, 126 & n1
Scherpenberg family, 126–7
Schlesinger, Arthur J., jr., 144 & n3, 145, 159–61, 182–4
Schlomo (Haganah guide), 89
Schmid, Carlo, 143 & n1, 145, 148
Schulberg, Budd, 170 & n1, 175
Schwarz, Solomon, 145 & n2
Scott-Watson, Keith, 88
Sergei, Grand Duchess of Russia, 180 & n1
Servan-Schreiber, Jean-Jacques, 149 & n2
Silone, Darina, 75, 77, 141, 147
Silone, Ignazio, 26, 75, 138 n1; and Berlin Congress, 141–2, 144–5, 147–8; disappointment with, 150; and post-Congress activities, 152
Simpson, Eileen (*formerly* Berryman), 187 & n1
Sinclair, Isaak von, 127
Sitwell, Sir Sacheverell, 19
Slater, Humphrey, 24 n7
Smith, Matthew, 19
Sontag, Irene, 30 n1, 49
Sontag, Mark Count Sontag von, 29 & n1, 30–1, 49, 68, 193
Sophie (Polish servant at Verte Rive), 111, 113, 115–16
Spanish Civil War, 3–5, 191 n2
Spender, (Sir) Stephen, 134–5, 138 n1, 161 n1, 170
Sperber, Jenka, 192
Sperber, Manès ('Munjo'): Koestlers meet in Paris, 40–1 & n3, 60–1, 99–100, 102, 149, 163; visits Koestlers at Verte Rive, 104, 114, 130, 132; political

views, 132–3, 160; book review, 190; on MK's clothes, 192; *Et le Buisson devint Cendre (The Burned Bramble)*, 176 & n1
Sprigge, Cecil, 75 & n2
Sprigge, Elizabeth, 75 & n2
Stalin, Josef, 5
Starkie, Enid, 138 n1
Stephens, Miss (of A. D. Peters), 184
Stevens, C. E. ('Tom Brown'), 20
Stockton, New Jersey, 163–71
Strachey, John, 159–60
Strauss, Eric, 53 n1, 150
Strunsky, Sheba, 145 & n2
Sulzberger, Cyrus L., 80 & n1, 81, 86, 89, 91, 104–5
Sulzberger, Marina (*née* Ladas), 80 & n1, 85 n1, 104–5
Supervielle, Jules, 118 n1
Switzerland, 25–8
Symons, Julian, 133

Tel Aviv, 84–5, 88, 91
Tempo Presente (journal), 152 n1
Temps Modernes, Les (journal), 60 & n4, 100, 102
Tennant, Peter, 147
Thorez, Maurice, 100 & n1
Tibermann, Frl. von, 125
Tito, Josip Brod, 114 & n1
Times, The (newspaper), 21
Tolstoy, Count Lev: *Anna Karenina*, 109
Torberg, Friedrich, 171 & n2
Torlonia, Prince, 141
Torres, Maître, 122 & n1, 128
Toynbee, Philip: *Tea with Mrs Goodman*, 64 & n1
Trevor-Roper, Hugh (*later* Lord Dacre), 144
Trieste, 77, 78–81
Trilling, Lionel: *The Middle of the Journey*, 117 & n4

Trotsky, Leon, 56
Tweedie, Michael, 82
Tzara, Tristan, 27 & n1

Union of Soviet Socialist Republics (Russia), 3, 4–5
United States of America: MK in, 22; AK plans to visit, 45–6, 113–14, 161–2; AK's 1948 lecture tour, 76, 78; Koestlers settle in, 163–91; AK's special residency bill, 166 & n6, 168, 177–8; standard of living in, 172–3, 180; AK's disenchantment with, 179–80; Koestlers leave, 192
Utley, Freda, 183 & n2

Valiani, Leo, 6, 40 & n1, 75, 77, 127
Vallon, Louis, 97, 102, 121–2, 139
Vallon, Suzanne, 121–2, 139
Veblen, Thorstein, 185
Venard, Claude, 119 & n1
Venard, Jacqueline, 119 & n1
Verte Rive *see* Fontaine le Port
Vilmorin, Henri de, 170
Vossische Zeitung (newspaper), 2

Waley, Arthur, 55 & n1
Walter, Gérard: *Histoire des Jacobins*, 65
Ward, Barbara (Lady Jackson), 161 & n1
Watson, Adam, 82 & n1, 114 & n1, 183, 190
Watson, Ann (Andy), 183 & n1
Weber, Alfred, 142 & n2
Weil, Simone: *L'Attente de Dieu*, 135; *L'Enracinement*, 116 & n3
Weisl, Wolfgang von, 130 & n1
Weissberg, Alexander, 5, 114, 117, 184–5, 189; *Conspiracy of Silence*, 188–9 & n1

Weissberg, Sophia (*née* Cybulska),
 5, 115 & *n*1, 117
Weisweiller, 120–1 & *n*1
Weizmann, Chaim, 21
Wilder, Thornton, 182, 184
Wiley, James, 33 & *n*2, 49
Willert, Brenda (Hon. Mrs Paul
 Willert), 33 & *n*1
Willert, Paul, 33 & *n*1, 128
Willert, Wanda, 33
Williams-Ellis, (Sir) Clough, 34
 *n*2, 36 *n*2
Wilson, Edmund: attachment to
 MK, 24 & *n*4; reads Betjeman,
 27; MK sees in USA, 164, 169,
 171, 180, 187; marriage, 171 &
 *n*3; *Europe without Baedeker*, 62;

Memoirs of Hecate County, 167
Wilson, Elena (*formerly* Thornton;
 née Mumm), 172 *n*3, 180
Winch, Henry, 30, 66, 68
Winkler family, 95, 108, 128, 134,
 138–9
Wolfe, Bertram D. and Ella, 163–4
 & *n*2, 190 & *n*2
Wolfe, Edward, 33 & *n*2
Woodcock (US trade unionist), 150
Wright, Richard, 138 *n*1
Wyndham, Richard, 18

Yakovlev, Boris, 145–6 & *n*1

Zimmermann (playwright), 124
Zuckerman, Solly (*later* Baron), 34